WHO COULD LOVE YOU, Astor Price?

Amy Jane Lehan

This first edition published in 2023

A CIP catalogue record for this book is available from the British Library

ISBN: 978-0-6456189-0-7 (Hard Cover)

ISBN: 978-0-6456189-1-4 (Paperback)

ISBN: 978-0-6456189-2-1 (E-book)

Cover Artwork by Cris Tea

amyjanelehan.com

CLOUDY DAY
PUBLISHING

A Note From The Author

I can say a hundred times over, I had a wonderful childhood. Summer days at the beach and moving the cows or sheep with my dad on the motorbike. I had dance lessons, birthday parties and sleepovers at friends' houses. But never at my house. Friends, if they came, didn't stay for dinner, let alone the night. As far back as I can remember, the words '*what happens in this house, stays in this house*' were repeated to me time and time again. They weren't said with love or kindness, but as a promise that there would be hell to pay if I spoke out of turn. Sometimes they were married with *'other people have it far worse than you do'*, and I took those in just as readily, letting them live rent free without question. Those words shaped my pre-teen, teenage and early adult years in ways I didn't understand for some time. They were with me in every morning after, in every heart racing moment I dared wear my long sleeves pushed up, and in every quiet night when I told myself it didn't matter. That I didn't matter.

A secret wrapped in a threat is not a secret you should keep, and abuse—emotional or physical—isn't a competition. There is no scorecard, number of days or degree of pain you must endure for you to matter. You are the main character in your life, and you deserve to be heard. Even when your words are nothing more than an uncertain whisper, when they are falling on unwilling ears or missed in quick moments. Tell your story again and again, I promise, it deserves to be heard.

While Astor and her story are works of fiction, it is all a part of me. Although this is aimed at a young adult audience, there is undeniably content that is not suitable for a younger audience.

For a full list of content warnings, please turn to the last page of the book.

To the person who told me that what happened in our house, stayed in our house; you were right, turns out I'm not any good at following the rules.

If you or anyone you know is suffering with self-harm or suicidal ideation, please know you aren't alone.

For a full list of content warnings, please turn to the last page of the book.

Because you deserve to be believed in.

WHO COULD LOVE YOU, Astor Price?
Amy Jane Lehan

Chapter One

The backs of my thighs were sweating against the carpet patterned seats, and it felt like I would eventually melt and become one with the bus. It was about one thousand degrees in this rolling death tube, despite the morning hour, and no one was happy about it. I picked at the fresh little scab on my hand and a bead of new blood popped, trailing into my palm. Dodging the glass of wine last night as it sailed through the air had been easy (though I owed Megan yet another apology for hanging up on her midsentence), but somehow during the clean-up, a small piece of said glass had embedded itself under my skin. Now I had a brand new scar on my body to join the others. I wiped my palm on my skirt and sighed. A year and a half of school left, then I could leave home. And mum.

The bus stuttered to a stop as I craned my neck around the heads in front of me to see my friend Dylan. His navy uniform shorts were halfway down his ass; a trend I would never understand even if I lived a thousand years. Sliding into his usual place behind me, he swiped his (very much from a bottle) black hair out of his eyes.

'Hey,' he said, cool chin lift included.

'Hey, how's it going?' I pulled my headphones out and slapped on a smile.

'Yeah, yeah, it's going. Troy is having a bonfire Saturday night, are you going?'

'Mmm if Megan is keen, maybe, yeah.' Even though I would rather throw myself into said bonfire than exist in the same space as Troy. He was repulsive, but his Mum was indulgent and let him have people over all the time, turning a blind eye to the drinking and everything else. I didn't really drink, but there was a good place to get high and hook up. So I dragged Megan along more often than not.

'Sweet. Text me when you get there and I'll come say hi,' he smiled, and his deep brown eyes held mischief. I knew what "hi" meant.

I rolled my own eyes and changed the subject. We passed the rest of the bus ride trading school gossip. We didn't hang out at school, but it wasn't huge, so all of our friends overlapped in some way. I wondered how often I came up in conversations like this between other people. I didn't exactly have a perfect reputation, not that I cared. You were only sixteen once so why not, but the rumour mill liked to be fed.

The bus came to a final halt, and we all staggered off into the sun. Dylan gave me another chin lift, which I interpreted as "farewell Astor have a wonderful day", and was gone, sucked into the mass of navy and white, moving as a group through the iron gates. I headed to the science block as I did every day, looking for my best friend.

Leaning against the brick building was Megan. Her hair was a haphazard pile of pale blonde on the top of her head, the bun so far forward it was almost at her hairline. Strands were falling out and if it were anyone else, they would look like they'd just rolled out of bed. Somehow though, it worked for her. She had her head down, undoubtedly trawling Reddit for some new variety of idiot to show me.

I met Megan when I was 12 and immediately shoehorned myself into her life, even though we were not the most likely pair to end up as friends. She wasn't much of a reader and didn't always love to go out, but came along anyway. She liked to watch movies with her dad, read forums online, and sometimes brought baked beans to school in a coffee thermos for lunch. When we finally graduated, we had plans. A little flat in another city, university and freedom. I wasn't sure what I wanted to study yet, but Megan wanted to be a vet nurse.

I wanted that future more than anything.

I stood right in front of her, toe-to-toe, but she was so lost in a thread, she hadn't noticed. I peered at her phone screen, but she was scrolling too fast that I couldn't make out the upside-down words. 'Hey dick,' I said by way of greeting, kicking my black leather shoe into hers. She managed to tear her eyes away from her phone to look at me.

'Oh hey! God you wouldn't believe these people. I'm about twenty comments into a thread on 'Am I The Asshole' about a woman who has a husband that is in love with his sister. HIS sister, Astor. Full blown blood sister!' She was quite literally vibrating with excitement at this.

'That's disgusting. And she just found out?'

'No, no. He told her *before* they got married! Now she's got the sister staying with them for a while and her husband can't stop drooling all over her. People are so fucking weird.'

'Understatement of the year, dude. Hey, uh, I'm sorry about last night.' I wrinkled my nose, embarrassed even though Megan knew everything anyway.

'Your mum?' she asked softly.

I nodded, eyes down, 'yeah.'

'You know it's fine dude. As. Are you okay though? What did Helen do this time?'

'Oh just the usual. It's alright. I'm alright. I just hate when I have to hang up mid conversation.' I hated flying glassware as well to be honest. I was ready to change the subject, I didn't like to dwell. 'So, anyway, moving on—,'

'Okay but—,'

'Nope,' I stopped her mid pity. 'Are you keen to go to this thing at Troy's on Saturday?'

I mentally crossed my fingers. I'd probably still go alone, but it was always better with her.

'Ugh, fine. I wasn't going to. But I feel like you're about to tell me that you're going and will require me to suffer alongside you.' She screwed up her elfin face in disgust. If I was pale, she was virtually translucent.

'You would be elevated to the status of best-friend-ever if you'd go with me.'

'I am your best friend ever. You do realise that it is you trawling for some guy or girl to get naked with, not *moi*.' She pinched the bridge of her nose, like I was exhausting.

'Yes, but you love me dearly. Imagine how dull your days would be without my presence. I am a gift, Megan. A joy. The ultimate thing in your life.'

'You're absolutely the reason I consider assuming a new identity and moving to Guam.'

I gasped, hand on my chest with shock.

'You'd abandon me? *Me*? Your heart and soul? Your reason to exist? In my time of need? My hour of pain? Well, more like five hours of pain. An hour probably won't suffice for a bonfire drinking thing, would it? Who knows how long it would even take these idiots to light the bonfire, I mean last ti—'

'Lord above Astor, I will go.' She rolled her eyes, the lenses of her black framed glasses making her hazel iris look abnormally large. I gave her my best (worst) smile and batted my eyelashes. I'd be lost without her really.

We made our way to our form class and our usual front row seats. While everyone else went to the back of the room to be 'cool,' we sat by the door so we could leave first. The room was fairly dated; vinyl floors and pale mint walls. The chairs were navy—to match our school colours—and plastic. Thankfully, we had air conditioning, even if it wasn't set as cold as anyone wanted it to be.

Megan was once deep in a reddit sub, trying to swallow her own laughter, so I opened my book up again, smiling as various people came in. As predicted, Nicole and Tash came in a mere heartbeat before the bell sounded. Nic—as she liked us call her—and Tash, were two other girls we tended to sit with but were constantly late. Tash was vibrant and outgoing, her toothpaste-commercial-smile consistently beamed and she never held back her opinion. She and Nic had gone to school together since they were in first grade, and while they didn't work on paper, they were a pair. Nic was always at her side and as quiet as Tash was loud, she didn't gossip like the rest of us did. Though not because she thought it was wrong, but simply because she didn't seem to care. I always liked that about her and never managed to get myself to that level. We sat together at break and in classes we had together, hung out sometimes at a party if our paths crossed, but we didn't do anything as a group otherwise. I gave them a wave as they dropped into seats behind us. Tash was leaning forward, her brown eyes wide and excited, likely ready to give us a breakdown of her weekend. Our form teacher, Mr Henderson, was two steps behind them however, and his no-nonsense face induced silence. His orange and brown sweater vest looked straight from 1975 and, given his age, it probably was. Despite his stern appearance, he was soft-spoken, didn't do more than take attendance and hand out any relevant newsletters before sending us to our lessons for the day.

Lunch was the next time we all got to be together properly, given that our classes were mixed over the entire grade and we didn't all take the same things. Nic and I stretched out on the grass, heads out of the sun so we didn't have to shield our eyes, but our legs stuck out into the light, willing a tan to bless us. Tash hadn't materialised as yet and Megan sat entirely in the shade, eating baby carrots and going over notes. As fair as her skin was, she was opposed to the sun generally. Her skin burned in about two seconds flat, and she had to drown herself in sunscreen for minutes of direct exposure. It was such a lovely day, the sort that came only as summer wound its way into autumn. Where out of direct light and the sun-soaked breeze, the air was curt. It fooled you with a whisper of layers; coats and woollen hats, then you stepped into the daylight and felt the sun in your bones and soles of your feet and forgot that it hadn't been there a moment before.

I played with the hem of my skirt, fingertips brushing the skin of my thigh, old scars flat and smoothed over. I reminded myself that last night I hadn't given in. I hadn't let the razor-sharp relief take over when home was hard. As a recovering self-harmer, any victory counted. I was fairly sure the others all knew I cut, but we never acknowledged it and I sure as shit wasn't about to let them—or anyone else—know how close I came sometimes. They knew Mum liked a drink and knew they weren't going to get an invite to my house any time soon, but only Megan knew what it was truly like sometimes. She was the first and last person to spend the night over, and without a single word exchanged between us, we agreed it wouldn't happen again. The fear she had tried to hide in her clear blue eyes was enough. So, I stayed with her, and we dreamed about life out of this town. And it was *everything*.

I looked over at Megan now, she was highlighting passages from her French notes, revising. She looked up and stuck her tongue out at me, crossing her eyes at the same time. Wanker.

'I know you're dragging me to the bonfire on Saturday night, but do you want to come to mine tomorrow after school for the night since it's a Friday? We can watch Rocky Horror and Priscilla...' Megan trailed off, words directed at me of course.

'Uh is that even a real question? You know I'm not going to say no,' I rolled my eyes and sat up, searching in my bag for my water. Megan cleared her throat, again, and I looked up. She wasn't done and judging by the wide-eyed hope on her face, I was immediately nervous.

'I've got this absolutely brilliant fool-proof idea for a bed canopy I'm going to need help with. I've got the wood, but I only have one set of hands, which is a hindrance I should have foreseen but did not,' she grinned. 'But I have you. And you have hands.'

Nic and I exchanged looks at the mention of wood and construction. As smart as Megan was, she was not entirely practical. Or seemingly sane.

'I'm sorry, wood? A canopy? What the dickens are you on about?' I paused, wondering what the hell I'd agreed to. 'But also, can we get takeaways, cause last time we cooked I spent the rest of the night pulling ceramic out of your rank foot with face pliers.' Knocking my drink off the bench, she'd jumped in fright, landing on the shattered mug. She had soaked her foot in antiseptic for an hour as she didn't want 'hoe cooties'. Her words, not mine.

'Tweezers. Just call them tweezers.' Right on cue, a long-suffering sigh escaped her, and she continued, 'as for the wood, well. You'll see, I have a plan. No nails this time, I promise, just rope. And you know I am always down for Chinese, so deal.'

Tash dropped to the ground next to Nic cross legged, shielding her eyes from the sun, and Megan went back to highlighting, happy with the Friday and whatever mayhem she had dreamed up.

'Did you see the new guy yet? I had him in my second class, and he was a delight,' Tash asked, her perfectly symmetrical face split into a grin.

I shook my head, I didn't even realise we had a new kid, and our school wasn't the biggest.

'His name is Matt, or Matty I think? He was with Troy.' Tash continued on. 'He is divine. I'm going to casually say hi after lunch.' She schooled her features, checking her nails like a bad teen film, mean girl and feigning demure.

'I thought you liked that girl that worked with you?' I asked, searching my memory for her name and wondering if I'd imagined her existence.

'Oh my god, Milla. I'm going to see her on Saturday at work. We really click, you know?' she insisted. Nic rolled her eyes as Tash continued with a list of things that made her and Milla a good match, new guy completely forgotten. I half listened, reading my book, wondering about the new guy. Mostly I tried not to be too concerned about all the wood and whatever Megan had planned.

CHAPTER TWO

I managed to fly under the radar at home that night, keeping to my room with my homework for company. My dad owned a mid-size long haul transport company but still drove the trucks himself when he was needed. Either in the office or not, he was always already at work when I left for school and often not home until after dark. He was the only buffer I had. My sister was a decade older and busy live, laugh, loving her best life across town. Callie didn't see mum like she got now, all her childhood memories involved mum falling asleep somewhere and maybe calling dad a prick at worst. She'd definitely levelled up over the past couple years.

I'd stuffed the new underwear sets Mum had left on my daisy printed bed in my bottom drawer with a sigh, not willing to look at any of it yet. She knew which nights were worse than just falling asleep with her jeans around her ankles on the toilet and would apologise with a gift. Drink too much, flip out, 'buy Astor a present and everything would be magically better' seemed to be her thought process. They'd live in my drawer for a month or so, then I'd add them into my rotation and that would be that until next time. There was always a next time. Keeping to my room wasn't a hardship. The walls were mint green, a classic white framed farmhouse window on one wall gave me a view of our winding semi-rural road and my bed was a haven of pillows I obsessively bought. Mum didn't like posters stuck on the walls so everything I had was planned and framed – nothing but pencil sketches of capital cities I wanted to be in, standing in places history had been made so long before I existed. A gap year in London with Megan was my dream and I was funnelling my allowance to one side for it. Mostly. That night I fell asleep with the soft light of the lamp on, letting me imagine the day I'd get to be there and not stuck in this house ignoring the snores of my alcoholic mother. Friday morning I packed my converse, some clothes, and other necessary things into a tote for the weekend. I stopped in the kitchen to rummage for something I could eat on my walk to the bus. Mum followed me in, putting her teacup in the sink to wash immediately because we didn't let dishes linger in this house.

'Morning Astor,' she smiled over at me, and I relaxed just a touch. It was hard to gauge what she would be like some times.

'Hey. Uh, I'm going to stay with Megan this weekend. After school. Today. If that's okay?' I didn't want to frame it as a question. I was old enough to stay at my friends' house without pre-approval, but she was still my mother.

'Of course! Do you need any extra cash? I don't think I have any actually on me, but I'm sure Dad can transfer some to your bank card?'

She packed her handbag for work, her voice light as she added sandwiches and her water bottle. Just another day.

'No, I'm good, thanks though. I may need a ride home on Sunday? If Megan can't drop me off that is.'

'Just text me and let me know. We can get something nice for dinner too then if we have to pick you up.'

She smiled at me again and I couldn't help but smile back. It all felt so normal. We talked a little while I made toast. She told me about some of the residents she worked with at the nursing home, their little quirks, and her favourites. I told her that Megan had a plan for some sort of wood-based build in her bedroom and she laughed. It was hard to reconcile this version of mum with the *drunken* mum of my nights. This one smiled at me, buttered my toast for me, slipped a fiver into my pocket as I walked past. This mum *maybe* loved me. I savoured these moments, saved them for later. For when I couldn't stand the sound of her yelling and needed to remember that she wasn't always this person. I gave her a wave and slipped out the door, ready for the weekend. Happy that mum liked me today.

School felt like a drag, somehow managing to be slower than usual for a Friday. I stood on the speckled path outside the gym, waiting on my sloth-like friends. Assembly was being held for the senior grades, but I couldn't see the three heads I was waiting for in the sea of people.

'Astor! Babes! Fancy seeing you here!' Troy had a voice like a brick in a blender and if it weren't for the value I put on my education, I would murder him. The regret of sleeping with this idiot was real.

'Troy. Given it is our year level assembly time, I would say I'm in the place you can expect to see me.' I turned to face him, surprised to see he only had one person with him and not his usual entourage. A person I didn't know either, so this must have been the new guy. Tash was correct, he was a visual delight; all-dark eyes and tanned flawless skin, his brown hair back in an artful swoop.

'You'll have to watch out for this one, Matty. She's a handful, if you know what I mean,' he elbowed new guy in the side, laughing at his poor attempt at humour. I opened my mouth to threaten Troy with bodily harm, but the gym doors opened behind me. Ms. Prendergast, our fearless leader, summoned us inside and ordered us to sit with our form classes and to move without sound. Megan, Tash and Nic snuck in just before the doors shut, grabbing seats at the end of the row, leaving me with Mandy, who had been the horse kid in primary school, and I suspected still gave the old four-legged gallop a whirl when she was alone. I couldn't stop myself from searching the crowded space for Matty. I didn't like to think I was terribly shallow—but maybe we all were sometimes—and he was particularly pretty. Two rows ahead and next to the very familiar head of Dylan, I found him. Undoubtedly feeling my giant eyes staring, both he and Dylan looked my way. Dylan looked at me with a raised eyebrow and gave me a wave while Matty flashed a one-sided grin that set my cheeks on fire. Resolutely, I turned away. Assembly was the usual collection of notices and presentations topped off with Ms. Prendergast giving us all at the end with a rousing speech about being the leaders of tomorrow and the mothers of the future. Clearly, she had never stepped out of the 1950s and this was just what every teenager wanted to hear before a weekend of poor decision making.

Megan's house was walking distance from the school. She was an only child and lived with just her dad, who taught primary kids. Her mum was never in the picture. She wasn't dead or missing, she just hadn't wanted to be a parent. Megan unlocked her front door and I stepped gratefully into the cool entrance of her little house. Whoever decided woollen skirts was the way forward for a uniform in a hot climate deserved to be left on an island with nothing but a spoon.

'So, I've brought the wood inside, and the rope.' Megan cut into my spoon island fantasies with her own brand of chaos.

'Huh?'

'The bed roof we are building. Like a canopy. God Astor, I swear.' She shook her head, looking at me out of the corner of her eye.

'Why are you staring like that? Have you had a funny turn?'

'Megan, I love you dearly, but please talk sense. Or as close to it as you can manage.'

'Rude,' she gave a very fake huff. 'Right, well. What we are going to do is attach the wood to each corner of the bed, sort of like a four poster. Then cover it in blankets so it's essentially a giant bed tent.'

'So...we're building a fort? You do recall we are almost adults, right? Probably a bit old for a fort.'

'Hush. It is happening. You've already said yes. You have committed.'

Megan's house was tiny, stuffed to the brim with a yard sale worth of things and super clean. There was an eclectic variety of paintings on the walls, colourful rugs with tasselled edges, and a weird collection of footstools dotted throughout. It was overwhelmingly homely and comfortable.

Until you got to Megan's room.

I followed behind her, forcing her bedroom door open wide enough to admit my body, barely. Clothes were all over the floor, not a scarp of the grey carpet was to be seen. Mixed in were art supplies, textbooks, shoes, and Lord knows what else. Her bed was unmade as usual, though to be fair, her bed was barely visible. It also was covered in a menagerie of items. I'd spent on average one night here every week for years, and while it was reasonable to assume that some of the clothing was mine, it was hard to say where exactly it would be. I let the familiar sight wash over me. The off-white walls dotted with polaroids and drawings and random leaves Megan had found and thought were pretty, all tacked up for her and anyone she let in to see. The faintest scent of the oatmeal moisturiser Megan used was worn into the space and made it feel more like home than my own room. I dropped my bags on the floor as always and sat on a suspiciously lumpy side of her bed. In the corner behind the door we'd just fallen through, stood four long planks of wood and a coil of thin blue and white rope. I rolled my eyes heavenwards, hoping for some divine intervention to save me.

Three hours, one shouting match, and some colourful language later, we had—somehow—turned her bed into some sort of rope-canopy-tent-fort-thing. I was 97% sure it would collapse on us in the night, and I would die under the weight of quilts and regret. Honestly, with the state of my life, I wasn't mad about that potential. Megan ordered our Chinese while I showered, making a mental will in my head. I pulled on some pjs and awkwardly, carefully crawled into the monstrosity we had created, shoving books and jeans onto the floor. In a moment of pure genius, we had pushed the drawers that held her TV and PlayStation to the end of her bed, and built the tent over the top. I hated to admit it but, once you were inside, it was kind of nice. Even if it did smell of cupboard blanket and we hadn't cleared the bed properly.

We ate watching *Priscilla, Queen of the Desert,* then sung along to all of *Rocky Horror*, standing crouched on her bed to do the time warp, careful not to take out a fragile fort wall or bed slat. Finally exhausted, we lay in the quiet dark, side by side and surrounded by junk we were too lazy to move.

'Astor?' Megan whispered from somewhere to my left.

'Yeah?'

'How are things at home?' the words were suffocated with her hesitation.

'Umm. Yeah, they're okay,' I shot for casual, but I felt nerves edging in. 'Nothing has changed really. Why's that?'

She paused, weighing her answer, 'The scars on your thighs. I haven't seen any new ones or anything, but we never talk about it either. I heard your mum the other night, before you managed to hang up. She sounded so angry, her screaming. And you sounded so scared, and there's that cut on your hand...I just...' her rushed words hung on broken notes between us.

'You just what...?'

'I just can't go to sleep and pretend I didn't hear her. I can't stop thinking about it. I can't not ask you if things are getting worse with her.'

I took a slow breath, stalling. I wasn't sure how to respond to her. What was I meant to say? *What happens in this house, stays in this house.* I could hear mums voice clear as day. Those words were a mantra, drilled into me since before I could walk.

'It's okay Astor, you don't have to tell me everything. Just. Just tell me if you're okay?'

'I'm okay, I'm always okay.' I made myself say the words. She was my best friend; we knew everything about each other. But mum and her drinking were mine to live with. I wanted to give her more, to know more but just not...all of it. I whispered: 'sometimes, everything feels really out of control.'

'What do you mean?' I could imagine her frown.

'Like, nothing in my life is my decision. I know it's being a teenager, I guess, and that this isn't forever, but it feels like it sometimes.' God, I didn't want to cry about this. 'We have all these plans to leave here, and I want them to happen so badly, but sometimes I can't see the way out when I just want it so bad.'

I could feel the burn of tears at the corners of my eyes at the sound of my own desperation. Megan's hand wrapped around my forearm, giving me a soft little squeeze.

'It will happen. We will make it happen.' I could hear the wobble in her words, determined and scared for me.

'I know.'

We had to.

'Can I ask something?' a few moments had passed, and her voice was back to normal. Still quiet but no tears.

'Always.'

'You'll tell me if you need to get out right? I'll come get you.'

'I will,' I said, not sure if I was telling the truth.

'I'm serious,' she sat up, looking down at me with her blonde hair falling around her face.

'I know you are. You're the only one who would come and save my ass anyway.' I forced a smile, not sure how much she could see it in the dark without her glasses.

'Yeah, you're right. I am.' She lay back down, wriggling back into my side.

'I know I'm right, I usually am.' I poked her in the ribs, letting myself relax. Silence was never awkward or uncomfortable with Megan, and right now it was sleepy, and peaceful.

'Goodnight As, I love your face. I hope you know that.' Megan mumbled, words barely recognisable as she fell into sleep.

'Love your face too Meggy,' I whispered. I knew she was asleep when she didn't smack me for calling her Meggy, a name she hated passionately. I lay in our weird little bed tent, listening to her breathing gradually even out, so very thankful I had her.

Chapter Three

I was a lot less thankful a few hours later, when I woke up with her arm across my face. Megan could sleep through a tornado tearing her house into pieces, so I had zero hesitation shoving her arm away and rolling out of bed, or rather, *trying* to roll out of bed. In my half-asleep state, I had forgotten the fucking tent. Fort. Whatever it was. Combined with the maze that was Megan's floor, it was pure miracle I survived. I found my phone sitting inside a running shoe and slipped out the door to the bathroom, before crawling back into bed with Megan. The day didn't need me yet.

When I woke next, Megan was already up, crawling around her floor in her underwear and a *Barney the Dinosaur* purple t shirt.

'What the actual fuck are you doing?' I asked.

'I swear I saw my favourite skinny jeans here yesterday, the ones with the knee rips?'

They all had knee rips. Megan loved a fake rip. She would probably sell her father for a pair of jeans with a good fake rip.

She looked up at me from the floor, noting my raised eyebrow. 'The ones with the swirly thing on the ass pockets?'

'Oh! Right. Yeah, I know the ones.' I did not. I surveyed the carnage, trying to spot any jeans at all. 'Look Megan, you'd be lucky to find a week-old corpse in here.'

'Well fuck you too Astor. It isn't dirty. It's just...I have a lot of things and they are all here where I can see them.'

'Just cause you take out your dishes doesn't mean it isn't dirty. You're one box of magazines away from an episode of hoarders.'

'I hate you and you have a spot on your chin.'

'You do not, and I don't.' I'd checked my face the first time I woke up, but when she returned to her head down jeans hunt, I may or may not have had a quick feel of said chin. Liar, liar.

'I swear to sweet Jehovah, they were down here. I saw them and thought "those are tomorrows jeans" and then we built the palace.'

I assumed by palace she meant the monstrosity. She was throwing stuff around now, so I dodged some leggings flying through the air and pulled my own clothes out. I shoved myself into my black skinny jeans and a Taylor Swift t-shirt, then left Megan to it. She'd either find them or perish in the hovel, but right now I needed food. Megan's dad was sitting at their scuffed, round wooden table. The entire house was warm and inviting, buttery yellow walls throughout the main areas, every fabric thing overstuffed and colourful. Chris was similar—well, aside from the buttery yellow bit. He was warm, inviting, colourful and overstuffed. The same pale blonde hair of his daughter, shot with grey here and there, was curling around his nape. He looked up as I came in, his smile wide and genuine.

'Astor! How are you, love?'

'Morning Chris, I'm good, thank you. Is it okay if I grab some cereal?'

'Honey, you've been here enough to be a part of the furniture. Help yourself. Where is my slovenly offspring?'

'Ah, well, she's trying to find an exact pair of jeans with specific rips, so we'll see her sometimes between now and 79 weeks. Assuming she isn't crushed by that tower of canvases, or something.'

I poured some cereal into a bowl and joined Chris at the table. He had paper spread out in front of him, child handwriting in pencil on each page, pictures on some of families and dogs.

'I'm marking my class's 'about me' assignment, I tell ya kid, some of these children aren't the brightest,' he sighed, shaking his head in faux misery. I knew he loved his job. He spoke about it all the time and you could just feel how happy he was, how much he loved his students.

'What age are they?'

'Seven. Think next year I might ask for an older class though. Anyway, what are you girls up to today? Into town?'

'We have a bonfire thing tonight with some people from school. Not sure what before then, though. I'm waiting on Megan.'

No sooner had her name left my mouth, she appeared. In holey black leggings, purple shirt still in place.

'Not a word Astor, not one.' She huffed past, pouring her own bowl of cereal, and joining us.

'Couldn't find them then?' I asked.

Megan kindly flipped me off.

Such love.

We cleared up our breakfast things—even though it was past midday already—then sprawled on the couch to watch trash tv for the rest of the afternoon. Being in this house, with its sunshine colours and thrift store finds, was the most at peace I felt, and I savoured it.

Chris left us standing at the end of Troy's driveway, making Megan promise we'd call him if we couldn't get a ride home. Uber was complete hit-and-miss around here, but we couldn't have driven ourselves. Megan had the propensity to bathe her liver in rum, and there was just no telling how or where I'd end up.

The rolling from the music Troy had on as we reached his driveway made it impossible to tell what was playing. We slipped around the corner of his big weirdly colonial brick house and the glow of the bonfire cast giant teenage shadows along the grass. It was a little bit of a walk to the paddock they were in, mostly flat and impossible to get lost. The first group of people we saw were girls from our grade, navigating the long-ish grass in their ill-chosen heels. They did however, kindly point us in the direction of the drinks and a folding table of snacks. Bless them. Megan and I moved from group to group, saying our hellos to people we saw at school daily like we hadn't seen them in a month. I sank into the atmosphere, accepting a joint from a pretty girl I knew in passing—but would like to know a lot better—and a beer from someone else. We were dancing and being social. The music was loud and the fire warm, we laughed at everything and nothing and everything in between. I was buzzed and happy. I picked a floppy black haircut out of a group of guys and made my way over, dragging Megan behind me.

'DYLAN!'

'ASTOR!'

We did a weird bromance type chest bump. I don't know why. He probably didn't know either, seeing as we saw each other daily and had been to bed together more than a few times. His arm snaked around my waist, hand on my hip and moving lower.

'Want to come back to mine later?' he lowered his voice, speaking into my neck. I assume he was aiming for my ear. Dylan and I had done this particular dance before, usually when neither of us found someone else to go home with. He was cute, sweet, and stayed my friend when the high receded. Hardly a bad decision.

'Maybe, no promises, kay?'

'You're a tease Astor Price, let me know when you decide. I can drop you back to Megan's tomorrow.' He gave me a lazy smile, easy going as always. 'Oh! Come and meet the new guy!'

He tugged on my belt loop and loped back to his friends. They had moved away from us slightly, taking Megan with them. I slipped in beside her, stealing back my drink before she could finish it. I hadn't even noticed she'd taken it from me.

'Thanks, Meggy,' I smiled sweetly.

'I am sober enough to kill you, Astor.'

She wasn't.

I looked around at the familiar faces, searching for the one I'd seen outside assembly. He was laughing at something Dylan was saying, lit up by the bonfire behind him, tall, dark hair. Our eyes met and though I couldn't make out their exact shade of brown in this light, I certainly saw them drag down my body and back up. He didn't seem bothered that I didn't have a perfect body, not at all. Not one to be shy, I went and stood with Dylan, facing the new guy, and gave him my best—actual best, not Megan worst-best—smile.

'Hey, I'm Astor. I didn't get to say that before assembly,' I stuck my hand out, like an idiot.

'Matty,' he shook my hand, laughing. He had a great laugh, deep and genuine.

'Are you new here or just new to the school?'

'We just moved from up north, Dad's firm opened a branch here last month, but this is my first week of school here.' He offered me the bong and I gladly took it, handing him a beer. Praying now wasn't the time I coughed my lung out like an amateur.

'Oh cool, and you've already had the misfortune of meeting these idiots, then?' I nodded my head at Dylan who was trying to assemble some sort of drunken human pyramid. 'I'd be careful, it's probably contagious.'

He gave that wonderful laugh again, turning to watch fools try to arrange themselves and running a hand through his hair. It was short on the sides, long on top, dark brown, and probably smelled delicious.

'I mean, those idiots invited me here tonight, which is where I've been able to spend some time with you. Can't really complain about catching idiots if you're the reward.'

I couldn't not laugh. Boy was smooth, I tell ya. I wasn't going to complain. We stood there for quite some time, talking books, enjoying the mellow weed provided, and maybe flirting. Megan materialised at my side, laying her head on my shoulder.

'Astor, can we go home now? Am tired.' Her eyes closed and she swayed into me. As much as I wanted to go home with Matty—hell, I'd even go behind a tree with Matty—Megan was more important. I tried to reach my phone in my back pocket while not letting go of her. Not exactly an easy feat typically, let alone now. I felt a hand ghost down my back and pluck my phone out. Matty handed it to me, a smile pulling up the side of his soft lips.

'Before you call whoever you're calling to collect you, can I get your number?' he cocked an eyebrow and, frankly, I was screwed. As well as jealous. I could never raise just one brow. Asshole.

'Yeah of course,' I rattled off my number and he sent me a text, a little kiss blowing emoji and an M. I saved it, blushing, and giving him a quick smile. Not quite sure why my stomach was doing somersaults, he wasn't the first person to give me his number.

'I, uh, better get an Uber,' I cleared my throat, nodding. Was I making this weird? 'But I'll see you around yeah?'

'You will definitely see me around.' Cocky bastard winked at me and walked away. Christ.

I opened the app and ordered us a ride back to Megan's, then dragged her sorry ass to the road.

'Jesus, Megan. Use your friggin' legs.' I was smiling, even though she was useless.

'I haven't got any ha ha ha,' she laughed like an idiot.

We made it to Troy's driveway and Megan dropped to her butt, legs out in front of her, and pulled out her phone. She started scrolling like she was a 75-year-old who had never seen technology before. According to my own phone, our ride was still a few minutes away, so I joined my considerably drunk best friend on the ground. Pale twirls of hair had escaped her ponytail and her eye make-up was smudged in the style of a raccoon. She didn't seem to notice me despite me having half-carried her there. She was typing something, each tap of her thumbs painfully slow, but a little smile was fixed in place.

'Hey,' I bumped my shoulder into hers, and I swear she momentarily levitated. She locked her phone and stuffed it into her jacket pocket. Now would also be a good time to have the ability to raise one eyebrow.

'Hey,' she said, flashing me a dopey, forced smile and hazy eyes. 'Can we go home now?'

'Yeah, our Uber will be here in a little bit. Are you okay?'

'Mmm just tired,' she put her head back on my shoulder, and I inhaled the faintly smoky scent of bonfire. The hum of the party rose and fell behind us as the car came to a stop. I got Megan clipped in, ready to be tucked up in her absurd bed, my thoughts already wandering back to Matty.

Chapter Four

'How was your weekend?' Mum turned around in the front passenger seat. Her hair was pulled back in a tortoise shell patterned clip and watery blue eyes fixed on me.

'It was good. Built a canopy thing over Megan's bed and watched some movies. The usual.' I shrugged, omitting my bonfire-based outing.

We all knew what I was up to and collectively were happier to pretend we didn't. Mum drove me to get the contraceptive injection every three months and that was that. She made a 'hmmm' sound in the back of her throat and turned around. She and Dad had just collected me from Megan's driveway. Megan was still snoring her face off while I'd been outside melting in the morning sun. Now we were apparently off to the only shopping centre in our town. We had a decent population in our spread-out town. The beach was on one side and rural farmland on the other. There were three high schools, a few primaries, and one big shopping centre in the middle. There was also the city centre, which we all referred to as "town" and that had a cinema, a few other stores, and restaurants, plus large public gardens.

I wasn't upset about going to the mall, despite being dead tired. I could always use more clothes. I shut my eyes and leaned my head against the window, the faint vibration almost lulled me back to sleep. Mum and Dad talked off and on and I tuned them out. Megan lived closer to town than we did, so it was only about a fifteen-minute drive thankfully.

I pulled my phone out to send her a message, so she knew where I'd gone. I did stick a post-it note to her face letting her know, but given the state of her bed, there was a more than fair chance it would be lost in the debris. Opening the app, the first message was Matty's from the night before. The M and emoji. I saved his number since I'd not done so last night. Opening the text window, thumbs poised over the keypad, I tried to think of what to say.

I was a little nervous. I was friends with plenty of people, many of which were guys. Matty wasn't any different and I was being ridiculous. He was just funny and so far, easy to talk to. He read seemingly a lot of the same books I did and, obviously a bonus, he was incredibly nice to look at. Faintly tan, tall, brown hair pushed back off his forehead, slightly wavy, the sort of hair you just wanted to touch and knew it would be silky and soft. Jesus. Gross lizard brain. I couldn't even explain what it was about him, really. Potentially, it was the allure of not having attended school with him since age 4 like most other people I knew. Maybe he'd be less appealing after a bit of time.

I typed every variation of 'hey,' 'hello,' and 'howdy' I could think of, plagued with indecision.

'Astor, get out of the bloody car,' Dad shouted.

Apparently, we had arrived while I was waxing poetic about hair. I was immensely thankful I wasn't contending with a hangover. The smell of the mall was not exactly roses as we entered via the food court side of things. I locked eyes with a girl my age working at a fried chicken store, the grease a visible sheen on her skin. Turns out I was also immensely thankful I wasn't required to get a job. We weren't exactly joining the country club and wearing monogrammed polos, but we were comfortable. Both Mum and Dad preferred I produced decent grades rather than getting a part time job. I got a regular "allowance" and helped out when asked, which kept dad happy all of the time and mum about 75% of it.

We went into a couple of stores, browsing racks of clothing but not really finding anything. Store number three had Tash situated behind the counter, sorting hangers from a large bin into baskets. My stomach gave a little lurch. Despite being friends with Tash since the start of high school, she'd not actually met my parents—as in, she hadn't met Mum. I had slammed to a halt in front of a table piled with jeans like a fool. I started thumbing through them, purposely not looking at the counter but glancing over at Mum, who was looking at skirts with Dad. Miniskirts—teeny tiny miniskirts—save me, lord. I knew logically that anyone could wear anything they wanted, you be you and all that, but seeing my 50-year-old mother wear glittered miniskirts designed with my age bracket in mind was a hard pill to swallow. I crossed my fingers that she wouldn't like anything, and we could move on without having to speak to Tash. Tash wasn't the most subtle of people.

'Hey As!' she said, surprisingly quiet. I turned to her, smiling. Her long honey blonde hair was braided over one shoulder, the shaved side of her head on display. She had an eyebrow ring, a black jumpsuit with Vans, and press-on nails with French tips, of all things.

'Hey, I didn't know you were working today?' Shit friend I was.

'Oh yeah, it was only meant to be yesterday. Short-staffed.'

'And you're alone?' I looked around, not having seen anyone else, or more importantly, Milla.

'Fuck no,' she laughed. 'My co-worker slash future bride is roaming about in the stock room. What's up? Are you here with Megan?'

'Nah, she's sleeping off last night still. I'm just out with my parents.'

Because I was incredibly cool, clearly.

'Astor did you find anything?' Mum said from behind me. Had I summoned them?

Mum smiled at Tash. She had a black and white striped skirt over her arm and, given the lack of fabric, it was indeed a mini skirt. Dad was half a step behind her.

'Mum this is Tash, you remember, from school. She works here.'

'Hi,' Mum said shortly. Her eyes were cataloguing Tash piece by piece, barely attempting to hide her contempt. She would undoubtedly have a comment or two after we left the store.

'Nice to meet you.' Tash smiled at mum and turned back to me. 'I better get back to it. I'll see you tomorrow at school, As.' She gave a tight little wave and promptly exited stage left. Can't say I blamed her. Mum was completely nonplussed.

'So, did you find anything you want? Callie just sent a message, so we're going to meet her for lunch.'

'Oh, just some jeans maybe?'

'Well hurry up, I haven't got all day.'

I handed her some distressed grey jeans in my size, and she handed everything off to Dad to pay for. Tash was nowhere to be seen and in her place was a girl a year or so older than me with beautiful dark hair, smiling away. Milla, I presumed.

Callie was already sitting at a chipped white Formica table waiting for us when we got back to the food court. Mum of course rushed over, and Callie stood to awkwardly hug her over the table. Her light brown hair was in an artfully sloppy bun, strands falling out around her carefully made-up face. Red floaty blouse, denim jeans and meticulously clean white shoes—standard Callie attire.

They debated back and forth about what we would have to eat, and I tuned out. I had no say at all.

Not that I really cared.

Dad went to order for us when they had decided, and I was left with Mum and Cal, already deep in conversation, like they didn't talk every single day. Callie was from Mum's first marriage and her dad had left when she was 2, making Mum a single parent for many years. They were incredibly close, and it was easy to feel like a big ol' third wheel.

I wrestled my phone out of my pocket, noting that there were no messages from Megan...or anyone else. I was tempted to open my book, but the overwhelming thrum of food court noise and the constant flow of moving bodies was distracting. The fluorescent lights lit the space up like a surgical theatre, exposing every sad, discarded French fry and black scuff on the grey tile floor. My phone vibrated and I almost dropped the bloody thing.

It was too much to hope it was Matty, right? I swiped it open, holding my breath.

D: come carry a tray

Ah, Dad. Not quite Matty. Decidedly less hair and entirely more related.

Bending my way through the table and chair sea to Dad, I took possession of a red plastic tray and wove my way back. Everyone was slightly less thrilled with my quiet 'excuse me' on the return journey, untrusting eyes glancing off the tray. Given that it was holding drinks in paper cups, and I was literally sailing them above various heads, the look was probably reasonable. Mum and Callie didn't seem to have noted my absence, but they sure as shit noticed my return when I slid the drinks onto the table. I'd like to say lunch was eaten in perfect silence, but Mum and Callie continued, Dad now chiming in too, between mouthfuls. I stuck to people-watching instead.

Until I heard my name.

'Astor's friend worked there. God-awful hair, that thing where they shave the sides off? Honestly, I don't know what kids these days are thinking. She could have been a pretty girl too.'

'Oh Mum, it's just hair!' Callie laughed. Like Mum hadn't just based her opinion of my friend entirely on her appearance.

'She's really nice actually,' I cut in. 'We hang out at school and have classes together. She's in my form group. People can wear what they want.' I felt myself frowning, trying not to glare at Mum.

'Settle down, I didn't mean anything by it, Astor.' She gave Callie a look like I was dramatic, like I wouldn't see it. 'Come on, we'll go to that little shoe place by the toilets,' Mum stood, leaving the table for the food court staff to deal with. Callie gave me a little smile and followed her, Dad in tow on his phone. I shoved my own phone back into my jeans and went to join them, my lunch untouched and waiting for the trash.

Three hours later we were on our way home. Mum and I were in possession of new summer wardrobes (which for me, wasn't too varied from my winter wardrobe) and aside from the lunch comment, it had been a nice day. I was reading on my phone when the car turned and came to a smooth stop.

'Just sit in the car, Dad and I are just going to get a couple things and we'll be back in five.' Mum said and opened the door.

A quick glance through the front window confirmed what I already knew. We were at a liquor store. I don't know why I felt disappointed when this was a daily reality. It was inevitable. My mother had a drinking problem and wine didn't just magically appear in the fridge. I opened my messages and sent Megan a quick *hey*. I had her saved as flicked through social media, leg bouncing, hoping she'd reply.

Megan: hey yourself bitch

Astor: nice to see you're alive. How's the head?

Megan: attached. thanks for delivering me to bed. What's up?

Astor: went to the mall with m+d and had lunch with callie. waiting in the car atm for Mum to get wine as usual. whats up with you

Megan: did Daddy get you an entire wardrobe again? for real, nothing.

Megan: I am vegetating.

Megan: did you get the new guys number last night?'

I startled as the door across from me opened. The car was stuffy, and much needed fresh air filled the space. Dad set a box with six wine bottles on the seat and another box holding beer on the floor for him. He gave me a smile, shutting the door and settling into the front where Mum had already got in.

My phone lay forgotten. Every melodic clink of the wine bottles bumping against each other on the drive home forced anxiety on a crawl through my stomach, threatening to wrap my insides like a vice. Six emerald-green bottles. Would that be six nights of mediocrity, the closest to peace I got? Some unkind looks, maybe "bitch" thrown my way at most, completely ignored at best. Seeing as I could barely remember the last time she only drunk one bottle, it didn't seem likely. Maybe three nights of name calling and snide remarks, uttered under her breath every time I walked past. Three nights of being stuck in the living room with her as she listed my numerous faults, unable to walk away as that would invite her into my room, forced to stay and stomach her words, choking on my own. Maybe I was in for the less common two-night event that six bottles could provide. The nights where I sat in the dark of my room, listening for her clumsy steps outside my door and counting my breaths until she left. Feigning sleep while she tore my entire being apart with her words, alcohol blurring the edges of each letter she spewed as she reminded me of the nothing I was, that I would ever be. I closed my eyes, nails biting crescent moons into my palms and hoped it would be option one.

Dad's friend Simon showed up with his wife Vanessa just after six that night. Vanessa with her own bottle of wine clutched in her taloned fist. Her nails were blood red, and her uncomfortably thin lips were painted to match. It all clashed magnificently with her box dyed 'plum' coloured hair, which she wore in an aggressive bob. Simon was big and burly, greys snaking into the sandy hair on his head. His flannel shirt was a permanent fixture, and the faint scent of cow shed seemed embedded in his skin.

'Astor! Hey honey, how are ya?' Vanessa asked enthusiastically.

Before I could get a word in, Mum came into the dining room, a teacup of wine in hand. She had started about an hour ago, though seemed to be pacing herself, undoubtedly for the benefit of their friends.

'She's doing so well at school, Ness. Got a 98 on her history test last week. She'll be something great, just you wait. A lawyer or something.' Mum blinked at me, smiling. Clearly unaware I had no desire to become a lawyer. Even though I had said more than once I wanted to be an editor. At this point I'd settle for lawyer if it took me half a world away from here.

'Sure Mum, something like that. I'm going to go and...do homework or something. It was nice to see you, Vanessa.' I forced my face into a smile and retreated to my room, set my Taylor Swift playlist up, and lay down on my bed.

It shouldn't bug me when Mum spoke proudly of me. Really, it should've thrilled me that she took an interest in my schooling, but I couldn't stop the way it turned me inside out. I wanted to make her happy, and I was proud of my grades, but that's all she ever told anyone about me. My worth as her daughter was seemingly entirely dependent on doing well at something. It made her look good, like an attentive parent. She never listened when I told her what I wanted to do when I left school. Well, if she did listen she was choosing to ignore what I was saying. Maybe I should consider medicine, I would love to cut out the part of my brain that told me to give a fuck about what she thought about me. I didn't think they'd covered that on *Grey's* either.

I pulled out my schoolbooks, choosing to sit on the floor with them spread around me, so I could go over my homework that was due in tomorrow and read through the rest of our assigned book for English. My phone lit up with a new message, likely Megan asking what was due tomorrow in our mutual classes. As crazy smart as she was, she frequently neglected to write down due dates for assignments.

Matty: hey astor its matty

Gasp. Matty had sent me a message. There was a little hand emoji, like a handshake. Like at the bonfire. Outwardly, I had frozen. Mentally my brain was that Homer Simpson gif with the monkey clapping the cymbals.

Message him back, fool.

Astor: hey matty its astor

I added the opposite shaking hand emoji. Good work me. I dropped my head back against the bed and looked blankly at my ceiling. He is going to think I'm an idiot.

Matty: so what does astor do on a Sunday nite?

I tapped out my response, knowing it sounded nerd-like, but it was the truth. I placed my phone on the carpet, out of my line of sight. Well, my direct straight-ahead line of sight. Mostly. I would not sit and wait for a message. I wasn't that girl. No Sir. From the dining room, the rise and fall of conversation seeped in. Like smoke under a door, it slowly filled my room, increasing in volume. I turned up my music. The opening bars of *Cruel Summer* drowned it out mostly ,and I forced myself to work through the schoolwork before me. One song rolled into another and by the third I just couldn't do it. My eyes were pulled to my phone, mocking me with its blank screen. I wasn't getting anything done like this, so I stuffed it all into my bag, hopeful that later would be easier.

I was obsessively looking at my screen now, like I was fucking unhinged. What was it about this guy? I felt like a fool, waiting on the cute boy to message me. Fed up with myself, I decided to shower, leaving my phone in my room so I didn't get it wet checking it every five seconds.

Ten minutes later and I was half drowning in fire water, having a stern conversation with myself. Level Astor was reminding Stupid Astor that this wasn't what we did. We didn't do the butterflies and the waiting. A boyfriend or girlfriend wasn't on the cards for me, and that was fine, I didn't need one. Sure, when I was 13 and my friends were getting asked out, I thought my time would come. It seemed like it was the most crucial part of school for everyone else. Four years later, I'd grown into my limbs and boobs, and I'd made peace with the fact I was a "for now" girl. I wasn't the one you wanted your friends to meet apparently. I had my own friends. I knew they liked me, knew they were happy to have sex with me and that was it. Dylan was my friend and frequently asked me home with him. Or rather to the tree house in his yard that had been there since we were 5, but same same. I just didn't quite make it to the dating part. And what did it matter? It was high school. It wasn't forever. I liked sex, I didn't need hearts and flowers and I wasn't going to stare at my phone like a fool.

There was absolutely no escaping the noise from the dining room the minute I shut the water off. My parents and their friends were all talking over each and the music, their voices rising as they fought to be heard. I quickly got dressed, braided my hair, and then allowed myself to check my phone. Praise be, he had messaged. I scowled as my stomach swooped.

Bad Astor.

Matty: you into school then? I like that. btw what do you do for fun?

Well that felt a bit flirty. That was flirty, right? I sucked my cheek in between my teeth, unsure what to say back, shower pep talk forgotten. I wanted him to like me.

Astor: oh, you know. The usual. Parties, pot, and penises. You?

I threw my phone onto my bed, watched it skate across the top and land on the floor. Fuck it. At least I'd hear it vibrate on the ground.

I went to the kitchen to get a drink and some sort of snack, then hopefully I could settle into bed and text Matty a little before sleep.

Cigarette smoke swirled in the air, their conversations sounded slurred and woven with 80s rock. The combination instantly set my teeth on edge.

'ASTOR!' Mum's voice was sharp, impossible to miss. 'Get me my wine!'

I knew better than to do anything other than comply. I found the bottle in the fridge door and took it over. A quick glance around the room showed that everyone was fairly well intoxicated. Dad and Vanessa were talking/shouting at each other about Steve Sanders. Simon's brow furrowed, concentrating on the ever-challenging task of flicking his lighter so he could have another smoke.

'Here, Mum,' I said, placing the bottle in front of her with a smile. Her hand wrapped around my wrist, halting my retreat. I waited.

'What are you doing,' she demanded.

I swallowed my snide remark about being an unpaid waiter and straightened my words before I answered her.

'Just going to go to bed, I have a test tomorrow,' I fibbed, wanting a quick escape.

'You think you're so fucking perfect, don't you,' she sneered. I could smell the sickly-sweet wine on her breath. 'I can see your face, you know. You think you're so fucking good, but you're nothing, Astor.'

No matter how often it happened, I never understood this. The way she could look at me and turn everything on its head. I hadn't *done* anything aside from what she asked me to do. My eyes were stuck to the floor, mentally tracing the wood grain. Mum gave my arm a shake, demanding some response and I bit my lip to keep quiet.

'I'm fucking talking to you. Say something,' her voice was louder. Drawing everyone else's attention and the atmosphere in the room swan dived.

'Helen, let her go for fuck sakes,' Dad sighed.

'No. I want her to tell me why she thinks she's better than us. Look at her. Prissy little bitch.'

I looked up at Dad, hopeful he'd say something more. He took a swig of his beer and kept his mouth shut.

'Ah well, we're gonna take off now. I'll give you a call tomorrow,' Simon drained his own beer, giving dad a nod. Vanessa swung her purse over her shoulder, not looking at me nor mum. Dad got up to walk them to the door, out of sight entirely and clearly nonplussed. Mum's grip tightened, like she *wanted* her fingerprints to be stamped on my skin. I finally looked at her face, green eyes against her soggy blue. Sober against drunk. Alcohol speaks the truth, doesn't it? That was the adage.

'Why do you hate me?' the question slipped through my teeth before I was aware it even existed. Pain softly dripped from every syllable, harshly underscored with desperation.

'Hate you? Little miss perfect you. Daddy wrapped around your finger. If I didn't love him, I'd never have had you. Perfect little Astor,' she spat, shoving me away. I stumbled a little, my feet not prepared for the motion.

I couldn't make it make sense, whatever had happened in her mind to start this. I'd just wanted a drink. She'd been fine earlier, singing my praises, and now my presence alone set her off.

'I…' I wanted to respond, but nothing would fall into place.

'Nothing to say? Waiting for Daddy to come back and tell me off? That's what you like, isn't it? You think you rule this house but let me tell you, you little cow. You are nothing. This is MY house.' She was shouting, vibrating. Disgust rolling off her. 'Fuck off. Run to your room so you can cry to that stupid fucking Megan or work out which stupid boy you're going to lay down for next.'

My cheeks were wet, tears coursing down my face. I wanted to go, I wanted to be back in my room away from her. But a part of me didn't want to give in and give her what she wanted. I didn't want to be so cut down by her words, I wanted to be strong and tune them out. I wanted to understand what I'd done wrong when it seemed like my only crime was existing.

She slammed her wine bottle down onto the table hard enough to leave a small moon in the wood and I ran. I ran away, pushing past dad and choking down a sob.

I shut myself in my room, back against the edge of my bed on the floor and cried. I was so confused and hurt and scared. I hated how scared I was. I hated that my fingers itched for the familiar feel of a razor in my hand. I didn't know how to be better, and maybe I couldn't be better. Maybe this was as good as I got and if this is all I would be then I had no chance. She would never love me back, and I didn't know how not to love her. It felt hardwired into my bones to love her.

A silver trinket box was in my hand. It was light, the only weight that of the consequences it held. I had it open in an instant, razor out and sliding across my thigh in half of that. Paper white giving way to bursts of red. Over and over I let the sharp bite of pain soothe me, fresh tears dripped off my cheeks, hitting the mess I was making. I closed my eyes, my head throbbing almost unbearably as I told myself that this was okay.

This was my answer, the how I got through life. How I slept. How I functioned at school. I was foolish to think I didn't need this to survive. I didn't want to die, not at all. I just wanted to feel better, and this made me better. I could control this, there was so much I had no control over, but

I had this. But it wasn't right, I knew it wasn't. I knew tomorrow I would hate this, hate *me.*

I shouldn't keep going.

I told myself I didn't want too anymore. I didn't. My skin was on fire, and I had to stop. It was repulsive. Depraved. It felt so right, the relief, but it was so very wrong. Pain twisted and spread, and I accepted it. I craved it, I needed it. My mind was a twisted mess and each violent stripe a balm.

Mum was banging around the house. I had no idea where Dad had gone to. I didn't care anymore, I didn't have it in me to. I curled up in that moment, built out of heartache and longing. Desperation. I breathed in the pain, hoping for peace. When I climbed into bed a while later, leg cleaned up and my mind silent, I remembered my phone on the floor. I found it half under the bed and swiped it open. Two new messages, both from Matty, who I had forgotten as swiftly as I'd let him take over my thoughts.

Matty: funnily enough, pretty much the same. I like a girl who just says it like it is.

Matty: I think I like a girl like you actually.

My heart skipped happily as I fell back onto the bed, starring at the ceiling once more. I touched my fingers to the scars and scabs on my thigh, souring everything.

I didn't think anyone could like a girl like me.

CHAPTER FIVE

My ass had barely hit the seat in form class before Megan had her nose half an inch from mine. Her wide eyes darted back and forth between my own two, her palms flat on the matte blue desk.

'Well?' she asked in a rush of minty breath. 'Did he message you? You think he's cute, right?'

'Hello to you too,' I greeted, folding down my umbrella. 'Yeah, last night. I haven't replied agai—hey!' Megan shoved her hand into my blazer pocket, fishing my phone out and unlocking it. We had long ago swapped passcodes, I had nothing on there to hide and there wasn't a thing I could say about her to anyone else that I wouldn't say to her face. A modern-day blood promise if you will. Not to mention it had come in handy more than once when we were out, since neither of us were particularly reliable with phone charging slash sobriety.

'Oooh this is cute. We like this. Yes, we do.'

She was talking more to herself than me.

'Just give it here, dick,' I said, grabbing it out of her hand. 'I don't even know what I'm supposed to say to that? Like, who even talks like that. We may be 16, but *Gossip Girl* this is not.'

'No, it definitely isn't. Your skirt would be about hip length if it was,' she paused, looking me over. 'And you'd have better hair. And nails. Yours are gross.'

'Thanks Megan. That's the ego boost I was after today.'

'You're welcome. But also, you need to text him back.'

'Yeah, I will. It's not a big deal.'

Liar. Such a liar.

Megan opened her mouth to speak but the—blessed—bell cut her off, Tash and Nic meandering in as it did, damp from a sudden burst of rain this morning. I typed out a quick *hey* to Matty and dropped my phone into my pocket. I wasn't all butterflies.

Not at all.

Tash and Nic were both in my first period class, so I fell into step beside them, listening to them talk about their weekends. A sliver of guilt crept up my neck as we wound our way around puddles that had formed in the shallow dips of the ground. Even though Tash had no idea what Mum had said about her, I knew. I hoped she hadn't noticed the dismissive way Mum looked at her.

'*Unlikely,*' I uttered under my breath.

'What?' Tash asked.

'What?' If I pretended that I had not spoken, maybe it would be true.

'You said unlikely? What's unlikely?'

I looked down at the murky little water pools as we walked. Far too shallow to drown myself in.

A shame.

'I was just thinking,' I peeked up at her quickly, curiosity on her carefully painted face. 'About how rude my Mum was to you and that it's unlikely you didn't notice,' I forced out. There were so many parts of my life I didn't talk about, or that I actively hid. My entire being was held together by a web of bold, open truths. So bright and distracting, tightly woven so the glinting wisps of secrets and lies couldn't be seen.

'Oh. Yeah, it's fine As. Like, she seems like a bitch, but she's hardly the first person to think I'm trash.' She shrugged her slim shoulders, seemingly not caring.

'Maybe you *are* trash. Just a thought,' Nic smirked. They traded insults all the way to class, each more absurd than the last, but full of humour.

The morning passed in fits and bursts, tedious and frustrated, and I was thankful when the lunch bell rung. I was ready to find the others. And complain.

I threw my bag on the now dry ground aggressively, tempted to throw myself with it.

'What is the ever-loving point of mathematics. If I need to do calculus as part of my future day job, please, somebody, push me into traffic,' I grumbled.

'Last week you said that calculus was super interesting and that you enjoyed the challenge.' Megan raised a slim blonde brow.

Rude.

'Last week Astor was wrong,' I said. 'As my best friend, you should have told last week Astor that she was wrong.' I kicked my bag closer to her, even if she had quite clearly failed me as a friend.

'Today Astor needs to stop talking in third person or today Nic is going to smack her,' Nic said, dropping to the ground and pulling out her lunch. I ignored her, what did she know.

'Also, can someone remind me why we decided that PE was the ideal filler class to take this year?' I lay on my stomach, poor abused bag forced to be a pillow. 'I fucking hate PE.'

'It's not that bad. I think Ms. Fisher has given up on us mostly. And by us, I mean everyone but Nicole.' Tash said. Nic was a natural athlete. She enjoyed the warm-up laps, the basketball drills, and the tennis workshops. It was disgusting, and I don't know why we kept her. We all decided that PE would be an easy grade for this year, and since this was our second to last year before graduation, there weren't many masochists picking PE, so we had all ended up in the same class. Nic was in her element, captain of the school hockey team, calm under pressure, and excited for a challenge. The rest of us? Not so much.

'I can't help but feel you dickheads would enjoy physical education a lot more if there was a lot less "physical" involved,' Nic said, her tone drier than a desert in a heat wave. She took PE very seriously.

'Wow. You're smarter than you look Nic,' Tash was on her back beside me, white heart-shaped sunglasses hid the fact that her eyes were closed. So, while I saw the apple Nic had been eating soar through the air towards her, Tash did not.

'Hey!'

'If you participated in class, you'd have caught that.'

'Fuck off Nicole,' Tash said, voice falsely sweet but cut with bitter.

I pulled my phone from my pocket, not at all helped by my chosen horizontal position, and barely supressed a squeal.

Matty.

He said he kept his phone off in class, only turning it on at lunch. I could live with that. I wondered idly where he sat, likely with Troy and his group, clear across the campus. I was typing out my reply as another notification appeared at the top of my screen, ominously displaying the words **'BROS AND HOES.'**

I was willing to bet that the severity of my eye roll would later be stated as my cause of vision loss. Dylan had created a group chat. I looked up to see the other three pulling their phones out as well, Nicole falling onto her back dramatically.

'I hate him,' she groaned.

'You don't. Nobody hates Dylan. He's a sweetheart. It'd be like hating Santa. A teenage sexy Santa. No one hates Santa.' Tash said, her eyes on her phone.

'Well I bloody hate Santa now!' I cried. 'Thanks Tash. Only you would ruin Santa.'

'Hey, some people are into that silver look. The beard. The suit. The big sack of joy.'

Now we were all gagging, Nic kicking her in the thigh as it all dissolved into laughter.

'For real though, why are we in a group chat. With Troy too. He's such an asshole,' Megan said, her exact words appearing in the group thread a second later. Troy insult included.

Dylan wanted to organise a group hang out for Saturday in town. I watched every agreeing message come through, hoping to see Matty throw out a yes. I turned to my friend.

'Megan, can I stay at yours this weekend?' I asked. Zero response. She was tapping away at her phone, a tiny smile quirked across her thin lips. I looked back at my own screen, expecting whatever she was smiling away at to pop up, but the chat rolled along without her.

'Meeegan, Megan.' I pestered. I was quite confident my maturity peaked at five. She read something and gave a tiny giggle, stopping abruptly like she'd caught herself doing something she shouldn't.

Interesting.

I typed her name in capitals and sent it to her, watching for the moment the notification popped up.

'What?' Sure enough, she looked up at me with her narrow face pinched.

'Hello friend, Megan dear. Thank you for your return. Pray tell, with whom are you messaging all your smiles to?'

'What? Can you talk like a normal person?' she asked, confused. Poor puzzled puzzler.

'If I must,' I sighed at the hardship. 'Who are ya talkin' to?'

'No one. Dad, actually. Just, uh, Dad...'

'Isn't your dad in class? Like, teaching?' I was fairly sure she was lying to me, but I couldn't work out why.

'Um, day off.'

She wouldn't look at me, her phone now tucked under her thigh. Tash and Nic were oblivious, bickering as usual and paying us no attention. I studied her face, as familiar as my own. Milky white skin, a little beauty mark on the crest of her cheekbone. Heat crept up her neck and bloomed across face. We didn't do secrets, it wasn't us. She was the most important person in my world though. Whatever it was she was keeping, I hoped she'd tell me soon.

'Oh cool. So, can I stay with you this weekend?' I asked, letting her story sit. She gave a tiny sigh of relief and finally met my eyes. Could I see the secret in hers?

'Of course you can, mi casa es tu casa,' she gave me a smile.

The bell cut off any need for me to reply. Three of us groaned, dragging ourselves off the ground for PE. One of us, a particularly lithe one of us with a shiny black bob and sharp grey eyes, leapt to her feet excitedly.

'It's PE bitches! Let's go.' Nic said, already walking away.

Fuck. Me.

We filed into the gym. Gleaming wood floors, the lines of the basketball court stark and white. It was warm, strokes of sunlight showing all the hidden dust particles and the air rich with the alluring scent of day-old sock and misery. I assumed the smells were similar.

PE class made my heart rate pick up from more than the physical activity. My shorts were about the same length as my uniform skirt, so my thighs were covered, but I didn't have to do cartwheels or climb a bastard rope in my skirt. My skirt stayed in place mostly. Good little skirt. I tried to keep the anxiety under wraps, being calm and having nothing phase me was how I preferred to come across. It was always harder in the days after I'd lost control though. My fingertips brushed the familiar pleated hem and the skin below. Warm to touch and unmarred. Always checking that nothing was visible so I could relax. Sort of.

We had two gyms, an 'old' and a 'new' one, as well as a space called "the activity room", which had a softer floor. Today we were set to continue with volleyball, which I did enjoy, despite my bitching and rampant anxiety. There was something deeply satisfying about spiking a ball towards Nicole. After a quick brief from our young, peppy teacher, we meandered into the changing rooms. In the actual room, it echoed like a tunnel. It smelt like chlorine, despite us not having a pool, and was rectangular with blue tiles from floor to ceiling. Everyone was pulling their PE uniform out. Bags were dropped without hesitation. Everyone tossing clothes and chucking shoes, eager to get back to the gym. I quickly redid my pony and changed out my shirt for my white tee with the school's name across the back. As soon as I lay hands on my shorts however, I realised I was in trouble. I had three pairs, all the same royal blue, the same repulsive, slippery material. Except one pair was shorter than the others. They were a slightly different style and cut higher, which was normally fine. Because normally, normally I didn't go full *Jason Vorhees* on my fucking thighs. There was no way they'd hide anything.

Around me the other girls were almost done, shoving their things away, heading back out to the gym, and I was locked in a mental loop. A hand landed on my bicep and my soul left my body.

'Hey what's wrong?' I could see my own panicked green eyes in the lens of Megan's glasses, eyebrows dipped together in concern. 'What do you need, As?'

I wasn't sure how to explain that my shorts were, in fact, too short.

'I can't wear these, they're...not long enough,' I stuttered out.

She looked me down and back up, her expression clearing as something seemingly made sense.

'Give them here then,' she held out her hand, palm up and I dropped them onto it like they were on fire. I'd like them better on fire. She pulled her own shorts down, replacing them with mine and handed hers over to me. 'Right, hurry up and put them on, cause I don't fancy running an extra warm up lap because we're slow, okay?'

She gave me a quick smile and went to join the class. I had no doubt she knew exactly why I was freaking out. I didn't deserve a friend like her.

I put on her shorts, stored my things, and followed her out. I told Megan to throw the shorts away after class.

I wouldn't make that mistake twice.

Chapter Six

Home wasn't too bad over the next few days as dad was mostly office bound at the moment, which meant office hours. Mum and I kept out of the other's ways for the most part, though she still insisted we all spent time together after dinner which consisted of watching two hours of tv as a family, while she steadily poured six-dollar wine down her throat. I felt like we were in a holding pattern, but I didn't know what for. I sat on the couch, pretending to watch what she chose and messaged Matty and Megan, excusing myself as soon as I felt it was safest to, so I could lay on my bed and do homework with Megan on speakerphone for company. Sometimes mum didn't care or notice if I left, and sometimes she called me a bitch and banged on my door on her own way to bed.

As always, Friday finally arrived. Dylan ambled down the bus aisle and dropped down next to me, rather than behind, just as I hit send on my message to Matty. We'd been messaging off and on, sending questions to each other at random. I was becoming mildly addicted, even if the questions were boring *get to know you, what's your favourite colour* type ones. I just wanted to talk to him alone, in person. Not at school in a dorky uniform.

'Texting Matty?' Dylan asked, eye-roll included.

'Yeah, just confirming he'll be there tomorrow.'

'Mmm yeah. Troy invited him.'

Distaste flavoured his words, though no one really seemed to like Troy. His wealth-driven arrogance made him one of the most popular in our grade, but also the one you endured simply so you weren't exiled.

'What did Troy do to you? I thought you were mates? Somehow...' I couldn't see how. He was an idiot.

'What? Troy's fine. He's a dick but he's always a dick. I don't like Matty.'

'What are you on about? He's lovely.' I was aghast.

'You're just saying that cause you think he's cute. He's a bit of a dick, man.' Dylan shrugged, like it was a foregone conclusion.

'He is cute, but he also likes to read and stuff.' My cheeks warmed, my fledgling crush more than obvious. 'Maybe you just need to spend more time with him?'

'Yeah, maybe. Obviously, you're a fan.'

His eyes studied my face, a little dip in his brow.

'Well, I mean, yeah. He's nice and...stuff.'

If my face were paper, it would be on fire right now.

'Hey, I'm nice to you.' He looked over at me and I promptly looked out the window. 'Dude, are you blushing. What?' he laughed. I refused to look at his brilliant, dumb smile. His voice dropped an octave, 'I'll try to like him if you do, As, for you, since you're my friend.'

We got off the bus, Dylan departing with his usual chin lift and setting off for his form class. I couldn't spot Megan anywhere but that wasn't entirely unusual. A bitch was sometimes late. Matty however, was leaning against a tree at the boundary of the school, trying to embody 80s rom-com bad boy, it would seem. I bounced on my toes a little, indecisive. I watched him put a cigarette to his lips and take a long drag. Mind made up, I made my way over.

'85% of head and neck cancer is linked to tobacco use, you know,' I said, smiling a little.

'Hello to you too, Astor. Is this your way of saying you care about my head and neck?'

He dropped the smoke on the ground, stubbed it out with his shoe and turned to me.

'I feel mildly invested in both, yes. I'm also not sure hospital gown chic is your style.'

'You wound me. I can pull off any look. Clearly.'

He held his arms out, quite clearly proud of his body. I wasn't going to turn down the chance of open perusal.

'Eh. You're okay.'

I shrugged, absolutely not willing to let him know I wanted to climb him like a tree. He laughed, loud and happy, and I bit my lip to fight my own smile.

'Are you still going tomorrow?' he asked.

'Oh yeah, I'll be with Megan. You?'

'I'll be there. Hoping to sit next to a certain girl.' He swung his bag over his shoulder, and we made our way into the school, cutting it mighty fine for the bell. 'Megan's the blonde with glasses and no tolerance for alcohol, right?'

'Yeah, that's her. She's wonderful sober. Way less tears.' I ignored the first part of his sentence entirely.

'So what are my odds then?' he nudged me with his elbow, playfully.

'Odds of what?' My heart rate kicked up a notch; I really hoped I was reading this whole situation right.

'Will you sit with me tomorrow?' his smile was crooked, a tiny bit shy and impossible to say no to.

'If you want me to, I'd like that,' I said, more serious than I intended, so I tacked a smile on.

The first bell sounded and Matty reached for my hand, giving it a little squeeze. 'Catch you round As, save me a seat tomorrow.'

He walked off to class, leaving me to scramble across the school to mine, even more excited to see him tomorrow.

Megan and I lay on her bed—in the fort that was somehow still standing—with some trashy slasher horror film on in front of us, though we were barely paying attention. I felt jittery, on edge. Like my blood was more alive than its standard version of alive. As much as I wanted to pretend that I didn't know why.

Matty.

Quite clearly, he was the cause. I was excited and nervous and it was weird.

We'd messaged more since yesterday, talking about books and movies. Arguing about books and movies mostly. I told him about the plans Megan and I had for London and a gap year. We discussed university pros and cons, and studying abroad instead of coming back. I couldn't shake the feeling that he was actually interested in me. As something more than a warm body to take to bed. Or car backseat, as was often the case.

He hadn't made a joke or anything when I'd told him I was pansexual. He smiled at me when he saw me at school, and he'd asked me to save him a seat tomorrow. Because he wanted to sit with me. That didn't count for nothing, surely.

Normally, our phones lay forgotten in our bags or lost in the tidal wave of crap on Megan's bed, but both of Megan and I had barely put them down since last night. I still had no clue who the heck she was talking to, and I was trying my absolute best to not steal glances at her screen, or try and read her facial expressions. Can't say I was entirely successful. I had watched a Shakespearean theatre worth of emotion flit across her face today alone. Her brows knit together in a negative line more often than I was comfortable with. I slid a little look her way again, we were hip to hip, with more space between our heads for the useful things like shoulders and arms. I recognised the familiar layout of Reddit and decided I'd take the moment to check in, as a good friend does. I threw my leg over her hips and sat up on top of her.

'Hey,' I grinned, as she jolted in surprise.

'Astor, I hate to fucking break this to you, but I'm actually quite fond of breathing.'

'If you managed to say that then you're fine. Anyway, I'm on your hips, not your chest. You are very dramatic, my friend.'

Smiling down at her, I chose to ignore her eye roll. She balanced her phone with its rainbow case on her forehead and looked up at me with a resigned sigh.

'To what do I owe this gross invasion of personal space, then. Do tell.'

'Real talk Meggy. Realz. The Z makes it real.'

I was fairly sure I could see the patience fading in her eyes. 'You know you can tell me things, right? We are two peas in the metaphorical pod of life.'

Large hand gestures, indicating said pod. Good work me.

'I know As, I tell you everything, always.' She looked over at the door, not happy with this conversational direction.

'Hey,' I lost the playful tone in my voice and turned her face back to mine, lowering my forehead to hers. 'I don't know who you're talking to, and that's okay. You're allowed to not tell me, to exist entirely outside this friendship. But I need to know you're okay, I need you to know this is a two-way street. And when—if—you're ready, I am here. You're my person.'

We were nose to nose, my hands on her cheeks, and her pale blue eyes dancing to catch mine. She let out a slow breath.

'I know. I'm okay. I just...need some time. You know you're my person too.'

'That's fine Megan. However...' I trailed off.

'What?'

'You can't like them more than me.'

'Oh for the love of—you're literally the most ridiculous person I have met.'

'FOR REALZ MEGAN.' I made my eyes as wide as I could, to convey the seriousness of this.

'I never will, Astor. Lord knows why, but you're my best friend, okay? Always.'

'Pinkie swear.'

'Fucking hell, are you six?'

'Yes.'

She wriggled her hand between us, forcing me to sit back so we could link our little fingers.

'Happy?' she asked, forcing a smile back.

'Promise me you're okay?'

'Promise. Now get off me. I want to show you the man with 75 stuffed rabbit toys hidden in his basement that his wife just discovered on Reddit.' She shoved me off, grabbing her phone and unlocking it with her face.

'Sweet lord Jesus. Gimme.'

After changing through both sets of clothing I had packed as well as half of Megan's wardrobe, we were absolutely the last to reach everyone. The group chat had directed us to the one cinema in our town, as through vote it had been decided we would be seeing a movie. The smell of popcorn seeped into our clothes the moment we stepped into the foyer, with its crazy patterned blue carpet and royal red walls.

Matty was easy to find, like familiarity with him from messages and brief contact somehow made the back of his head recognisable in a crowd. I was happy to see Dylan talking to him, in his typical animated fashion. Hands waving around and lean body moving in sync with the flow of whatever he was saying and feeling. We made our way over, there were about ten of us in total, including Tash, Nic and Troy.

Dylan's face split into his familiar easy grin. He wrapped his arm around my waist, pulling me in for a quick hug.

'Hey Dylan. Matty.'

I gave Matty a little smile, nervous to see him. What if I wasn't really what he was attracted to? If he suddenly noticed that I had hips and shoulders and boobs. I wasn't blonde like Tash, willowy like Megan or Nicole. Or—as I confirmed with a quick look over my shoulder—seemingly unlike every other female here. I felt like a potato, and not a cute one. Dylan squeezed my side, and I came back down to earth a little. Megan was the one who made me feel free, but Dylan somehow grounded me. Matty's steel grey eyes were focused on Dylan's arm around me, his hand on my hip.

'Hi, I'm Megan. We didn't really meet properly at the bonfire as I was testing my alcohol holding abilities,' Megan announced, Matty's eyes snapping to her face.

'Hey, you okay?' Dylan's breath tickled my neck as he whispered in my ear. I gave him a nod and a smile and stepped out of the circle of his arm.

'I'm good,' I said. Quiet enough for just him. 'Just nervous.'

Megan and Matty were talking, though Matty barely looked away from me and Dylan.

'So, what are we seeing then?' I asked.

'That's what we were trying to decide, actually. Dylan was telling me about some new dinosaur thing that's out soon, but I think right now there's only an action car chase one on at this time,' Matty said, blatantly looking me up and down as he did so.

I felt heat creep up my neck and into my cheeks.

'Oh well. Ha. That one sounds quite swell. I mean, good. I think, anyway.'

Why on earth was English suddenly hard.

'You alright, Astor? Don't think I've seen you quite this red before.'

A hand came down on my shoulder, a hand connected to Troy. Was I too old to say "ew cooties"? Cause that's how that felt.

'Please don't touch me, Troy. I don't want to have to bathe in bleach later.'

I stepped away, and he barked out a laugh, though his eyes narrowed at me. It was nice to know I wasn't his favourite person either. Dylan cut off whatever Troy was planning to say next, herding us to the ticket counter and then snacks. I said hi to a few of the other girls, making small talk about classes and the gossip that was currently making the rounds—a teacher and her supposed "relations" with a student. Matty was a sort of ghost at my side, offering me soft smiles when our eyes caught, but talking to the others.

We filed into our row in the cinema, chairs a plush maroon on the worn black floor. Drinks were carefully settled into cup holders, and feet already kicked up onto the row in front of us. I focused on opening my Skittles; a steady thrum of excitement coursing through me at the prospect of being in the dark with Matty for two hours.

We sat Megan at the end, then me, Matty, Dylan and so on with Troy at the other, nicely far away. The lights dimmed to that in-between level of dark, and the ads and previews started rolling. The rest of our group becoming seasoned movie critics from one heartbeat to the next.

'Can you not suck face with Matty in the dark, cause I feel like I'll hear you and I don't want that. Please and thank you,' Megan stage-whispered into my shoulder. Not even remotely quiet.

Dylan's head popped forward, inky fringe swinging out and a frown above his eyes. I dared a quick look at Matty, hoping the building would fall on me, or a lightning strike, perhaps. Literally anything. He was tossing popcorn into his mouth, eyes on the screen. Oblivious. I thanked baby Jesus for doing me this one small favour and glared at my so-called best friend.

'Can you shut up? Flipping hell, Megan.'

'What? I'm sure it's no surprise to him, dude.'

She helped herself to a fistful of my Skittles, shrugging.

The lights dimmed further, ready for the main event, so I wriggled back into my seat to get comfortable and snuck one last little look at the lovely silhouette of Matty's head. Our eyes met and once more my face was a brilliant crimson. Thankfully, he couldn't see that. I gave him what I hoped was my best smile, and his teeth flashed in return. Lord, I couldn't deal with this. My stomach was practicing the floor routine of an Olympic gymnast and we had barely begun. Two hours felt like an entirely too long prospect now.

The movie was heavy on the car chases and explosions, and low on believable plot. It stumbled along well enough, the occasional blinding flashes of white breaking up the darkness and throwing Matty's profile into view. His sharp jaw, straight nose, hair artfully styled. It was almost rude how lovely he looked. A smile would pull up his lips sometimes and I knew he could feel my eyes on him, but I couldn't resist. Sitting in the dark like it was just him and me felt almost like a date. As the movie worked its way to the predictable finale, Matty's hand slid across my knee. Softly, a gentle squeeze, before he turned his hand over in the open invitation to join mine with his. His fingers were long, bigger than my slender ones, almost uncomfortable to be linked together. I didn't care. I was holding his hand. He had reached for me. I wasn't imagining it. Megan nudged her knee against my other, reminding me that we weren't actually alone. I couldn't make out her face entirely, but I could imagine the raised brow and smirk she would be wearing, knowing her as I did. The lights came on as the credits rolled, and Matty stood immediately, dropping my hand into my lap. Dropping my heart into my stomach just as fast as I watched him stretch, not even a brief look my way.

We stood outside blinking in the brutal reality that was natural daylight, and decided to all walk down to the park via Hungry Jack's. Megan and I dropped behind the group a little, their dissection of the film was not something we needed.

'*Matty and Astor sitting in a tree, K-I-S-S-I-N-G,*' Megan sung under her breath, complete with audible kiss at the end.

'Someone will have you murdered one day and I, for one, won't be sad.'

'I saw you, holding hands.'

'Yeah...but he basically dropped it like I was on fire when the lights came on. I don't think he's even looked at me since,' I said in a single breath, unable to hide how I felt from Megan, dork or not. 'Like that's weird, right?'

'Dude we just sat there for two hours. He probably just wanted to have life return to his body again.'

'Yeah. Yeah, you're right. Ugh, why am I being this person.'

'Cause you like him, dickhead.'

'Okay, but I've liked plenty of people before and not overthought it this bad.'

'Maybe you like him a bit more than usual. Which is fine. Personally, I can't see the appeal,' she coughed a little. 'Anyway. You're fine, As. You're good. Just go with it.'

'I fucking hate when you're right,' I smiled at her and pulled open the door to Hungry Jack's.

We'd barely made it in, when Dylan forced us to a halt, brown paper bag in hand.

'I have obtained fries and onion rings. We don't have to stand in here with the lesser folk,' he said, as he gave the bag a shake. 'Let's go.'

'I love onion rings. Thank you, friend. You are a king amongst men, Dylan.'

I held the door open once more, giving him a small bow. Happy with his little smile in return.

By the time everyone else made it to the park, Megan, Dylan, and I had eaten the contents of the bag and were lying on the sharp grass, heads together. Laughing at Dylan and his bullshit stories and watching the sky strip out of its afternoon colours and into its dusky evening wear. Matty dropped to the ground next to me, lazy grin breaking out across his tan face.

'Hey.' I bit my lip, not used to feeling out of my depth but, lord, did he make me feel that way.

'Hey yourself.' He reached forward, running his finger down the bridge of my nose. 'Want to go for a walk?'

I hadn't noticed the group had thinned, Troy and a few of the others must have left. Dylan and Megan were laughing about who knew what, and no one else seemed to be looking our way. I gave him a quick nod.

'Sure, sounds good.'

I stood up, brushing non-existent grass and dirt off my ass. The park had walking trails, winding through water features, little ponds, and paths of overgrown trees. I followed behind him slightly, appreciating the view of his denim covered butt, and accepting that he was in control of destination. I wasn't stupid. Well, not entirely. I'd been asked the walk question before, at parties typically. When my nerves had been given a chance to swim in alcohol and mellow. Right now though? Right now they were swimming in cola and onion rings. Onion rings. Jesus.

He wandered down a path where the light was weaker, snuffed out under the canopy above us. The trees whispered, tired and weary, leaves laced together. Some were older, trunks bowing forward, as ailing branches tickled the pebbles of the ground. Matty stopped and looked at me, eyes soft, that easy smile. Hand outstretched. I laced my fingers with his once more, praying my palm wasn't sweaty with nerves, and that all of this was leading where I hoped it would.

He tugged me down on the park bench, grey from weather and witness to many first moments, I was sure. I sucked my lip between my teeth, eyes on my knees but flicking up to meet his.

'Astor,' my name was an exhale from his lips.

It wasn't full dark yet, just picturesque, intimate. A beautiful place for a kiss. A first kiss between two people. I let myself study his face, the smooth plains of his cheeks and kissable lips, the top one fuller than the bottom. This was a book moment. A stomach swooping, toe-tingling moment.

His hand cupped my jaw, fingertips in my hairline. Leaning into me with his eyes closed, lashes against his cheek. I didn't close mine until the last second. Wanting to savour a kiss that wasn't fuelled by desperate hormones and vodka. My own picture-perfect moment, for once. My heart rate hummed in my veins.

My eyes slid closed as his lips met mine. Softly, sweetly. One little kiss. Two. Then three. His hand tangled in my hair, his tongue into my mouth. I waited for the fireworks, for the tingles and the swooping. My scalp stung where my hair was pulling, he tasted like fries and cigarettes. It felt like any other kiss. He bit my lip in what I imagine was supposed to be a sexy way, but just smarted. I pulled away, schooling my face into a smile. He ran a thumb over where his teeth had just been.

'Sorry As, you're hard to resist,' he smiled at me, his lips red from our kiss, smile in place but eyes lit up.

'It's okay, just took me by surprise,' I smiled back. Disappointed. Not with him, not at all with him. Disappointed that the Disney moment wasn't real.

Here sat this beautiful boy, tousled hair, and bedroom eyes, wanting me as much as I wanted him, apparently, and there was no magical earth-shifting moment.

How on brand for my life.

Lost in my own thoughts, I didn't realise when he had stood.

'Let's go back. Wouldn't want the others to have to come find us.'

He threw me a wink, turning back the way we'd come. I trailed behind him, reliving the kiss and searching for sparks.

Chapter Seven

I was still turning the kiss over in my head the next day, sitting in the front seat of Callie's piece of shit Honda, as she drove me home. I opened my messages, scrolling to the one I'd received from Matty a couple hours ago.

Matty: hey babe how r u? im still thinking bout that kiss

Three flame emojis that followed his text. Clearly, he wasn't facing the same uncertainty I was. Though there was a fair chance I was just over-thinking everything.

'Hey Cal?'

I was going to employ my sister for wisdom. That's what they were for, right?

'I'm not stopping so you can wind the window down. It's not my fault it's jammed and needs to be pushed down from the outside as well as wound. She is old Astor. *Old.*'

She looked over at me, eyes wild like she was possessed. The faded patch-work blue hatchback didn't quite fit her beach babe aesthetic, but our parents had bought it, so she didn't complain.

'Don't worry, I've long accepted that I will simply run out of breathable air in this disaster,' I sighed.

'That's really offensive to Hortensia.'

Callie gave the steering wheel a fond rub and I resisted an eyeroll, barely. I wasn't questioning the name again. I didn't need another ten-minute spiel about how the name called to her after she watched Matilda. Again. As an adult.

'Uh huh. I actually just wanted to ask, maybe, about a dating thing? Maybe.'

'I'm listening,' she grinned.

What was it about saying all the words out loud that was making me sweat? Maybe just the fact that this absolutely felt like a little girl crush, and I was an idiot. Probably that. And the whole admitting *I liked him* thing, I guess.

'Um, do you think when you uhm...kiss someone you're meant to...be with, that it feels different? Like it means more, so it feels special or something?'

I focused on the chipped black polish on my nails, flaking little pieces off. Not looking at my sister.

'Nah I reckon it's all the same.' I felt her eyes on me briefly and my hopes did a pathetic leap before she ploughed on. 'Kissing's pretty gross when you think about it. It's all *hey I like you, let me lick inside your mouth.* Or maybe I've just never kissed anyone worthwhile. It could be either. Dating is shit and I don't recommend it.'

'Gross Callie, what the hell,' I screwed up my nose, not entirely sure what I had expected. That definitely wasn't it though. Callie was dreamy candlelit dinners and *The Bachelor* marathons sort of girl.

'I'm going through a dry spell and could be the tiniest bit salty,' she frowned.

'Sometimes the "half" in "half-sister" is glaringly obvious. Now, for example.'

I watched her roll her eyes, smiling to herself.

I considered what she'd said, salty or not. Maybe I'd just built it all up in my head. Maybe it was a perfectly fine kiss. Maybe it was just me.

The world passed by as I stared out the window, thinking. The familiar shapes thatched together, ribbons of vibrant greens and earthy browns marking the change from town to country. As we got closer to home, the changes in myself felt more pronounced. I fought down my hair-trigger temper and all the future words I had. Silenced the version of me that danced in the kitchen with Megan and laughed like the world wasn't on fire. Coming home was a matter of slipping one mask off for another. I'm sure if you studied them side by side you'd see their differences, folded into their faultless alabaster structure. The studious set to my brow, neutral smile fixed in place—smooth and faultless—the false perfection that 'home Astor' strived for.

We pulled through the gate, and Callie turned the car off. We sat in silence for a beat, as I think most people do, staring blankly at the dulling sky.

'I think for some people—maybe most people—there's a moment. Whether they're dating or know each other or have just met, there's a moment where they just *know* when someone is something special. Special to them. I don't know if it's a kiss or a look or a touch. I'm not sure if it feels like fireworks or butterflies or whatever other cliché things we're told.'

Her voice was quiet, the easy-going tone from before non-existent. I sucked on my bottom lip, letting her words sink in. 'It could be one person in a lifetime, or it could be a dozen. I don't think there's a rule to how many people you can fall in love with. But that's just what I think anyway.'

She got out then, leaving me to wonder if there'd been a moment between me and Matty and I'd somehow missed it.

Dinner was quiet and went predictably well. It felt so normal and like a family with no boozy skeletons in the proverbial closet, simply because Callie was there. It wasn't often she came for one, so Mum had put in a bit of effort. Table set and dessert included. Mum had been sipping from her familiar teacup since we'd gotten home, though she was perfectly happy, and Callie being present kept her so.

I felt a little closer to Callie after the car conversation. Usually it was like a gulf lay between us, about a decade wide and seemingly impossible to bridge. I wanted to be close, like "real" sisters with inside jokes and secrets to keep. I wanted that more than I would ever say out loud. But we were different in so many ways that even if we tackled the age difference, the path to sisterhood was littered with many other things.

Mother, for one.

I helped Callie wash and dry the dishes, answering her questions about Megan and school. Side stepping the pointed ones about relationships, with the intimacy of the car removed from the equation. She would tell me about her few friends, all like her with big smiles and perfect tans. Like I knew their names and faces well. I did not. I didn't think I'd even met half of them. Presently, she was telling me about her new co-worker. She worked as a medical receptionist for a swanky specialist in town, all chrome and glass and Botox. The new girl kept getting lost in the building, turning up on the wrong floor continuously and Cal was laughing her ass off as today the poor thing had somehow ended up in the basement.

'So she gets back to the desk, hair stuck to her forehead, and she looks at me and goes: "Callie I swear I'm not this stupid, it has to be the elevator!" And I swear, Astor, she absolutely has to—'

Whatever the new girl had, I didn't get to find out, as mum's voice snapped through the house.

'Fuck off. I'm not going back to the fucking doctor!' the slightest slur tainting her words.

We both turned toward the living room, Callie still elbow-deep in dirty sink water washing the final pan.

'Some things never change,' she gave me a small, indulgent smile, rolling her eyes and returning back to the pan.

I bobbed my head, agreeing with her and drying without thought.

Some things never change.

Callie let the water out and started to help dry, wilfully oblivious to the rising tones. I placed the plate in the cupboard, dropped the towel on the bench, and went immediately to my room without looking back.

Some things never change.

How many times had I tried to tell Callie that things, in fact, *did* bloody change? Had changed. How many times had I called Callie asking to be picked up? Maybe they were just arguing like every other couple likely does, but I knew that this was the tip of the iceberg. There was no way to tell if this would end in mum crawling into bed angry or her, *oh I don't know*, chasing me down the road with a knife.

I shoved in my headphones, sliding the volume on my phone up as high as I could bear, and started stripping out of my clothes. Callie's indifference was infuriating. I didn't care what time it was, I wanted my pjs, my bed, and loud music. Or maybe I'd get some reading done.

Stepping into my sleep shorts with all the grace of a newborn mule, I barely noticed my door opening but I sure as shit felt the pinch Callie delivered to my upper arm.

'The fuck?' I yanked out my headphones, anger ratcheting up at my sister's intrusion.

'I was coming to see if you were okay, since you ran off. And to say goodbye. Then I saw your leg,' she sighed, pinching the bridge of her nose. 'I thought you'd be past this shit. You're 16, for Christ's sake.'

'What do you mean "*past this shit*", Callie?!'

Heat crawled up my neck and into my face, fuelled by shame and sealed with anger. I wanted to meet her eyes, to sound confident and defend myself somehow, but my voice was a frustrated whisper.

'Don't be stupid, you know what I mean. The "*poor me pity party*" you've got happening on your thigh.'

'You don't get it, Cal, what it's like here. What she's like when she's had more than one bottle. How much she hates me.' I forced my eyes up, the blatant disbelief in hers giving my tears permission to spill over. 'Callie...she really scares me.'

My voice fell apart under the weight of what those five words meant.

'Oh she does not. God, you're beyond dramatic. Our mother drinks a bit, Astor. So do a lot of people. A slap is nothing. Did you stop to think maybe she's got bigger issues than you? Maybe you should be less concerned about yourself and more about how you can help her. She does everything for you.'

She turned back to the door, done with our conversation. Desperation filled me, clawing its way up my throat. I needed her to understand.

'Callie, please,' I reached for her arm. 'She doesn't just fall asleep. You don't know what it's like when she comes into my room at night and yells at me. She's always telling me how she hates me, doesn't want me. She hurts me. She does, I swear. I wouldn't make this up. She throws things at me, her glass and my books. She pushes me into the wall and squeezes my throat, and I'm scared. Please,' I pleaded, each word tasting like desperation on my tongue.

'Astor,' she sighed, exasperated. 'She isn't perfect, but this is ridiculous. You only have one mother, and you should love her, and be kind to her. You're almost an adult. Time to grow up. Stop being so dramatic and stop making stuff up. Half the words from your mouth are a lie, I swear.'

She pulled away from me and left, shaking her head. My hand dropped to my side as I sank down on my bed. I just wanted her to listen, to hear me. Any sisterly closeness I felt earlier was gone. I let her words play in my head without restraint. Testing how they felt. Maybe I was being dramatic. I wasn't the easiest person to like. I knew that, and mum was never awful to Callie like she was with me. She adored Callie. Maybe it was me. I was where the fault lay.

I focused on the carpet under my feet, trying to count each little thread, and not feel the consuming sadness twisting in my chest. Not the whisper on its heels telling me relief was available, that mental freedom was razor-shaped and within reach. I shut that down immediately, rolling onto my side and stuffing my headphones into place.

Mum and Dad were still fighting, entirely oblivious to what had just taken place between Callie and me. Their voices rose and fell, the anger from Mum crystal-clear compared to Dad's almost monotone. I closed my eyes and fought to bury tonight in the recess of my mind. I didn't need to cut. I'd do better, and then Callie wouldn't look at me the way she had tonight, like I was beyond hope.

My head throbbed, and the music certainly wasn't helping, but there was no way I could turn it off and listen to them arguing. Weighing up my options, I decided that slipping down the hallway to the bathroom, and ultimately some ibuprofen, was worth being near my parents. A bare two minutes later, and I was dry swallowing the chalky white pills and avoiding the mirror at all costs. I didn't need to see my puffer fish impersonation up close.

No thank you, sir.

I stepped out of the bathroom, ready to sink back into music and bed, when mum lurched out of the separate toilet and straight into me.

'Why the fuck are you standing here?'

Her eyes were slightly unfocused, and she'd spilt something down her front. Her slow blink and sneer made for an unmatched pair on her ageing face. Dad came up behind her, tired and drawn. Before I could get so much as a word out, he put his hand on her arm, talking to her in what I imagine he thought was a soothing tone, but one I knew would absolutely set her off.

'Helen, just leave her alone, she isn't doing anything.'

'Don't you dare tell me what to do, she's my daughter,' she growled, eyes trapping me in place, though I knew I needed to get out of the way. 'MY daughter. She is the reason I'm this way and you know it.'

I should have been used to it, after all this time, but no matter what I told myself, her words mattered to me. Each one was saved, preserved as a whole and tucked away. Saved for me to pull out and try to unravel when I was alone in the dark. When the only things awake were dying stars and nightmares.

'Helen...' Dad sighed, igniting her fuse in that pale-yellow hallway.

'No! I had her for you. Not for me, for *you*. You wanted a kid, and here you go. One fucking kid. One kid who has been nothing but work from the start.'

Tears rolled down my face and fell from my jaw rapidly, unstoppable at this stage. She stepped closer and we were eye-to-eye. I couldn't help but search her face, desperate for a glimpse of...something. Some flicker of love, of sober mum.

My mum.

'You ruined my fucking life,' she snarled.

And my heart skipped. 'Fuck. You.'

The words wavered between us for a single, naked moment before they're swept out of the way as her arm cut through the air, palm cracking against the damp skin of my cheek.

Chapter Eight

My face was on fire, the sting from her hand lingered, and I wasted barely a breath before I fled to my room. I could hear dad yelling behind me and I had no idea if it was at me or her. I couldn't believe I did that, telling her to fuck off. I was such a fucking idiot, letting my stupid mouth go that way. I wished I could bleach the words out of my head as I crawled under the covers. I had ruined her life. She had me to keep dad and I had ruined her life. I'd heard it before, not quite like that, but what if it was true?

Dramatic. Pathetic. Ruined her life. Grow up Astor.

My hand shook as I touched my cheek, hot like day-old sunburn and humming with the memory of her hand. The front door slammed at the other end of the house, and I knew dad had gone out. I wondered, just for a moment, if the thought of taking me with him even blinked in his mind. Did he think of me at all?

His face in my own mind was weary. Tired and worn down from the gradual uptick in mum's drinking and ranting.

'ASTOR!'

My name was slurred and punctuated with the sharp sound of mum's fist on my door. I barely had time to scramble out of bed before she was in my room. Her eyes were wild and rimmed in red, as she swayed on the spot, glaring at me. There was no way to tell what she wanted. Sometimes she came in to call me a bitch, and sometimes she wanted to rant, get in my face so I could smell the wine that drowned our lives in this misery, or throw her glass across a room. I didn't have to wait long. Her hands slid into her hair, fingers digging into her scalp, and she screamed. Unadulterated and inhuman, one long cry of hatred before she lurched towards me. I stepped back and turned, desperately trying to unlatch my window and jump free, while her hands curled into my shirt.

'Mum no, please, get off me,' I cried and her nails bit into my skin. I pushed myself out of her grasp and into the night, while she yelled that she would get me and that it would be the end of me.

I landed on my hands and knees, the shock shot through my shoulders and dropped me onto my tummy. Our house was slightly elevated, enough that you could jump out but not climb back in, and the ground was hard as hell. With a groan, I rolled onto my back, looking up at the silky black sky. Artificial light poured from my window, ruining its perfection. My chest ached, my stomach was threatening to come up, I felt so sick and so very tired. But mum was still yelling, her voice fading as she moved through the house and took her vile words with her.

And I knew, *I knew* like the sky was blue and the grass was green, that she was coming to get me.

In her head, she could drag me inside because I was *hers*.

I knew I needed to get up and move before she got to me, but my phone was inside. My keys. My legs and feet were bare. All I had on were panda printed sleep shorts and a t-shirt—hardly the ideal attire to be out of doors in the middle of the night. Indecision was keeping me stuck in place, unsure if I should hide, sneak back inside, and pray mum forgot about me...or what? Run? I looked around, the dark, a hindrance and a help when again, my name was shouted. Closer than I wanted.

Around the corner of the house came my mother, no shoes, jeans undone, and a brief glint in the dim light tore my eyes from her sunken face, taking in what she had in her hand. Her grip was tight on a handle, the steel, a gentle curve to the tip.

For now at least, the knife pointed to the ground.

Oh God.

All her vile words from earlier were obliterated as she filled the empty space between us with new ones.

The entire scene before me was completely surreal, like a B-rate slasher film come to life. Except in this particular slasher, I was the intended victim.

Decision made, I jumped to my feet and took off out our farm-style front gate. My feet pounded against the road, little loose stones biting into the soft soles, not at all used to the unprotected beating they were being subjected to. It was just under a kilometre to the next house, and I had not entirely worked out what I was going to do when I got there. If I got there.

'Don't you run away from me you little bitch!' The voice of my mother felt like a whip in the night.

I could hear her footfalls behind me, heavier and less coordinated, but still coming faster than I expected. For a fall down drunk, there was truly very little falling taking place there.

My lungs were on fire, burning from the crisp night air I was forcing in. Every inhale sharp, I could practically feel the adrenaline frantic in my veins. Trees rose up beside me, leaching even more colour from the already soulless night—boxing me into this nightmare. A tiny flash of light flickered through their branches and, honest to God, hope exploded inside me. Mr. Sanders's house. Steve. He was dad's friend and he'd let me in, I knew it. Then I could call Megan and she would come and get me. Tomorrow I'd tell dad and pray he listened.

Steve's driveway split through the wall of trees, his large white house was to one side, and in the daylight, brightly coloured rose bushes lined the path. Right now it looked cold and dark, save for one small glowing window. I almost missed dad's truck parked to one side, and seeing the familiar shape stopped me in my tracks for the scantest of heartbeats, until the sound of mum behind me pushed me forward.

God, I was so close I could almost feel the light on my sweat clammy skin. I flew up the wooden front steps and slammed my palms hard against what I knew to be a forest green front door.

'Dad! Steve! Help me! Dad are you here? Help!' I hit the door again and again, frantically looking behind me as the sound of my mother grew closer. 'Let me in, please! Dad! Steve! Somebody, PLEASE!' sheer desperation strained every word.

Please, please let them be here and not out in Steve's car at some fucking pub.

I didn't know what I would do if they weren't here. I pulled back to smack the door again, another plea on my tongue but the door wasn't there anymore. Blue flannel pants and sleep in his deep brown eyes, Steve stood in front of me, whiskey tumbler in hand. Dad stood behind him, brow furrowed. I took one quick peek over my shoulder, then pushed past them and into the safety of the house.

'Shut the door please, God, shut the door. I don't want her to find me, please.'

Tears were drying on my cheeks and my voice shook as I fought to catch my breath.

'Astor? What the hell is going on?' Dad asked, his voice gruff.

Steve quickly locked the door, then turned to look at me, confusion and a touch of anger marred his weathered face, and his greying brown hair was sticking up in all directions. I couldn't remember anything about him other than his name and that he was a widower with no children.

'Mum. She came at me with a knife. I jumped out my window and ran. I didn't know what else to do but run, I had nothing on me,' the words fell out of my mouth in a rush. 'She's going to kill me, she hates me so much she actually wants me to die. I didn't know what to do, I'm sorry. So, so sorry.'

For the barest of seconds, dad just looked at me, while Steve sighed and downed the remainder of his drink. I was practically bent double in his kitchen trying to desperately calm my breathing at one in the morning.

'ASTOR! WHERE THE FUCK ARE YOU! COME ON ASTOR, IM NOT GOING TO FUCKING HURT YOU!' Mum screamed, alcohol still more than evident in her voice as she moved towards the house.

Steve sighed again, 'John, what do you want to do. I can call the police?'

'Let's just see what she does. Turn the lights off and she might just go home, easier for all of us.'

Biting back an argument, I sunk to the floor. After a beat of hesitation, his eyes locked on my father, Steve flipped the switch and plunged us into darkness. I curled up on the cold wooden floor, as close to the counter as physically possible and wrapped my arms around myself. Steve sat down next to me, not looking at me or dad who stood with his back against the wall. Together, with only the sound of my still racing pulse ringing in ears, we waited. Mum had reached the steps now, the dull thud of her footfalls were clear in the tense quiet. With no way to actually see her, I strained to hear what she was doing and where she was as she moved around outside.

'Astor! I know you're in there, you twisted little bitch.' The door shook as she tried to get through. 'Let me in, you little slut. I am your MOTHER!'

My *mother*. This wasn't how a mother was supposed to treat her child. My stomach riled and I tried to make my body as small as humanly possible in the dark lemon-scented kitchen. I could hear her feet scuffing across the porch and back down the steps and I prayed that she was going. I peeked up at Steve and we locked eyes, but if I had hoped to find some sort of comfort there, I wouldn't. He looked away quickly, and I felt alone even though I wasn't.

Mum was making her way around the outside of the house now apparently, banging on the windows and walls, screaming for me to come out or to let her in. The minutes stretched on until finally there was silence. We continued to sit in the dark for a while longer, it felt safe somehow, the dark keeping all the monsters hidden. Turning the light on would throw all of this into reality.

I needed time to try and shove all my wild thoughts into some sort of order, to work out what next. I wanted Dad to finally do something. I had wanted him to go out there to tell mum to leave, to call the police. To do anything at all. I wanted Steve to tell dad he was weak and tell him to help me, but he didn't. He'd gone with what dad wanted, his friend. This wasn't normal. She had never chased me like this before, never used a knife. Never said she would kill me and had the weight of conviction bringing each word into reality. But because she drank every day and was a good time with everyone else, this was okay?

Fuck this.

Steve stood, awkward from the long stint on the floor and turned the lights back on. His house was stacked with boxes, a maze I hadn't noticed when I had forced my way in. Moving, I guess. Dad hadn't moved, his features stoic, not so much a glance my way. I told myself it didn't hurt.

'Can I have a word, John?' Steve got his attention, dad's eyes snapped to his. 'Astor, go down to the living room. We won't be long and then your dad can take you home.'

I was moving before he had finished speaking and let myself sink into the velvety peach couch in the box filled room, pulling my knees up to my chin. I kept turning tonight over in my head, trying to understand where I'd gone wrong. What I could have done different, so that I didn't end up here. I shouldn't have told her to fuck off. Sometimes my frustration with her got the better of me and I knew that. But tonight, tonight she really wanted to hurt me, and I didn't understand. She was my mum.

Dad and Steve were arguing. I couldn't quite make out everything he was saying but managed to catch the odd word from their library volume fight. 'Astor,' 'knife,' and 'drunk' all featured. I closed my eyes, embarrassed about everything that made me who I was and focused on deep breathing the faint smell of furniture polish, as my heart rate settled. Back to normal and not "running for my life" rhythm.

Maybe Steve seeing this was a good thing. He was my witness now, my proof. It wasn't just my word against hers, but someone else who had witnessed what had happened. Had heard her screaming at me, trying to get to me. There was no way dad could ignore this; it wasn't like anything else she had done. This time, it was a big deal. It *felt* like a big deal. This wasn't my fault, and it was stupid to feel embarrassed. Dad would see. This was different.

I was sleepy, warm in the fuzzy sofa and heated house. Abruptly, the voices stopped, and dad stepped into the room, Steve waiting behind him.

'We're going,' Dad said, voice void of emotion.

'What's happening?' I asked, looking between them both. 'Can I call Megan?'

'Nothing. And no, don't be ridiculous. Your mum is just having a bad night. Let's go.'

I don't know what I expected and, really, it was stupid of me to have expected anything other than this, but I had. My eyes burned viciously with tears.

'John,' Steve spoke from the hall and his tone was harsh.

'Thanks Steve, but I'll just grab her and be out of your way. Sorry we bothered you this late.'

His words were slow. Deliberate and careful, like he was fighting a simmering rage. His deep tone was so familiar to me, but not what I craved. Not the comfort I was desperate for. He was just going to take me home. No mention of where mum had gone.

'John, Helen was out of control tonight. I'll say it again,' his arms folded over his barrel chest. 'Get her into rehab. Don't make me call the police.'

Dad said nothing. He motioned for me to follow, turned, and made his way out through the kitchen. It all felt surreal, like I hadn't been on this floor half an hour ago with my heart in my throat. My eyes were wet as I moved on autopilot.

Dad faced Steve briefly. 'Thanks again. We won't bother you again. Come on, As, get in the truck.' Without another word, or even a glance in my direction, Dad turned and made his way back to the driver side.

Steve looked at me and shrugged his shoulders, a deep sigh escaping. He'd tried, I guess. He gave me a small grimace and went back inside his warm house, the door snicking firmly shut behind him.

As quickly as hope had swelled up inside me earlier, it was even quicker to leave. It didn't matter that I had run for my life tonight, that the soles of my feet were a web of cuts from stones viciously breaking through my skin. Dad was going to take me home and this would just be another night in the books for him. Bile raced up inside me, and I sent a silent 'sorry' to Steve as I emptied my entire stomach contents onto his lawn. With a shaky hand I wiped my mouth. I was utterly, devastatingly crushed. Dad was the person who should protect me, should put my wellbeing before alcohol and his friends and her. Mum was slowly destroying his only daughter and somehow, *somehow*, she could do no wrong in his eyes. I was just there, on the sidelines, waiting for it all to end.

I looked up at the sky again, the swirl of stars, magical and infinite. I wanted so much more than this. University, a gap year in London, a life and love and feelings that were vibrant and hopeful. That was what I wanted.

But how?

It felt as though the very seams of who I was were violently tearing apart, each fragile one worthless and discarded. This was it. It would always be this and right now it felt terminal. Dad banged his knuckles on the window, letting me know he was done waiting. I took a deep breath, then another, and crossed the cold lawn to his truck.

The drive was short. Too short to come to terms with my mother wanting me gone and my father not caring.

Chapter Nine

I tried to focus on my book, but my mind kept drifting off to stand in the hallway of last night, my brain determined to keep that particular movie reel crisp. Frustrated, I shoved the damn thing back in my bag, knocking my raw thigh in my haste.

'Motherfucker,' I hissed out, eyes screwed shut.

'Not what I'd call lady-like, Astor. I expect better from you.'

Dylan stood at the end of my seat, arms stretched holding onto the bar above and all of his perfect teeth on display.

'I think we can both agree that the chances of me ever being lady-like are about the same as you developing humility,' I smiled back. It was hard not to with Dylan.

'You are so rude. It wounds me. Shame really, as I have a gift for you. Milady.'

He dropped into the seat at my side and presented me with a small container of what appeared to be brownies.

'Is this your dad's triple chocolate double layer brownie?'

My eyes grew wide in my face, which given their size was quite a feat. One of Dylan's dads was a chef, and his brownies were to die for. The other was some sort of engineer, decidedly less beneficial to my stomach.

''Tis indeed, but do we think you deserve it?'

I popped my lip out in a pout. I wanted it. He studied my face, then gave a sigh, handing over the container of joy. I may or may not have hugged it.

'Mine, mine, mine.'

'You're pathetic, As, it's just a brownie,' he said, shaking his head at me.

I knew in my soul he didn't mean it the same way, but I couldn't stop Callie's voice echoing that same sentiment the night before in my head. I closed my eyes and fell into the memory of it, her words soured under my skin.

'You okay?' Dylan prompted.

I looked up and plastered a smile on my face, hoping it would smooth out the concern on his and forced that particular mental door shut.

'Yeah, I'm good. Thanks for this, I really needed it today.'

I tapped the lid, then added it to my bag to have later when I was alone.

'You're welcome. Are you sure you're okay though? I know I'm a bit of a dumbass and we have that whole "friends with benefits" thing, but you can talk to me. I'm your friend first, you know...' his voice trailed off. Soft and without the usual humour that was so trademark Dylan.

'I know,' I spoke to my knees. 'I'm okay. Sometimes things are just. Hard, I guess. Callie and I had a fight and then, mum. Ugh. I'm fine.'

I made myself look at him properly, his brown eyes serious, tracking the shape of my face.

'I'm sorry As, I—'

'It's fine. I'm fine. Always am, Dylan. Sisters fight, right? Plus now I have brownie.'

I cut him off and pretending it was just Callie. I knew he wasn't lying; he would listen to me empty every crawling black secret from the depths of my heart if I so wished. I also knew it would change how he looked at me. He'd never admit it out loud, but he would pity me. He would pity me and I would suffocate in it. He watched me for a moment longer, then his face split into a smile and his shoulders relaxed.

'Okay As, whatever you need. Word on the street is you're basically off limits now anyway. No more after-party rolls in the hay, then?' he literally winked at me.

'Ew, who under the age of 60 says "roll in the hay" now? Why would anyone want to roll in hay, naked or otherwise. It's not exactly feathers.'

'Nice try, you can't actually avoid me, we are stuck on this rolling rust bucket for...' he checked the time on his phone. '...11 more minutes.'

'All we did was kiss, that's hardly "off the market" and you know it.'

I rolled my eyes, pleased for the subject change but not what it changed to.

'I doubt he sees it that way. Astor Price is fairly delightful. Mostly. Sometimes?' he squinted and stroked his non-existent beard like he was trying to reach a conclusion as to my level of delightful. Honestly, he was absurd.

'You have literally had the full Astor interactive experience and don't see it that way, dork.'

'Mmm, now who said I didn't, though?'

I stared into the mirrorless brown pool of his eyes and the thread of familiarity between us lit up. I'd known him since my first day of school, knew how he had finger-painted and climbed trees. I knew what his hands felt like on my bare skin and his breath against my neck. It was a kaleidoscope of memories and moments and, for a second, I couldn't look away. He twirled an imaginary moustache, and I snapped out of it. I wouldn't trade his friendship for anything.

'Like you'd be able to survive all of this personality Dylan,' I grinned and nudged my shoulder against his. 'How was your weekend, anyway. Tell me all.'

I let his tale take up all the time we had left on the bus, clearing my mind of anything else.

Megan was late, sliding into the desk next to me in our first period history class with her glasses askew and her hair swept into a bun held together by a big metal bull clip.

'Oh my god Astor, I couldn't hear my alarm. It was buried under—'

'Megan Parsons, I know that isn't you talking, after waltzing into class late on this fine Monday morning.'

She screwed her petite nose up at me, the teachers voice cutting her off mid-sentence and drawing the attention of the entire class.

'Of course not Sir. It was Astor.'

I kicked her under the table. Cow.

Judging by the way he raised one of his bushy black eyebrows, it was safe to say I retained my angel status and he saw Megan for the dirty liar she was. He dropped a textbook on her table for our new topic and returned to his desk, tapping his fingers on the board where he had written "chapter 1 + Q&A" so Megan knew what we were doing. She hastily flipped to the correct page, glancing up briefly as she tore a blank piece of paper from her notebook. She scrawled a message and pushed it across to me.

did you hear from matty yesterday???

I quickly wrote my reply, not sure why this was suddenly a pressing issue.

we text a bit why?

just wondering. you guys were all good?

dude what

I think I saw him with some girl

My stomach dropped as I let Megan's barely legible words sink in. A girl? I bent forward to write my reply, but my pen was pulled right out of my grip. I looked up to the disapproving scowl of Mr. Braddock, this time absolutely directed at me.

'Really Astor? This absolutely does not look like notes on Women's Suffrage, unless of course this 'Matty' is somehow a suffragette? Pivotal member perhaps?'

'Sorry Mr. Braddock, I'll put it away now.'

I screwed up the paper Megan had passed me and dropped it into my bag, properly chastised.

'See that you don't get it out again, alright?' He gave both Megan and I the same weighted stare that only a teacher can pull off.

As soon as he turned away, I looked over at Megan, trying to establish some sort of telepathic link that would enable me to find out what the hell the rest of the story was. She stole a quick glance at the teacher and mouthed 'sorry' at me.

The remainder of the class crawled by and focusing was hard when my mind was so helpfully providing me with images of Matty strutting about town with *Karlie Kloss* clones on his arm. The minute the bell sounded I practically threw myself at Megan.

'Tell me,' I demanded.

She sunk her teeth into her lip and nodded a little to herself.

'Okay but we'll have to walk and talk cause if I'm late to French I will literally be turned into Gorgonzola.'

'That's Italian. Honest to God, Megan.'

I could not with this girl some days.

'Huh. Makes sense. I always thought it didn't sound like a French word. I guess I should say make me into Camembert, then? I just don't really like Camembert...'

'Megan. Focus. Matty.'

I shoved my books into my bag, resisting the urge to massage my temples.

'Right, yes. Sorry. So you know that sushi place next to the dog groomers that Dad really likes even though I tell him it's probably got some sort of dog cross-contamination thing happening?'

Deep breath.

'Yes, I am familiar with the one sushi place your dad likes in this entire city. Please, the point.'

'Well he wanted that last night, so we went there in our *Oodies*, and while we were waiting, I saw Matty with some other people, and he had his arm around a girl who was absolutely not you.'

She pushed through the door and set off to her next class, leaving me to basically jog beside her.

'Are you sure?' I asked. Not that Matty and I had defined what was going on with us or anything. I just sort of assumed if he had his tongue down my throat, it wouldn't be near anyone else.

'Well she was thinnish and blonde, from what I could tell. She had her back to me mostly, and you're—'

'Not about the girl, about it being Matty.'

'Oh. Yeah, I'm pretty sure. I definitely saw Troy cross over to them. He flipped me off. Hate that asshat.'

We were outside her class now, so I only had a couple seconds.

'Scale of one to ten, how sure are you it was Matty?'

'I mean...like a nine? I dunno, As, I looked up and it was him. Maybe you can ask him?'

'Yeah, I think I will. We've not really gone out or anything though...' I shrugged. I wasn't really sure why I was pretending to not care.

'I'm going in now but just...he's made it pretty clear he's interested in you, Astor. Don't let him be another asshole who treats you like a commodity.'

'Five-dollar words, you must be serious,' I forced a smile.

'I am, you dickhead. Something feels off about him, Astor, and this—I don't know. Ask him. I have to go but lunch time, yeah?'

She gave me a tight smile and disappeared into her class. I hurried to mine with my mind swimming with Matty.

Calculus was more gibberish than it had ever been today. I was beyond being able to concentrate. I knew I didn't have any sort of claim on him, but I liked him, and I thought he liked me. I didn't think I had misread things, so I was confused as to what was happening. Fidgeting in my seat, my skirt caught on the fresh cuts on my thighs, a delightful constant reminder of the previous night. Just to add to the mental soup poor little brain was drowning in.

Dropping my head to my desk with an audible thunk, I worked to shove everything into some sort of mental box. I suspected that most people had metal boxes, whereas mine was more of a soggy cardboard. Likely due to the soup. I only had to get through the rest of this lesson and then maybe I would message Matty and see what was up. Except that was a bit needy, wasn't it?

It was, I decided. I needed to wait and not look like I'd lost my marbles entirely. So lunch time it was then. With a small, very warranted groan from the effort my life required at the moment, I forced myself to focus. This entire day would drag if I obsessed about Matty and didn't actually do anything else.

Each lesson somehow felt longer than the last. When the bell finally sounded for the start of our lunch hour my stomach was writhing with nerves. Nic and I rounded the corner to our usual spot, and I mentally composed what I would send to Matty.

'What the fuck,' spilled out of Nic's mouth and I couldn't really blame her.

The usual spot where we had sat since day one of attending this god-forsaken school, had been infiltrated. Dylan and Megan sat side by side, swapping food. Tash and Matty were talking, a couple of other people from their group—who I knew mostly by name and how they looked sans clothes only—were also present and talking over each other.

'What the ever-loving hell is happening, Nicole?'

'I don't know but I'd like if they left.'

She somewhat stomped through the group and sat down on Tash's other side without another word. A real people-person our Nic was.

Megan and her zero-chill waved me over to sit next to her, though she immediately turned back to talk to Dylan. I elected to sit opposite them, which had me within talking distance of Matty. How convenient.

'Hey As, how's it?'

His smile was cute and crooked and sent my nerves spinning.

'Hey. Not bad. Bloody long day, though,' I smiled back happily, though a certain faceless blonde was climbing out of the aforementioned mental soup box, reminding me she may or may not be between us. 'Uh, I just wanted to ask ab—'

'Do you want to do something on Friday after school?' he cut in before I could finish, and his question caused the blonde to falter.

'You want to go out with me? Like...alone?'

'Yes? Is that okay? We just had all these Muppets with us on Saturday, and I'd rather be alone with you.'

'Yes. Yeah, I'd love that.'

Well shit. I had a date. I had a date and internally I was doing cartwheels. Megan and her raised eyebrows were opposite me, however, reminding me of the blonde and the arm that may have belonged to Matty around her waist.

'Uh, so you aren't seeing anyone else then?' I forced myself to look into his eyes, convinced that the truth was under that layer of storm cloud grey.

'No of course not As. I like you,' he said, smiling easy.

Megan gave a pointed cough, clearly audible, even though the entire group was talking. Clearly listening in.

'Oh well. I like you too. I just heard you were seeing a blonde girl, maybe?'

'Sorry what? Do you mean Chelsea? She's just a mate. I have a few of those, Astor.'

Who the fuck was Chelsea?

'Ha, yes. Of course you do. Sorry. Just didn't want to step on any toes or anything,' the words tripped out and my cheeks burned. We weren't even a "thing" and I was coming across as some needy nutcase. 'Friday would be awesome. Bus into town, then?'

'Sure. I'll text you,' he shrugged and turned back to Tash, who evidently watched our entire conversation play out.

Her strong features blank, but she managed a little smile before diving back into talking with Matty. I forced all my confusion and questions down, and just let the excitement roam freely in my mind. I focused more on Dylan and Megan; happy things were moving the right way with Matty now, hopefully.

I walked through the back gates of the school when the final bell sounded, Megan at my side.

'Why's your dad picking you up?' she asked, balancing on the edge of the path like a small child.

'Fuck knows, he messaged me and said he'd meet me by the church and not to catch the bus, but my phone died, and I didn't see what his reply was when I asked why.'

I was incredibly curious as to what was going on. I could count on one hand the amount of times dad had picked me up from school. Hell, I didn't even need a hand since it was a total of never.

'Want me to wait with you? Not like I have any pressing things to do, may as well sit with your lame ass.'

'Well if you wouldn't mind, that would be great. Perhaps together we can make one whole functional person.'

The church was just down the block from school, old red brick with a squat matching fence around the perimeter. It didn't really fit the neighbourhood of newer houses with manicured lawns and walls of glass, and some committee or another had attempted to drag its historic ass to the present, with new gardens of flowering bushes and a big gaudy sign. Predictably, this made it stand out even more and it was just referred to as *The Church*, cause everyone knew which you meant.

Megan sat on the wall, pulling her phone out and opening Reddit. I checked my watch, hoping Dad would be on time and ready with an explanation for this routine variance.

'So there's this *'Am I the Asshole'* thread where a woman has said her boyfriend left her, and she's asked if she crochets too much and I am living for the replies,' Megan was scrolling away, presumably searching for the crocheting singleton.

'Crochets too much how? Like...does she spend all day doing it or is she making everyone couch covers? What are we talking here?'

'The latter. Ugh I can't find it and now my phone is being a dick and not loading. Piece of shit,' she threw her hands up, never not a complete drama of a person, inadvertently sending her phone flying behind her. It landed with about as much grace as its owner possessed, and Megan scowled at it over her shoulder.

'Do you think that maybe the lack of care you give to it contributes to its piece of shit status?'

I climbed over the wall and went to pick it up for her. 'I'm just going to send Dad a message since I can't use mine.'

'Just pass it here, or just leave it. It's fine Astor,' she said in a rush, climbing over the wall too. I picked her phone up and looked at the screen, there was a message notification from someone called "E" and I expected it to unlock as usual. However, it did not.

'Dude why doesn't it know my face. It always knows my face,' I asked, confused. We had always had each other's passcodes, finger ID and facial recognition. 'And who is E?'

'I just changed things and...didn't add you back to it. It's not a big deal, okay?'

She grabbed her phone from my hand, swiped the notification away and shoved her phone in her skirt pocket.

'Right... and who is E?'

'Just a friend.'

'From school? Do I know them?'

'Astor. It's just a friend, for fuck's sake,' her jaw was tight, and she wouldn't look at me.

'What the fuck, bro. I was just asking.'

I was not entirely sure what has flipped this particular switch.

'Fucking hell, it's not always about you all the time.'

'Don't be a dick Meggy, I was just asking. I worry about you, okay?'

'DON'T call me that! Mind your own business, Astor.'

Her words hit like another slap to my face, this time dealt from my best friend. She stalked back to the wall, leaving me standing in the church garden, feeling as out of place as the church itself.

'Megan...' I started, not sure how to follow it up.

'Your dad is pulling in. Bye Astor.'

She threw her bag over her shoulder, the loose strands of her hair trapped under the shoulder straps and power-walked away without so much as a backward glance.

Dad's horn sounded and I hurried to collect my things and get in.

What the fuck.

CHAPTER TEN

We were halfway home before Dad said anything beyond hello, though I wasn't complaining. I was busy replaying the fiasco with Megan to try and work out why I was such a moron. Everything in my life just seemed so chaotic right now and every version of myself felt it.

'You need to try more with your mother.'

His openers left a lot to be desired.

'Sorry, what?' I spluttered, sure I had misheard him.

'You know it's not really her, As, it's the wine.'

I kept my head forward, watching the road rush towards us out the windscreen, the painted lines skipping past as rapidly as my thoughts.

Was he serious right now?

'Are you serious? You know it's more than the wine, dad. Jesus,' my disbelief boldly staining my words.

'Tone, Astor,' his voice stern, softening with his next words. 'Seriously. I know she loves you. You know she loves you. It's just that addiction is a disease. It makes her crazy.'

'She chased me down the road, Dad. Screaming she wanted to get me and I didn't even do anything wrong!' I couldn't hold back my anger.

He finally sees something happen and just tries to explain it away?

I wasn't dense, I knew drinking was an addiction. Her addiction just happened to want me gone apparently.

'She wasn't going to hurt you Astor.'

'Dad, come on.'

Was he for real right now?

'Just listen. She is very sick and needs help, so I need you to pull your shit together and stay out of her way so we can do that, okay? She doesn't need you swearing and defying her when she is trying to get her drinking sorted. Go to school, keep your grades where we expect them to be, and stay out of the way.' His words were final and allowed for no argument. 'Seen and not heard, Astor.'

My eyes burned at the effort of keeping every single tear behind the meagre gate my lashes created. I would not cry in front of him, not over this. Not over mum.

'I love you Astor, you know that. I don't want you upset either. This is just best for everyone.'

I nodded. Every time he spoke it was a door slammed shut on his chance to make this right, to help me, until nothing was left but the echo of the father-daughter relationship we had when I was small. The one I still wanted.

'Okay dad, I'll do better,' I forced out, each syllable perfectly controlled.

'That's a good girl, As.'

He smiled over at me, another door swinging shut as he did.

My phone vibrated on my side table just as I climbed into bed later that night. I hadn't dared look at it since we'd gotten home, not wanting to see a cancellation from Matty or, more importantly, nothing from Megan. This was neither.

Callie: Im sry 4 the other nyt. I h8 her drnkng 2 I jst dnt wnt u 2 upset her 2. Ull undrstnd wn ur older bt sh luvs u.

Me: I'm sorry too.

Lord knows why she messaged like vowels personally offended her, but I fired off my reply and settled in my nest of pillows. Between Callie and Dad, I felt like it was a coordinated attack. The anger at them both for not once listening to me, believing me, was pure fire in my veins. But guilt was its quiet companion, insistent whispering doubt. I pushed their words around, turned them inside out. Maybe I was at fault. I knew she was sick and that it wasn't as simple as deciding not to drink. She was an addict. An alcoholic. I traced the angry, raised cuts on my thigh, easily able to tell the new ones from the older. If I hadn't talked back to her last night, she wouldn't have slapped me. I knew that, knew it was my own words that invited her open palm. I closed my eyes and let other moments filter through. It was always me, my mouth, my actions, that tipped the balance. Guilt raised its head, bold and sure. Consuming, relentless, and barbed.

My leg itched where the skin had started to heal, so I rolled over, trapping my hands in order to preventing scratching. I could hear mum snoring across the hall and resolved to try harder with her. I would do better, be better.

I could do that.

Each day for the remainder of the week, I made myself stop and say a proper good morning to mum. I got myself ready and out the door with time to spare each day and every afternoon when I came home, I asked about her day. As night crept in and dinner cleared, I would retreat to my room. I only listened to music with headphones, I didn't watch tv and I made sure all my homework was done. The results were somewhat mixed. Tuesday and Wednesday; she didn't seem to notice or care where I was, the lack of conflict had given me hope that maybe I had stumbled upon the perfect amount of contact between us. By Thursday, the cracks were showing. She didn't return my good morning and at night she stood outside my door, calling my name in every tone, from rage to despair, for over an hour. Even though Matty had messaged to shift our date to Saturday and was seemingly chatty, Megan hadn't said more than a handful of words to me since the church fiasco. We had never gone so long without talking properly and I still couldn't figure out where exactly I had gone wrong so far as to deserve the almost silent treatment. So Thursday night, when mum decided to practice saying my name for 73 minutes straight, it took a lot of self-restraint to not tell her to piss off. I kept my headphones in, though she often was louder and forced myself to stay silent.

By Friday lunch I had had enough. Mum had been a cow that morning, Megan had said not a single word to me, and I was done. I stalked to our lunch area and came to a halt quite literally right in front of her.

'Hey.'

She looked up at me but didn't take a step back.

'Hi Astor,' she said, looking down at the slightly too long grass she stood on.

'I am quite done with this, Megan. We don't do this.'

I gestured between us. I wanted to sound angry, but every word was just sad.

'I know,' she sighed. 'Can we go for a walk and just...talk for a minute?'

I would go through hell for her, I thought. But I gave a simple yes in return. We wandered along the fence line for a couple of minutes, neither of us talking. Neither one knowing where to start.

'Meg...'

'I'm sorry, Astor. I was way out of line.' She stopped walking and leaned against the chain fence. 'I went too far.'

'Dude you didn't. I shouldn't have pushed. I told you to take your time telling me, and then I was pushy. I'm sorry.'

'Maybe we both were a bit shit, really,' she said, finally looking up at me. 'I am sorry As, I missed you.'

'Me too.'

'I just. I just want to say that I will tell you everything. I just need a bit more time.'

Selfishly, it wasn't what I wanted to hear. I wished she would tell me, but I had to wait, and I would.

'You don't have to explain. Just when you're ready.'

I reached for her, hugging her quick and tight and kissing her hair.

'Piss off Astor,' she laughed. She laughed and it was like the past few days hadn't happened.

'Wanna go sit back down? I hate to say it, but I don't hate that the others have joined us now,' I admitted, turning back and assuming, rightly, that she would come with.

'I know, I know. Same. But don't tell them.'

'Never!' I laughed.

'So date with Matty?'

'Oh my god, yes. I don't think it's anything major, but still. Not my usual fare, is it?' I almost squealed. I was excited, sue me.

'I hope it's good then.' I could feel her frown without even looking.

'Meg, it will be, trust me.'

'I do, I'm just not convinced about him. Being a reader doesn't make him a unicorn.'

I bit my tongue, not willing to start another argument over something like this. She'd see that he was great, I knew it. She just needed to give him a chance.

Saturday afternoon came, and I had been waiting for Matty for five minutes now. Sitting on the bench we had first kissed on, knees bouncing as I scrolled through my phone. I opened up the app to send Matty a message. I was prepared to wait a bit longer, though I didn't really have a lot of time, when he practically burst through a row of trees opposite me.

'Astor! Hey babe!' he waved and came over. Hair styled in the now familiar way, a red bag on his back ,and beat-up Vans at the end of his jean clad legs. 'Sorry I'm late.'

'Late? Nah, you're fine,' I smiled, enjoying the one he gave in return. 'Uhm, I do have to leave early though, I was going to stay with my sister tonight but she's sick, and Megan has something on so...yeah. Mum is picking me up in about two hours.'

I watched his smile melt away, like I was Dorothy and I'd just doused him with water.

'Well. That isn't long, is it,' he frowned at me.

'Sorry Matty, I can't help it.'

I chewed on my lip, waiting to see what he'd say next, almost able to see his mind turning this over. Just as quickly as it had gone, his good mood was back. Eyes bright, smiling wide, he pulled me to my feet.

'Let's go get a couple of milkshakes and then go for a little walk. Sound good?'

'Yeah, let's do it,' I grinned at him, ready to begin the date.

We barely made it out of the store, milkshakes in hand, when we bumped into Tash hand in hand with someone I couldn't quite place. Though I knew I had seen them before.

'Tash! Hey! What are you two up to? Aside from the obvious,' I waved my drink at her, still trying to place who she was with.

'Hi Astor. Matty. Milla and I were just going to get an ice cream,' she smiled at her friend. More than friend maybe, judging by their hands. 'What about you guys?'

'Just going for a walk, nothing major or anything,' Matty said, almost dismissive.

'Oh shit, Milla this is Matty. And Astor. They're both friends from school.'

I watched her pale thumb make circles on Milla's hand as she made introductions. 'Astor, I think you came into work when Milla was working once. With your rude mum.'

'Oh! That's where you're from! I've been trying to place your face.'

I ignored her comment about mum, it wasn't like she was wrong.

'Can we move this along, please? We don't have much time,' wisps of frustration clear in his voice.

'Sorry Matty. Tash, we'll see you at school then. And Milla! I hope to see you again soon.'

I waved my cup again, this time in goodbye, and followed Matty back down the road to the park, hoping we would be alone a bit now.

'No. I'm not saying he could be a *DC* villain, but even if he were just playing, he'd still be destroying the city AND he would need to be neutralised by a superhero. Probably Wonder Woman. Because Gal Gadot is visual perfection, and I will fight you,' I smiled at Matty, confident in my argument.

'*Clifford*.'

'Yeah.'

'*Clifford* the *Big Red Dog* from those books and cartoon?' he sounded confused. Adorable, really.

'Yeah, just picture it.'

'I worry about your little brain, Astor Price. *Clifford*.'

His head shake was affectionate, like I amused him.

'Why? Do you know another one?' I gave him my best smile. We were having a wonderful time, wandering through the park. I let myself relax into it, happy to be there and to just get to be me. We wandered back down the same path we had started on, branching off on a little hidden trail, a shortcut that took you straight to the biggest pond. The ground squished with leaf litter, unable to dry out under the canopy tree, and the sounds of people and traffic faded.

'I haven't been down here, have you?' Matty smiled over his shoulder at me, good mood reinstated.

'Oh yeah, of course. I've lived here my whole life so I'm fairly sure I've seen every hole this town has to offer. If you keep going along here, it comes out—'

'Cool, yeah. Can we stop a second?' he cut me off, swung the bag off his back, unzipping it as he did. I wasn't sure what he had planned. We were about halfway along the trail and there was nothing much here but trees and leaves. I wanted to keep moving and not stop on some sunless path. He pulled a picnic rug out, red tartan on one side and a waterproof fabric on the other. The low-level annoyance I had been brewing evaporated as quickly as he flicked the blanket out on the ground. He had gone to the effort of planning a picnic for us, and here I was worried about him being a bit snippy.

He sat down with his legs out in front of him and pulled out a little plastic supermarket box holding two cupcakes.

'Sit Astor, come have a cupcake with me.'

He patted the ground next to him. You didn't have to tell me twice.

'Sorry about Tash earlier... and having to cut our date short.'

I didn't really know why I was apologising, I hadn't brought Tash here, but she was my friend and I felt somewhat responsible, I guess. Matty shrugged and handed me a cupcake. He licked the frosting off the top and threw the rest into the tree line.

I was, admittedly, a little stunned.

'Dude, that was a perfectly good cupcake. What the fuck.'

'The top is the best part. Like you eat the good bit and just throw the rest away. Then it's always perfect,' his smile was wolfish, watching me try and eat cupcake like I had manners hidden away.

We talked about school and the latest episodes of a zombie show he was watching. Laughing and enjoying ourselves without anyone else. It was lovely and peaceful.

I wasn't oblivious, I knew he was moving closer the more we talked. He sat up properly, legs crossed like he was five and eyes roaming my face and body. I closed my eyes, trying to summon excitement for this moment. His mouth met mine and he let a little moan slip out, pulling me into him.

It was...okay.

It was better than last time at least. His hand slid down my side and under my shirt, tickling my side and round to my spine. I returned the favour, the warmth and soft skin of his back new to me as he deepened the kiss. A wolf whistle, the kind that involves putting your fingers in your mouth and makes your ears hurt broke through the little clearing.

'Astor getting it ON! You go girl!' I rolled away from Matty with zero grace, my cheeks burning.

'Shut the fuck up Troy,' Dylan snapped. His familiar voice angry, but so welcome right now.

I looked up, searching for his familiar head, and realised we had been joined by half a dozen people. All of them staring down at us. I wasn't a prude by any stretch of the imagination. I had definitely been in a similar position with a few of the present company, Dylan included, but I scrambled to my feet, nonetheless. Matty's anger seemed to match Dylan's, though he seemed to be trying to control himself.

'You fuckers ruin everything,' his smile was forced. Annoyance crystal-clear and twisting his handsome face.

'Well, fuck. Forgive us for using a path to get to the pond,' Troy said, rolling his eyes. 'Just come with us. Astor won't mind.

'Astor does mind, thanks Troy.'

Though I wouldn't mind the chance to push him in the pond. I looked over at Matty, silently asking his thoughts.

'God, whatever then, let's just do it.'

His face was a permanent scowl as he shoved the picnic rug back in his bag, ignoring the others and me.

'Hey,' I lowered my voice, leaning into his neck a little. 'We can set up another date. If you want.' I kissed below his ear and stepped back, holding my hand out for his. He looked at me for half a beat, took in my flushed face and outstretched hand.

'Okay, yeah. Let's do that. Are you free tomorrow night?'

He twined his fingers with mine and we made our way after the others, heading to the pond.

'I'm sure I can work something out. Can you pick me up from my parents?' I bumped my hip into his.

'Yeah, that's fine. Should we try see a movie?' he asked.

'A movie and maybe dinner? Like a proper, proper date?'

I crossed my fingers, mentally anyway.

'Sure why not. If that's what you want. I'll text you with a time later.'

'Yes!' I squealed a teeny bit. 'I'm excited.' I gave his hand a squeeze, then tried to reign myself in.

A proper dinner and movie date were, admittedly, extremely exciting. And to be picked up?

Dreamy. I was happy.

'I can tell. Come here and give me a kiss, babe,' he demanded, his tone playful as he pulled me in. Another just perfectly fine kiss. I knew that we would get our moment, that connected feeling. I wrapped my arms around his neck, pressing one final quick kiss to his lips.

'And hopefully, we'll be all alone tomorrow, with no interruptions.' My voice came out lower than I meant for it to be, but his wicked grin in return told me he liked it.

'You bet. Come on, let's go cause you'll be picked up soon.'

Coming out from the trees, everyone else had spread out around one side of the pond. Someone had produced a few beers and cigarette smoke swirled around Troy. Matty dropped my hand, leaving me to go and sit with him and share a smoke. I checked the time, half an hour 'til I had to meet mum, which wasn't much. I lay down next to Dylan, happy for his presence.

'Astor,' his voice a smooth rumble of a thing.

'Dylan.'

'You okay?' he asked, turning to study my face.

'Gosh why do you always lay down, I think I'll fall asleep,' I fight a yawn. 'I'm fine, Dyl. Ask me why.'

He rolled his eyes and I felt it cross the space between us. 'Why Astor. Do tell.'

'Dylan, good sir. I have secured myself a very real proper date.' I fought down the squeal again but couldn't resist a little happy wriggle. Dylan gave me a little smile.

'Hey, don't you think that cloud looks exactly like *Patrick Stewart*'s head?' he pointed at the sky, seemingly more interested in the clouds than talking to me. But whatever. I was excited and he couldn't kill that.

There was very little fanfare when we parted ways. Matty gave me a kiss and said he'd message. Dylan waved and everyone else either gave me a chin lift or looked right through me. It was a mixed bag. Mum didn't say a word the entire drive, though I did catch her looking my way more than once. Something felt off and I didn't enjoy this sort of anticipation in the slightest. As soon as we were home, I retreated to my room, immediately messaging Megan to let her know what had happened that afternoon and how I had a dinner date for tomorrow. Heart emojis were liberally used and I wasn't sorry. Dinner was quiet and I couldn't shake the idea that something was up with mum. I had stayed out of her way, I'd done my homework and my chores, and not said a word out of line all week. But it all just felt off tonight.

'Mum, are you alright?' I asked, hesitantly.

'Fine, Astor, just go to bed. That's all you do now anyway, isn't it. Lazy.'

She sounded almost bored, tired maybe, but I didn't need to be told twice. My room was clean, calm, and orderly, and I already spent the bulk of my time there. Hardly a prison sentence. I gave mum a tight smile and shut myself away, happily diving into my book and pretending I lived anywhere else. I wouldn't let her mood sour today.

Barely an hour later and the sound of shattering glass ripped me from the welcome pages of my book and dumped me in the living room, where mum was. Kneeling in front of the window she had broken, blood dripping into the carpet and running down her arm, Mum cradled her hand against her chest.

'Oh my god, are you okay?' I reached for her hand, watched her recoil at my touch and swallowed. 'Mum?'

'I fell over Astor,' she slurred, not quite full-blown drunk, but definitely heading that way.

'I know, mum, can I just have a quick look at your hand?' I kept my voice quiet, her pale blue eyes seemed a thousand miles away as she swam towards sobriety.

She held her hand out, a cut freely bleeding along the side of her palm. It didn't look too deep, so I grabbed some kitchen paper roll and held it to the wound, mum's hand in mine. I couldn't tell you the last time she held my hand. Her skin was papery, the kind that's associated with old age and not your fifties. Down on the floor like that, surrounded by the shattered glass of the window she'd fallen against, and her wine soaking into the carpet, she looked so small.

'I'm going to rehab,' she said, her words joining together to make one long one. 'I don't mean to be a bad mother.'

She swayed in place, closing her eyes like it'd help. I wasn't sure what I was meant to say anymore. I'd had the same words in a dozen birthday cards. Cried through closed doors. Written on paper and shoved in my grade five lunchbox. It never amounted to anything. It never changed anything. So what did I say? Thanks? Great? That's cool, until next time? Nothing seemed sufficient.

'Will you...stay the whole time this time?' I practically whispered, frightened of breaking the little bubble we had created.

She nodded, closing her eyes. 'Yeah? I'm going to rehab, and I'll stay this time,' she slurred again, nodding to support her claim.

I used a couple of band-aids to secure gauze, making sure it would stay in place, and sent her to go have her dinner, happy to clean the glass up alone. I let Mum's words sink in, trying against all reason to not get my hopes up.

To be realistic.

But hope, hope was a violent thing. Hope crashed through the walls you built with no regard for what it cost you to build them again. And right now, hope was front and centre, walls crumbling around it, telling me that this was the time. This was the one that would work. It had to.

I got everything tidied, vacuumed, and put away before climbing into bed.

My mum was going to rehab, and Matty was taking me on a date.

It felt like maybe things could only get better from here.

Chapter Eleven

I bounced on my toes and tilted my head back to look up at the inky sky, my long hair falling down my back in waves. I was stood on the side of the road where I usually caught the bus from, waiting for Matty to pick me up for our date. *Our dinner date.* Until yesterday, I'd never been on any date, let alone one that involved dinner and nice clothes. There were always plenty of group meet-ups or parties to go to, and I'd had my fair share of hook-ups and messy midnight backseat kisses. No one had ever made the effort to take me on a date though, even if it was just dinner and a movie. I was beyond excited that Matty seemed somewhat serious about me, as serious as you could be at 16 and 17.

Smoothing out my clothes, I touched my fingers to the wide neck of my striped tee and traced along my collarbones. I'd stepped out of my safety blanket jeans and right into a high waisted skirt. Bottle green and swirling around my knees when I moved, I was a little in love with it. I actually felt pretty, which was exceptionally off-brand for me but here we are.

The quiet hum of a car rolled through the dark, headlights jumping with every dip in the road. Matty pulled a tired, faintly brown station wagon to a stop, almost perfectly in front of me and I watched the window roll down. Manually.

'Astor? Jump in, babe. We don't want to be late,' he said, his voice gentle and warm.

I wiped my palms on my skirt discreetly, hoping my nerves settled, and slid into the car, looking over at Matty's now familiar face. His blue shirt was done up to his neck, short sleeves with a little pattern I wasn't able to make out in the half light. I was quietly pleased that he seemed to have put a little effort into his clothes as well. Maybe he was excited for this too.

He reached out and gave my knee a squeeze, his eyes were taking a quick tour down my body.

'You look pretty, As,' he smiled. His crooked smile that felt like it was just for me.

I blushed slightly at the compliment and played with my hem, compulsively making sure my scars were covered. He pulled out and headed in the general direction of town, while I let my gaze roam around the car. It was older, upholstered in a frankly terrible shade of maroon. The back row of seats had been folded down, turning the rear of the car into a vast, faintly musty maroon cave. I found myself looking back to Matty, wondering if maybe tonight, now that we were going out on our date, we would have *a moment*. The sparks and goosebumps.

He turned and I squinted through the window, positive he'd gone the wrong way. I caught the sign at the last possible moment.

'Why have you gone this way?'

'Just taking a shortcut, don't worry,' he smiled at me.

This way wasn't quicker, everyone knew that. He hadn't lived here long though, so maybe he didn't, or maybe someone had given him bad directions. Had I given him bad directions?

'Oh, well. It's not exactly a shortcut, though. You can turn around here and it's still quicker to go back the other way. This way could make us late,' I explained.

I had plans for movie theatre popcorn and no desire to miss the beginning of the film, or the hand holding I was hoping for. I didn't want my first proper date to be over before it begun.

'Relax, As, we can always get the next showing, I just thought we could talk a bit first. I mean, we keep getting interrupted by your friends, don't we?' he looked over at me, his half-baked smile exuding sarcasm.

'Oh. Yeah, okay, I suppose that's fine. I mean, yesterday wasn't so bad, was it? Even with the others around.'

'Hardly the same. Tonight we're going to have a lot of fun though.'

'Yeah, sure. Where are we going then? Did you have somewhere in mind?' I smiled.

'I thought we would park down the end here, no one can bother us, and we can just chat a bit yeah?' Matty glanced at me, and his deep brown eyes seemed flat in the dark. He smiled once more.

Easy. Calm.

Wrong.

My stomach curled into knots and my skin prickled. Something didn't quite feel right. It sat uncomfortably on the edges of my mind, like the tune of a song you couldn't remember the words to, but couldn't get out of your head either. I shut down those thoughts. It was just nerves and the change of plans that had thrown me a bit. Of course I wanted to have time to talk to him.

We drove down the empty road, past the turn off that would take us to town and not another car to be seen. The gaps between the dotted lights of houses stretched, and the chilled fingers of the dark outside seemed to creep into the car. I suppressed a shiver, not convinced it was the cold alone setting my nervous system on edge.

'Matty where are we going?' I asked.

'Just a little further, babe. One of the guys from school told me about this cute lookout. I thought you'd like it. You'll like it right?'

He looked over at me, his features arranged in a question. It felt like a mask, artfully placed.

He turned the car down another side road, narrow and winding steadily upward. Brief flashes of light in the wall of trees hinted at houses tucked away from sight down long driveways.

The trees seemed to grow larger, houses disappearing altogether and, at the crest of the hill, he pulled to a stop. Without looking at him I asked.

'Where are we?'

'There's a river out there or something, apparently. Probably better in the daylight. But we can still...get to know each other.'

I kept my head forward, trying to hear the water, but the world outside was still and dark. Moonlight dragged sombre shadows from the ground, quietly setting the scene for this moment. My heart skipped ahead, my pulse trying to outrun itself as well as the silence that sat between us.

This wasn't right. None of this felt right.

The interior light snapped on and startled me out of my own head. Matty gave a low laugh and I looked over at him again, out of the corner of my eye, not wanting our eyes to meet. He turned his much larger body towards me, his hand stretching out to softly brush my cheek. I wanted to lean into his palm, but I hesitated, then pulled away.

'So, what did you want to talk about?' I cleared my throat.

'Mmh. How about we start with a quick kiss? Just to make us comfortable?' his fingers traced my jaw, down my neck.

I wondered if the hum of my heartrate was obvious to him. He smiled—all his teeth—but it wasn't the same. I bit my lip, unsure of what was happening, what I was missing. Desperately trying to quiet the whisper that said I needed to go home.

'I don't know, could we maybe just go to the movie theatre? We can talk over dinner afterwards?' my eyes darted from Matty, to the window and back again, insides knotting.

'Come on, Astor. Quick little kiss. You were into me yesterday, why are you being like this now?'

His was voice lower, needy. This wasn't what I expected. It wasn't what he had ever been like. My mind raced, tripping down dark alleys of panic. I didn't know what to do. I didn't like the way he was looking at me, the pleading tone he used. I wasn't even sure what was wrong. I could kiss him, just a quick one. I leant forward, the centre console between our bodies, and I brushed my lips against his. His hand gripped the back of my head, holding my mouth to his and his fingers twisted in my hair.

'I'd really like to go now, please,' my voice trembled as I pulled away, pushing my back firmly against the door, wide eyes fixed on him.

'We haven't even done any talking. Isn't this what you wanted? Spending time together? You're so sweet Astor.'

His thumb brushed over my cheek.

I felt sick. This was what I wanted, wasn't it? The date night and the alone time. He touched my knee, fingers stroking the skin of my thigh and I desperately wanted to pull away. He had no sweet smile for me now. No warmth or affection.

I wanted to go home.

'You led me on yesterday, didn't you? Such a little tease. And then left me hanging so you could go hang out with Dylan. I know what you're like. I had a taste and I want more. I know you're into me.'

'I want to go home, please.'

My stomach sunk at his words, I hadn't led him on at all.

I didn't summon everyone to crash our picnic.

'Don't be ridiculous. I've driven all the way out here to get you, and I just wanted a little one-on-one time first, you know? It's not like you haven't done it before. I know what everyone says. Heard plenty of little stories.'

'Just take me home, please. I just want to go home now,' I fought to keep my voice from shaking as much as my hands were. His words hurt because they were true. 'Please Matty.'

'Fine, just fucking fine. You have to do something for me first though,' he growled, venom on a razors edge. 'You and I are going to move into the back, and you're going to make up for leading me on with your mouth. Don't pretend you're not okay with this, Astor. I know how many boys you've let between those legs,' his hand pushing at my hem and his eyes crawling all over my body. 'I'll take you home. After. Otherwise you can get out right here and walk, for all I care.'

My eyes burned, I was such an idiot. How had I fooled myself into think he wanted me as a girlfriend.

Idiot, such a fucking idiot.

I looked past him into the engulfing darkness outside. I wasn't sure where I was, how I could get home from here. I hadn't paid enough attention.

My fault.

'Can you just tell me what the road is called, and I'll get out,' I fought to keep control of my voice.

'Yesterday I had you laid out next to me, finally. I wasn't done. Just get in the back.'

He ignored me, his voice frustrated and angry. His hand squeezed my knee hard enough to leave five round finger marks to remember this moment by.

'Promise that you'll take me home? Just a little kissing like yesterday and then you'll drop me home?'

I couldn't bear to look at him, my fingers twisted anxiously in my lap, knitting, and dividing. I wanted to go home.

Deep breath in, As. You can do this and then you can go home.

'Yes Astor, Christ. I will drive you home after. Stop being difficult, you're hardly a blushing virgin.'

Embarrassment flashed up my neck and coloured my cheeks. Was I just being difficult? I could kiss him. I'd done it before. I'd wanted to do it with him. Not like this though. Every single cell in my body revolted against this, and I hated seeing under the mask and how vile he was.

I gave a sharp nod and climbed into the back, trying desperately to keep my skirt down. I tucked my legs under me, ignoring the faint smell of damp and weed, and focused on my hands. I felt him settle next to me, but I couldn't look up. I could feel his anger filling up the space, raw and unbridled. He forced my face up, then looked me over head to toe, like I was some prize he had won but didn't really want. I tugged on my skirt, like somehow it would grow and cover my legs. Cover *me*.

Our eyes met in the half light, any trace of humanity in his had seemingly been erased in such a short time. Was the Matty of yesterday an act?

His arm crossed the short distance between us, and he pushed me down by my shoulder, not even trying to be gentle. Bile burned the back of my throat, clawing its way up, and I fought to blink back the tears that relentlessly threatened to spill.

'Just kissing, right. I don't want to do anything else. Just kissing and you'll take me home, right?' I could hear the desperation in my own voice, my eyes locked on his as I pleaded with him.

He was silent for half a beat, staring at my lips. He rushed forward with a growl, pressing his mouth against mine, unapologetically rough and demanding entrance. I turned my head to the side, trying to get away from the intrusion. His hands snaked up my neck and held my head still how he wanted. On my next gasped exhale, he shoved his tongue into my mouth. I gagged on the sour taste of his breath. His teeth scraped against my lip as I tried to move and push him off my body. He had somehow managed to slide his knee in between my thighs, teeth biting at the skin of my throat. I was trapped. My heart pounded, blood roaring in my ears as fear threaded itself through every cell.

This wasn't happening. I didn't *want* this.

'I think I'll just get out, Matty. I'll call someone else to come and get me. Let me out please.'

I pushed against his chest, pushed him away. He barely moved, bigger than I was.

'Don't be an idiot, Astor. We're just going to play around a little. I know you want it, why else would you be all over me yesterday? Why would you basically beg me to let me pick you up?' He put his lips to my collarbone, biting down then sucking the skin into his mouth. He pulled off with a little pop. 'This isn't so bad, is it?'

His laugh was a chill against my overheated skin, his mouth back against my cheek and his hands held my head.

Did I deserve this?

He wasn't wrong. I definitely wasn't a virgin, hardly picky about who I had slept with in the past. I just wanted to go home. *Home, home, home.* I *couldn't* do this.

'No, stop. Let me up, I'll find a way home, just let me out.'

I tried to make my voice sound firm, but it wasn't really. I tried to wriggle free but couldn't move from under him. Fear strangled every syllable I spoke, wrapped around every part of me.

Matty surged forward again. His lips were dry, rough, and unrelenting. His breath was foul and filling my mouth. Again, I tried to turn my head and his hand flexed at my throat, forcing me to still. His free hand made its way under my shirt, roughly pulling the cup of my bra down, pinching my nipple hard. His thigh pressed up between my legs, holding me in place as he thrust against my hip. He bit at my lip, pulled it roughly between his teeth; a small whimper escaped when I felt the skin tear.

This is really happening. This is happening and I can't stop him.

His hands moved down my body. He pushed my skirt, my pretty swirly skirt, up to my waist, exposing the plain black cotton underwear I had on. Sneering down at me, hands holding my hips in place. Shame and terror fought for control in my mind.

How did I get myself into this? How fucking stupid are you, Astor.

I was desperate to move but couldn't. My body betrayed me, and I lay there as my mind screamed at me to go.

'Please Matty, I don't want this, please,' I begged, my desperation somehow spurring him on.

He pushed his own pants down and pulled out a condom. I didn't want to see, squeezing my eyes shut tight. Tears rolled rapidly down my face as Matty yanked my underwear down. His rough hands pushed my legs apart and pulled me too him. My mind went blank as his hips snapped against mine, pushing my head into the side of the car with each painful thrust. I watched the condensation form on the window, followed the beads of water as they rolled down, cutting a pathway to nowhere. There were discarded shoes. School books. Paper and clothing. A miscellaneous audience with front row seats to my humiliation.

I waited, numb. Exposed and silent.

With a guttural groan he rolled off me, giving my leg a pat, like I had done well.

'See, not half bad, was it?'

I said nothing, I couldn't.

'Hurry up and put your fucking clothes on, then. I'll take you home,' he bit out, apparently oblivious to how desperately wrong all of this was. He smacked my thigh right over the healing cuts. 'You're more fucked up than people said,' he laughed.

His touch was live wire, enough to spur my traitorous body into action. I quickly tugged my underwear on, brushed my skirt down and clambered into the front seat. I curled my aching body against the door, and willed the tears to leave. To leave and take all this shame and fury and weakness with them. I knew they wouldn't, they would all be companions now.

My stomach felt hollow, empty and nauseous.

'Home please, Matty,' I forced the words past my torn lips, a whispered mumble into the window frame.

'Yeah, I fucking said I would, didn't I?' his voice was so unbelievably different from the gentle tone I was used to. Two separate people seemed to exist inside the same body, and I didn't want to know either of them.

He started the car and pointed it in the right direction.

I continued to cry, my head against the window as I tried so, so hard to quiet the sniffing. I didn't want to make him angrier or have him stop driving.

A half mile from my house, Matty pulled over again. My entire body went rigid, I could barely breathe, each pull of oxygen felt unnatural.

'I seriously cannot take your fucking bullshit crying and snivelling anymore. Get the fuck out, this is close enough. Stop acting like you're too good for me.'

He leaned across me to push the door open. Before he could quite reach, though, I was gone. I had the door open and dropped out into the night, my hands stopping me from falling on my face. I couldn't breathe, I needed to breathe. Why couldn't I breathe? I got to my feet and stumbled forward on weak legs. Behind me I heard the car door slam, Matty throwing the car into gear and roaring as he took off into the dark. I turned, hoping the dark would swallow me entirely as I stood there watching the taillights disappear. Goosebumps sprung up all over my skin, tears chilled on my face and new ones painted their own tracks over them. I looked around, trying to work out where he had left me, a new panic joining the flavours I already had. The longer I stood alone in the endless dark, the clearer my mind was. I recognised the area—not hard given the size of our town—and finally felt the barest hint of relief, knowing I had a direction to go in. I pulled my phone out and found her name in my contacts, sending her a short message asking if she was home. I didn't wait for her reply, I couldn't. I wrapped my arms around myself and set off toward her house.

I couldn't stop crying, little sobs slipping out on every other breath. I needed to shower, to wash the feel of his hands off my skin, his foul breath out of my hair. I felt dirty. Used and discarded. I felt like a fool. I tried to force every second of tonight into the soggy mental box in my mind, just lock it away where no one—myself included—could see it.

I wasn't convinced that I could make it all fit.

CHAPTER TWELVE

Nic was silent as she opened the sliding door to her room, ushering me in. I had been wildly unsuccessful at stopping my tears on my walk to her place. She took one look at me and pulled me into a hug.

'Oh Astor, what happened? What can I do?' she stroked my hair softly.

Nicole liked her personal space so I knew I must have looked a wreck. Her quiet voice reopened the floodgates, and I buried my face in her shoulder and sobbed. I wasn't sure how to put into words what had just happened at that moment, I wasn't entirely sure I ever would. She pulled me over to her perfectly made double bed, covered in schoolwork, and told me to wait, disappearing out her bedroom door. Her room was a basement flat type of setup, under the main house. It had its own little bathroom and a microwave on her dresser which I knew she used to heat giant cookies in before she ate them. The carpet was red, and the walls were white painted brick, covered with posters and pictures she'd drawn. I wiped my eyes and nose on my shirt and received a massive smack of cologne, twisting my stomach violently to the point I thought I would be sick. I doubled over, breathing deeply, and trying to hold it together. My skin was unbearable.

Uncomfortable, like it had shrunk in the past hour and would never again fit the same.

'Here, I made you a hot chocolate. Which probably isn't what you need right now but my mum always says, a cup of tea in times of stress. But you don't drink tea, do you? So I made this...uhm here?'

I looked up to a mug in my face and a nervous Nic.

'I'm so sorry, I'm trying to get it together,' I sniffed, wiping my face then taking the steaming drink from her.

Nic dropped down next to me, her leg bouncing up and down.

'Can you tell me what happened? I thought you were with Matty tonight?' At his name, fresh tears rolled out and my whole body ached. 'Please As, I'm worried,' she said softly, hazel eyes wide.

I knew I had to give her something, but I didn't know what to say, or even how to say it.

'Matty...uhm,' I cleared my throat and forced a mouthful of boiling hot chocolate down. 'Can I shower, Nic.'

I studied my shoes. Black ballet flats with a little bow. I thought they were cute when I put them on earlier. Now I wanted to burn them, and everything else I was wearing.

'Oh Astor, what can I do? Should I call your parents? Oh god, are you hurt? Do you need the hospital? The police?'

Every word was pure pity. I was shaking my head before she had even finished. 'No, God no. None of that,' I laughed a bitter laugh.

'Let me call someone.'

'Nic, please. I just want a shower.' I needed to wash him off. 'I'm fucking disgusting.' I got to my feet, frustrated, threading my hands into my tangled hair. I could feel his hands on me again and I wanted to tear my skin off with my bare hands. 'Please can I just shower.'

She studied my face and nodded solemnly.

'I'll find you something to wear.' She stood and squeezed my hand. 'Just go get in and I'll come leave them on the toilet for you, okay?'

'I'm sorry Nic, I just. I didn't know where to go. I'm so sorry,' I cried and tears fell anew. The frustration breaking down as quickly as it had arrived.

'It's okay, we'll work it out. Just go hop in.'

I turned the shower as hot as my skin would allow and then a little more. This scene had been shown a hundred times on TV and in film. The hot shower, the crying. Never once did I consider that this would become my reality. I scrubbed at my skin, scrubbed until it was red and raw, desperate to erase the sins on my body. The scabbing cuts on my leg were torn open, blood and tears and conditioner swirling at the bottom of the shower.

How was I such a fool to think he wanted to date me. Such a fucking idiot.

I don't know how long I had stood there with my mind spinning in circles. Trying to pinpoint when I should have figured it out. The water had cooled, my skin chalk white, marred with sweeping red patches where I had tried to clean off his scent.

The flimsy blue shower curtain pulled back and my heart leapt forward in fright. I wrapped my arms around body, desperate to hold myself together.

'Astor?' my best friend in the world stood there. Megan said my name like a question and a sob tore from my chest. 'Oh Astor. God.'

She kicked off her shoes and fully clothed, climbed into the tub with me, flinching a little at the temperature of the water. She pulled me to her, and something snapped inside. My hands grabbed at her back as my soul tore with every exhale.

'I don't understand. I want to understand,' I pleaded with her for an answer I didn't have a real question to. My body ached and I shook violently in the cold.

'I don't know, As, I really don't. Let's get you out of here, okay?' She took a step back and I clung to her hand like a lost toddler. 'I'm not going anywhere, I promise.'

One handed, she snagged a towel from where Nic had left them—unnoticed by me—and awkwardly wrapped it around my shoulders. My teeth chattered and I let her go. I didn't want her to be cold too. Nic had left us both sweatpants and hoodies and I got dressed mechanically. I felt cleaner, but I didn't feel *clean*. I was exhausted, completely cried out, but unable to stop crying, asleep where I stood. I couldn't look at Megan, ashamed by how broken I was over a guy. Over sex.

It was *just* sex, wasn't it.

Nic was sat on her bed again, seemingly waiting for us, but I couldn't look at her right now. I kept my eyes on Megan.

'So uh, I'm going to go sleep upstairs, but you guys are welcome to stay down here. I changed the sheets...I...didn't know what else to do, sorry,' Nic said and I was grateful. As lovely as she was, I just wanted to be alone. Or with Megan, which was sort of the same thing.

'Thanks. I'll make sure we head back to mine early tomorrow. I think she needs to sleep right now,' Megan was talking quietly.

I was embarrassed, waiting pathetically behind her. I closed my eyes and immediately felt his hands on my hips again. I careened into Megan and twisted my hand in the cream fleece of her sweatshirt, needing an anchor in reality. Shame hummed in my veins, painted my cheeks crimson, and forced my head down.

'Night Astor,' Nic said softly. I nodded, unable to look up.

I climbed into the bed and curled up on my side. The fresh laundry smell and the weight of the blankets were unfamiliar, another reminder that tonight had not been what it ought to have been. Megan turned off the main light and a whisper of fear curled through me. She reached her arm around the door of the bathroom to turn that off too, and the whisper burst into a scream.

'No!' I sat up in the bed, the word stolen from me before I could stop it. 'No, Megan, leave it on. Please?'

I didn't want to be in the dark, with its secrets and monsters hidden in its quiet folds.

She stared at me for half a moment, that familiar pale brow pinched and concerned.

'Whatever you need, As. Anything,' she said.

She left the light on and slid in beside me, just like we had done countless times before. I wriggled down, pressed my forehead into her shoulder and inhaled the comforting scent of my best friend. Her hand found mine under the covers and she knit our fingers together, keeping me in the present where she was, and I could breathe.

My eyes fell shut and I let sleep take me.

I felt warm, too warm. The familiar shape of Megan curled into me, her ridiculous blonde hair in my face. The real world brushed against my sleep-infused mind as it crawled to consciousness. I was suspended in those moments between asleep and awake where the world is calm and free of conflict. I opened my eyes and reality exploded into full high definition. My chest was tight, each breath painful and heavy. I scrambled out of the bed and bent over the toilet, emptying the minimal contents of my stomach. I closed the lid and dropped my head to the top, as last night played a mental highlights reel.

Yay for me.

I felt frail and I didn't want to be. I didn't want this at all. I washed my face with some of Nicole's cleanser and swirled some mouthwash round, managing to not look in the mirror even once, unsure what I was going to see on my own face if I did.

'Astor?' Megan called through the door, her knock sending my nerves into orbit. I made eye contact with myself and was sure the mirror must be fucked. My skin, normally pale without any effort on my part, was grey and washed out. The bags under my eyes severe enough they looked to hold a lifetime of weighted problems and not just last night's. My bottom lip was a little swollen, the dark red line left by *his* teeth stark. Added to my present electrocution hairstyle, I was divine.

'As? Are you alright?' she knocked again.

'Yeah,' I cleared my throat, hoarse from the all the crying I managed to cram into one night. 'Coming out now.'

I rifled through Nic's drawers to find a hair tie and threw the nest up in a ponytail. I'd deal with it later or shave my head. It was anyone's guess. I opened the door and Megan was dancing in place, evidently needing to pee.

'Thank fucking Christ, I was about to burst!'

She pushed past me into the bathroom and dropped her pants.

I sat down on the bed and waited for her to come back out. Last night when she magically appeared, ready to hold me together and catch the falling fragments of who I was, she hadn't said anything. Hadn't demanded answers to the questions I knew waited. I wasn't sure I had them to give. Last night felt like a bad scene from someone else's life. I could almost believe it was, until I closed my eyes and his hands were a ghost on my skin, his breath a wretched whisper against my neck. My pulse tripled.

'Astor?' she said my name and I could hear the unease. 'Can you tell me what's going on?'

I looked at her, my one true person, with her blue eyes and blonde hair, pale face pinched in concern. I could tell her, she was Megan. I opened my mouth to speak, and she smiled, small and encouraging.

'I...uh...' the words I needed to say clung to the sides of my throat. I swallowed forcefully.

'It's okay, As, you can say.'

No, I couldn't. I couldn't say.

How do I tell her what had happened last night at all. *Oh, well, I climbed into the back of his car and we had sex and then he dropped me off walking distance from Nicole's.*

I didn't scream for help, I didn't bite him or scratch him. I did what I do best and just took it.

'Nothing Megan, I just don't think Matty and I will work out.'

I forced myself to keep eye contact, my face smooth and mask in place.

Inside I was screaming.

'Astor, I have seen the aftermath of many people and you not working out. Not once have you sat in a shower until the water was colder than the fucking snow in the Arctic Circle and cried like that,' her voice wobbled at the end, caught on the word cried. 'Please don't lie to me. What happened?'

I pushed to my feet and paced the room, twisting my hands in the long sleeves of my borrowed hoodie. 'Nothing. Just let it go.'

'I can't. Not this time.'

I walked in circles, red carpet, white walls. Posters and soccer boots and textbooks. I shook my head. Felt the tears in the corners of my eyes. The match was lit, just waiting to fall.

'Please,' she whispered, the concern so blatant in that one tear-soaked word. Breaking me.

'I told him no. I swear, Megan, but I didn't fight back. I didn't scream. I didn't fight, and I won't ever, ever get him off me, will I?'

I heard her gasp, saw her as her hands covered her mouth. Her wide eyes swam, and a river flowed from my own. She took two short steps, and I was wrapped in her arms. I let myself lean into her for a minute, maybe two.

I couldn't do this forever though, couldn't expect her to carry this too. I forced myself to step away, wiping my eyes on my sleeves.

'What do we do now? What do you want to do, As. Anything, and I'll be here. Did you call the cops?' She lifted the hem of her shirt to wipe her own face.

'I want to go to school.'

Megan's eyes looked like they were about to fall out of her face in shock.

'Astor...we should go to the police. You need to tell them wh—'

'I don't need to tell them anything,' I said, harsher than I'd ever been with her. I could read her disagreement in the twist of her mouth and the groove that appeared between her eyes. 'You know as well as I do that they won't believe me.'

'Well, no, we don't know that. You're a good student, and Nic and I saw you last night. Aren't we like some sort of witnesses? I'm sure that's a thing.'

'Christ Megan this isn't an episode of SVU! What am I going to say? *Hi officer, I had sex I didn't want last night with a guy I've been trying to date?*'

You didn't have to be a genius to know how things would go, one look at my social life would speak volumes. Telling the truth didn't automatically mean you were believed, and few things stood against you more than being a teenage girl. And on the off chance that they did believe me, that they overlooked my reputation, and the clothes I wore and the make-up I applied with care, on that chance, my entire life would be dissected, privately. Publicly. Because things like this didn't stay tucked away on black lined notebooks in detective pockets.

I also didn't have to look too deeply to touch the embarrassment that curled its way through me. I was stupid to think he had wanted more with me. Stupid to not fight back, to not give every ounce of who I was to get away. What would happen when police interviewed my family, when they realised my mother could barely stand me and my sister thought I exaggerated everything? That my dad didn't care about what happened to me.

No, this was something I would get over on my own. There was no upside to saying anything.

'Astor...' she paused, mentally preparing herself for whatever argument she was going to use. I wrapped my arms around my middle and cut her off.

'Please. I can't. I won't. I just want to go to school and pretend last night never happened.'

'You know he's going to be there too,' she said.

I knew he would be there, but we didn't have any classes together, and I simply would find somewhere else to sit at lunch. I needed to keep busy and for my life to just...stay the same.

'Oh fuck, I don't have a uniform. And my phone is probably dead. Mum and Dad will have noticed I didn't come home. Fuck, fuck, fuck.'

I buried my head in my hands, digging my nails in. I didn't need to deal with them on top of that fresh hell.

'Okay. Okay, we can go to my place. I drove here so that's not a problem. I didn't think of your phone though, sorry, and Nic doesn't have an iPhone.' She pulled her own phone out of her pocket and offered it to me. 'You could text your dad?'

'...no, I think I'll just wait 'til I can use my own. I can borrow your charger, yeah?'

She nodded her head, messaging someone herself. Nic appeared a moment later and I immediately looked away, feeling my face flood with heat. The way I was last night—so unlike any version of myself—I was mortified. I was sure she had some idea of what would have happened. It wasn't rocket science to figure something had happened between Matty and me. I studied the chipped polish on my nails, trying to suffocate my shame, so I could thank her. Megan was talking in a low voice, the familiar tone kept me in the moment and not drifting in my memories.

I forced my head up. I knew I had to get a handle on this shit. It was just sex. I'd had sex before, plenty. It was just like that. Just sex.

Hello new mantra.

'Uhm Nic? Thank you.' I injected as much sincerity as I could manage into those few words. She had such an open face, watching me like I was a puzzle to solve before replying.

'You'll be okay Astor.'

I nodded, making peace with that being my set response for the time being.

'I'll wash everything and get it back to you, Nic,' Megan said. 'Can we just grab a bag to throw all our clothes in?'

Things moved quickly after Nic returned with the bag. Megan bundled everything up, ushered me into her car and we drove to her place to change into uniforms. I tried to focus on anything other than last night but couldn't quite silence the little voice saying I should have known better.

We sat in her car down the road from the school.

'Dude, are you sure this is a good idea?' Megan asked, sounding unsure on this whole school plan.

'Yeah. I just want to keep things normal.'

Nodding, again. How many nods before it's a signature move?

'We won't go near the group, okay? We'll sit somewhere just the two of us.'

'Can we just go?'

I didn't wait for her answer, getting out of the car and setting off at a brisk pace. I didn't have any books, my phone was dead, and I wanted to throw up. For all my insistence that I would be fine, I absolutely did not feel like I would be fine. The idea of seeing him again curdled my stomach and made me want to run as far as possible in the opposite direction. Megan huffed up behind me, trying to zip her bag shut at the same time.

'I put a binder in that bag for you, and a couple pens. Sorry all I had was a *Finding Nemo* bag.'

'It's fine. Thank you.'

I knew I owed her so much more than a simple thank you; she deserved more in a friend than I was ever able to be.

The closer we got to the gates, the more my skin prickled, and my stomach twisted. I grabbed her hand and gave it a squeeze, stopping us both.

'I don't know how anything is meant to be now. I'm so scared to see him. I know I said I wasn't but I am.'

She blurred behind the tears burning my eyes. I clung to her hand and my body shook. I couldn't work out why this was affecting me so severely when I went home daily to a mother who frequently wrapped her hands around my neck. I knew Matty wasn't going to touch me at school. Logically, I knew that. And yet, bile ripped its way up my throat at the reality that I would see him today.

'Fuck it, Astor I'm taking you home. Come on.'

'No, no. I can do this. I need to,' I said. My voice was a plea and a sob hastily sewn together.

'As, sometimes it's okay to just...not be okay. There aren't any rules for how you feel.' She took a steadying breath while I tried to gulp down air. 'I think we should tell Dad.'

I pulled my hand from hers and backed away, fear warping into panic.

'No. No, no, no. I don't want to tell *anyone*.'

'Astor. You haven't done anything wrong. You were ra—'

'NO!' I yelled at her, yelled with enough force I stunned us both into silence.

The world narrowed to just us. Just us on the footpath, standing between childhood and the adult world. A line we danced along so frequently as teenagers. We painted our faces and our nails. Stuffed our feet into heels and drunk until life was a kaleidoscope of laughter and colour. We made choices we weren't old enough or smart enough to make. Then we came home and climbed into *Care Bear* pyjamas and slept in beds our parents bought and went to schools they chose for us. Never knowing when our own decisions would creep into our days to trip us up and remind us that our years were few.

A lifetime had passed in that moment. I don't know what she saw on my face or the secrets seeping from my eyes, but she held out her hand. No judgement or anger.

'I'll take you home and we can do whatever you want Astor. You always have me.'

I knew with no question she meant it.

CHAPTER THIRTEEN

No one was home, but I knew they wouldn't be. Megan wanted to stay and wait with me, but I was exhausted. I hadn't done anything except sit in the car and cry, but my entire body felt like it was falling apart.

'We can watch a movie and just hang out for a while. I'll go before your mum is back from work,' Megan said as she made her way into the living room.

'Meg, honestly, I just...want to have a nap and maybe another shower. Wash my hair properly,' I smiled at her, tried to make my face convincing.

'I'm not sure you should be alone right now. God, your mum really likes plants, doesn't she? It's like the Amazon in here.'

She was trying to distract me, so I wouldn't insist that she leave. She also wasn't wrong. Mother enjoyed a ficus more than most.

'Please, I want to be alone for a bit.'

She looked me over head to toe, assessing what she saw and passing some sort of judgement. Eventually she gave a curt nod.

'Okay. But there are conditions,' she said. 'One, you call me if you aren't coping. Two, you have something to eat and send me a photo as proof. And three, wash your hair, you look like Bob Ross.'

She ticked each point off on her fingers, smiling at herself for the third. Clearly pleased at her own sad humour.

'Fine, that's fine.'

She pulled me into a fierce hug and I tried to ignore how pathetic I felt.

I watched her climb in her little car and drive away. I was alone for the first time. I decided to shower, hoping that being clean and in my own comfortable clothes would ground me somehow. I moved through the house I had lived in since the day I was born, focused on my next actions only. My room was as it always was. Bed perfectly made, every drawer shut tight. Not a speck of dust or random sock to be a seen. Last night I had walked out of this room with excitement thrumming in my veins, completely unaware that I would walk back in with my soul raw. I wish I could go back and continue to see the world through the eyes of Astor from last night.

I pulled out my favourite green pyjama pants, a tank top, and a cardigan big enough for two people to wear at once.

I took stock of the disaster that I was in the full-length mirror. Megan's spare uniform was a little too tight, the plaid skirt short and the button unable to close. My hair was a riot. If you squinted it sort of looked intentional, but I knew I would be using a bottle of conditioner in penance for not brushing it last night. I turned to walk away, to go and bond with the soap, when a little burst of red caught my eye. Forcing me to a dead stop, heart included.

Where my neck sloped down into my shoulder, the usual gentle curve with its faint and sparse freckles, was now marred by a purple-red circle.

His mouth on my skin wasn't something I was likely to forget, and yet I had missed this detail. Or maybe I had hidden it from myself. What the fuck else had I hidden from myself?

I stripped then and there, standing in front of my mirror in the full light of day, looking for what marks were lying in wait on my skin to catch me off guard.

An oval on each hip, where his thumbs had pressed into my skin. The corresponding finger marks seemed like faded ink blots, when I twisted my body to look at my back. I traced the marks with my own smaller thumbs. Disgust and confusion and wonder battling for prime position in my head.

I thought I knew him. But these marks said otherwise, and I knew I would see them as clear as they were now long after they had faded. Nausea twisted through my stomach, and I tore my eyes away. Balling up my clothes, I walked to the bathroom and started the shower, resolute on not looking at my body again any time soon and determined to be clean.

Again.

I was curled up on the overstuffed sage green sofa watching a mind-numbing third hour of *Catfish*, when mum came home from work. The door banged shut, and the familiar sounds of her emptying her handbag pulled me from the fog I'd gratuitously slipped into. I braced myself for her anger. I was going to tell her Megan was sick and had needed me last night and

I'd forgotten to charge my phone. I didn't want her to yell but I knew it was inevitable, so I let myself focus on the small sliver of hope that was her committing to getting sober. At least I had that, and I had to hope that would lead to something better. Anything had to be better than what I lived in now.

The TV show dragged on as I waited for her. Countless people claiming that they'd found "true love" with strangers online. Strangers who never turned out to be who they said they were. I loved that show, I loved how they were all so unable to see the obvious. And of course, I thought of Matty and how I hadn't seen a thing but what he'd wanted me to. Again, I was taken back to the inside of the salmon-coloured car, the stale air, and engulfing dark. The snapshot moments. I wanted to set them all on fire and eliminate them from my mind for good. All I could really do, however, was to just focus on now, and right now was this mindless MTV trash. Then I would have dinner. And after dinner I would read, then sleep. Dinner, read, sleep. I knew I could manage those few things. Just had to keep focusing on the next things.

'ASTOR!'

I was sharply smacked back into the living room, Mum standing across from me. The stern set of her lips and her crossed arms told me I had been even less present than I'd thought.

'Sorry…' I said, forcing myself to pay attention.

Mum didn't smile, she merely stood taking in my pjs and TV binge. 'Want to let me know why I have a voicemail from school claiming you didn't show up today? Did you over-sleep or just go to Megan's?'

I sort of knew in the back of my mind that school might call her when I didn't attend, but it hadn't occurred to me that my not-coming-home last night would go unnoticed. I pulled my phone out from the crack of the couch and opened the call log. No missed calls from her or Dad. She was talking at me, a carefully measured tone, words barely restrained in their anger trying to pierce the hum in my head. Anything could have happened to me last night. Anything *did* happen to me. And when would they have noticed? Dinner time? Tomorrow morning?

'Well? What trivial shit was more important than school then?'

'Are you fucking kidding me?' I snapped out.

'I beg your pardon. Don't you dare take that tone with me!'

'You could at least pretend to care about me!'

Anger blistered beneath my skin. Mum scoffed, rolling her eyes.

'I always care about your education, Astor. And when the school calls to tell me you didn't bother to even show up, you can bet your ass I'm going to have questions, young lady!'

Fitting. She cared about my education. Her status amongst the happy drinkers she called friends. What my success said about her to a group of middle-aged friends.

But how did you not notice your teenage daughter had failed to come home?

'I'm not doing this,' I said to myself more than her.

What was the point. Without so much as a backward glance, I headed to my room, vaguely aware she was calling my name and following me. I needed to snap out of this, whatever the hell this was. Each step away from Mum was making it all worse, but I couldn't stop. I wanted to crawl into bed and bury myself in a book. Leap off the unstable cliff of my life mindlessly into the pages of another.

'Astor! Don't you dare walk away from me. Hey! I'm talking to you. Stop!'

'No.'

Mum was properly shouting now, demanding I stop and look at her. Her voice harboured no negotiation. I let my head fall forward against the closed door of my room, sucking in a breath. Forcing myself turn, I was unable to give her more than a glance. I felt the burn of tears lighting their path down my face. Whatever Mum had planned to say died on her exhale as she took in my sorry image before her.

'Oh Astor, what is going on?'

I couldn't stop the way my body flinched at her outstretched hand any more than I could stop the sigh she let slip.

'I don't want to talk about it.' I wasn't sure how I would talk about it ever. 'Please Mum. Not today.'

She studied me, taking in all the soggy details. Trying to find insincerities in my tears.

'Are you hurt?' she asked. I shook my head. Not daring to speak. 'Okay. But we will be talking about this. I know I haven't been...the best mother. But I'm working on it. And I won't have this shit in my house. You go to school every day. Understood?'

'Yeah. I got it,' I nodded, desperate to slip into my room.

'Okay. I'll knock for dinner.'

I gratefully retreated, my bed an island refuge I crawled onto, and buried my face into the pillows, letting go of each restrained sob. I had lived my entire life with the idea that freedom was attainable. That one day I would walk out the front door and away from Mum and this house. Away from all the poisonous barbs I couldn't escape just yet. Under the mask I wore outside these walls, however, something I couldn't escape had slipped in. Venom coursed throughout and changed everything it touched. My life would move on from Mum and here. A house was just a house. But last night? I suspected that this I would have forever.

When Mum let me know dinner was ready, I forced down a few mouthfuls and stole back to my room. A flicker of happiness that she had postponed her first glass of wine until dinner time in an effort to drink less. A step toward sobriety. I gave her a wobbly smile as I fled. In my room I turned on my light as well as my lamp, needing artificial daytime as the night edged in.

Focusing on what I needed to do before tomorrow, I made a mental list. Uniform checked. Assigned reading. Homework completed. The idea of sharing space with Matty had me screaming down a maze of panic, but it was entirely unavoidable. If I wanted to claw back any semblance of who I was, I had to go. I would go.

As I lay in bed, unable to turn off my lamp knowing full well what lurked in the dark, my eyes found the little metal box that hid my razor. My painful companion. Could it take this away too? The way my skin felt filthy, and my entire body used and discarded, completely different to the way Mum made me feel, but unwanted all the same. Could that little piece of metal fix this too? I wasn't sure I wanted to find out. I forced myself to open my book, committed to reading until I feel asleep, no matter how long it took.

I wasn't doing this.

The morning was bleak. Sleep had evaded me for some time. My eyes didn't shut until the sky was shredded with bursts of pink and birds insisted there was something worth getting up for.

The house was quiet as I got dressed, muscle memory currently my best friend. Mum had left a note tapped to the toaster, her twirly scrawl making it clear we would be talking soon. She did, however, sign the note with a couple of hasty looking x's. I couldn't remember the last time she had given me a kiss—written or real—and with care, I folded the note and slipped it into my pocket to keep.

I had to have breakfast, brush my teeth, and lock up. Bus ride and then school. It was easier to keep my mind on task, I had found, if I focused on what was next.

The walk to the bus stop was crisp, my breath curled in the air and the mist draped across the road in front of me. I knew Dylan would want to know about my date, so I had to work out what I was going to say to people. It was hard as I had no idea what Matty would say to people himself. Whatever it was, I doubted it would be flattering. I stood at my stop, lost in a web of anxiety and indecision, when a familiar car pulled to a stop.

'Do you have any idea how fucking early this is for me?' Megan shouted through the window. I couldn't stop the smile that split my face or the warmth, inside and out, as I slipped into the front seat.

'I think I have a fair idea,' I said. 'What are you doing here?'

'Clearly I am picking you up? I thought we could go together. Moral support and all that.' Her smile was bright, but her face gave away her concern. 'How was last night?'

'It was okay, but I don't think I slept much.'

'Mmh. Well, half of today's classes are likely nappable so you can catch up. No one will care.' She hit play on her Spotify and *Flower Face* flowed smoothly from the speakers. She drove in silence, letting my mind rest in the safety that was Megan's bubble.

Too soon for my liking, she was pulling into the student parking lot, muttering curses as she wished death upon our classmates. Apparently, all were incapable of parking comfortably between the painted lines.

'Ohhhh boy,' nerves sprinted through my body, colliding with the butterflies in my stomach and making me nauseous.

'Are we sure this is a good idea? We can just go back to mine, Dad will be at work now,' Megan asked. She reached out and gave my arm a little squeeze, reminding me she was there.

I felt fragile, damaged in a way I couldn't close my eyes and wish away. I lived with mum, my own flesh and blood who was hardwired to love me. Not just passively, she was meant to love me *unequivocally*. Without terms and conditions and beyond what anyone else could. My mother who tried her best to tear me down routinely with her wine-tinged words and vicious hands. Day in and day out I looked into the eyes of contempt personified and yet, yet it was this 17-year-old boy with soft hair and a tilted smile who had obliterated who I was.

Can't say I liked that.

'Yeah, let's go. Fuck this.' I got out of the car in a hurry, not wanting to linger with my thoughts, any of them.

Student parking was located across the road from one of the school's side entrances, so we had to join the bottleneck of identically dressed people waiting at the crossing. Megan was pressed into my side, her warm body a comfort and keeping me from sprinting back to her car like my ass was on fire.

I looked at the kids around us. Some my age, some a little older. Plenty younger as numbers tended to dwindle in the senior levels of school. I wondered if I stood near another Matty. Was there a female version of him? Was there another me, standing in this little group as the light flickered red and we all awaited the green that permitted us to walk. What would they be like if they existed. Or was it just me? Would I ever stop thinking like this?

We made our way into our form class, Megan stopping at our usual front row desks and shrugging off her bag. Suddenly the front row felt like a stage and I didn't want to perform.

'Can we, uh, sit at the back. I don't want everyone looking at me,' I mumbled. She raised an eyebrow but didn't complain, merely grabbed her things, and moved to the last row and the corner furthermost from the door. 'Thank you.'

'Anything, As.'

I gave her and pulled out a notebook. There was no way I was letting this brain free-range with the thinking, while we sat through form class. I was weighing up what I could—poorly—draw when my phone vibrated in my skirt pocket. I expected Mum, demanding some sort of explanation for last night and pulled it out.

I was wrong.

Matty: are you okay

I stared at his name at the top of the screen, the yellow heart emoji next to it bright and hopeful. I don't know what expression was on my face, but Megan snapped her fingers to get my attention, confusion clear on hers.

'What?' she asked.

'It's him,' I whispered. 'Why is he messaging me?'

'Show me,' she demanded, not waiting for an answer and relieving me of my phone.

'Fucking asshole.' Her fingers moved deftly over my screen before she handed it back to me. 'I deleted his contact and blocked his number. No more surprises.'

Relief.

'Thank you. I saw his name and my brain switched off. Or over to hyper drive. I don't know.'

She smiled at me before something at the front caught her attention, I looked up to see. Tash and Nic had just arrived. Tash's voice carried to the back where we sat currently unnoticed.

'Skipping again. She's ridiculous,' Tash said, sitting in our usual place. Nic sat cross-legged on the desk next to her.

'I'm telling you man, she wasn't right the other night. I've never seen anything like it.' Nic reasoned.

'And I'm telling you, Matty said they had sex and she was weird after, so he dropped her off. Like she has any right to act like a prude.'

'Don't be a bitch.'

'Whatever,' Tash changed the subject then, talking about her next class, and side-stepping any further criticism.

Tears pricked at my eyes and my body felt like lead. I had known this was what people would think, that it was his story against mine. What proof did I have? Nothing except my word, which meant nothing. *Less* than nothing.

'Ignore her As. You know what she's like,' Megan said, not bothering to temper her volume in the slightest. We watched Tash freeze at Megan's voice, not turning to look back at us. A brief moment and she threw herself into conversation again. Nonplussed apparently.

Mr. Henderson came in with zero fuss and took attendance, handing out notes to the relevant kids and sending us on our way when the bell sounded. Time for first period, which also meant time for me to be without my human-shaped safety blanket I lovingly called Megan. We were the last to leave the room and I turned to her just outside the door, but she got in first.

'You'll be fine. You've got this. One class at a time.'

'Yeah. Okay. I think it'll be okay. As long as I'm not free to think, it's okay. And I'll see you at break. By the music block,' I forced a smile and tried to halt the panic poking at my heart rate.

'Right. Now go.'

She fist bumped my shoulder in a truly odd gesture of support and left for her own classes.

It wasn't as bad as I thought it would be. I focused on the work I was given, not letting my attention slip for even a moment. I told myself that this was the proverbial silver lining, my grades would soar surely. I was thankful we didn't have assigned seats and I was able to sit in the back of each class, happy to fade into the background.

Megan asked me to quiz her on French words during break, even though I knew she was in no need of revision, but grateful she offered the distraction.

Lunch time had passed without issue, Dylan joining Megan and I, as we walked around the running track talking nonsense and planning what we would do after we graduated. Dylan seeming to know not to bring up the date and to keep things light.

Tash had ignored me in our mutual classes, but that was fine. I didn't need her. I made concise notes and paid attention to every word each teacher spoke. Completely focused.

By the time the end of the day rolled around I was feeling okay. I took my time when the final bell sounded, packing my books into my bag and setting everything just so. I wanted her well shot of the classroom, so I didn't accidentally overhear any more of her opinions. I slipped out the door and made for the stairs, not taking in the couple at the bottom of them until I was practically on top of them.

'Shit, sorry!' I apologised, orientating myself and realising who I had bumped into.

'Hello Astor,' Matty said, smiling. The familiar one-sided grin was more of a smirk as he raised an eyebrow. Like he dared me to share the secret he knew we had together. Tash was with him, her face a mirror of his expression. I thought she was my friend, in some way. I didn't understand what her problem was with me or why she had one at all. I wish I didn't know what he had told her. Or maybe what I really wanted was to know every little word, so I could pull them apart and examine them. How did each word sound to him.

Was it different to how they sounded to me? I wanted to know what I was meant to do now. How did I gather all the notes of who I was two nights ago and arrange them into a version of me that I could live with?

I didn't say anything to him—to either of them. I turned on my heel and took the long way to get to the school bus, trying to erase that twist of his lips permanently from my mind.

Chapter Fourteen

Megan picked me up again Thursday and Friday, not content with letting me sit on the bus without her. Murmurs of what had transpired with Matty were threading their way through the student body now. Torn paper swapped hands in class, half-truths and full lies scrawled by eager pens were pushed into waiting palms. My peers fed off secrets and falsehoods, each new version spurned their turned necks and cocked heads as they tried to lift what was real, straight out of my mind. Megan and I no longer sitting with our group seemed to confirm that their fourth-hand version of whatever bullshit Matty had spewed was the truth. Tash didn't so much as look my way, and Nic stayed at her side, except in the one class we had together. Both days, she had dropped into the seat beside me, an apologetic smile pulling at her lips but not a syllable of conversation extended. School, a previous haven, offered me little peace now.

Home was a whole other beast. Mum committed to drinking less in an effort to make rehab easier when a space opened up for her. However, the apparent trade-off of less booze was that her mood was acerbic, day and night. Her words had lost their fangs, but they made contact more frequently as she wrested for control. I held my tongue, minded my manners, and slipped into my room the moment I could. My desperation to keep my thoughts occupied saw my homework completed to perfection and library books cleared, as fictional characters fought all of my troubles as well as their own. Night would slink in and set the stage for a midnight pantomime. A cast of violent thoughts tearing through whatever mental peace I had created, determined to drag me into the back of that car. Where light was scarce and the only touch I felt were unwelcome hands and a heavy exhale on my skin.

I slept with my lamp on.

The dark held demons I wasn't brave enough to face.

I had no desire to socialise with anyone on Saturday, not that anyone outside of Megan was interested in my company. Megan had said she was busy this weekend, which wasn't unusual, but I couldn't help but feeling that this weekend tied into her secret messages, somehow. Anxiety and I didn't usually spend so much time together, but we were apparently besties now. A weekend at home seemed like the best choice, however, by Saturday afternoon I was well and truly sick of myself. I had flipped through every streaming service on tv, started and discarded half a dozen books and gratefully completed each chore Mum presented me.

'What can I do now?' I asked, quietly desperate to have a task.

'What is going on?' She was suspicious and her words were curt. Understandable since I didn't typically bend over backwards to do housework.

'Um, nothing. I just want to keep...active...and help out.'

It sounded like a lie to my own ears.

'Since when?' she demanded.

'Since now, I guess?'

'Why aren't you at Megan's? You're always at Megan's.'

Yeah, she'd heard the lie. Her tone got my back up, justified or not, I was annoyed by her questions.

'I just wanted to stay home. At my home. God, is that okay?'

'Don't be ridiculous, Astor.'

'I'm not! For God's sake,' I half-shouted, hands in my hair. I needed to calm my ass down. I closed my eyes and tried to settle my flaring temper. 'Can you just give me something to do. Please.'

'Fine. Callie is coming for dinner. Go peel potatoes, she'll be here soon.'

She turned her back, effectively ending the conversation.

Callie waltzed through the door not long after I had cut my final potato, brown hair in a braid and stretchy blue yoga pants on her legs. I was willing to bet money she had, in fact, never done yoga. I hadn't seen her since our argument at the previous dinner and I tensed, waiting for what she would say.

'Hey As, how's it going?' Callie sounded like her usual breezy self, and she gave my arm a squeeze, dumping her bag on the counter. 'Are they making you work for your dinner, then?'

My body unlocked, relaxing at her words. I was grateful she was here to throw variety into the day. I also couldn't shake that underlying need for her approval.

'Oh you know what they're like...ha ha...' I said. I wasn't going to admit I had been begging for housework like a depraved Cinderella.

'Well, I think you'll be pretty happy with them, tonight, if I do say so myself,' she grinned.

'What do you mean?'

'You'll see soon, and you will love me for this.'

She flounced off to find Mum and I trailed behind her, my curiosity piqued. Both Mum and Dad were in their room, Mum putting laundry away and Dad sitting on their wood framed bed, the floral duvet not quite to his tastes.

'Oh Callie! Hello sweetheart,' Mum's face split into a smile, one I was sure I hadn't seen directed at me.

Don't be bitter Astor.

'Hi! What's for dinner? When can I tell her the news?'

'Come on, let's get out of here, I'd rather not stand around.'

Mum shooed us back out the door, not bothering to answer Callie or clarify what she was on about. We sat down at the dining table and despite how excited Callie appeared to be, apprehension snuck in. Surprises didn't tend to pan out for me.

'Okay, so,' Callie started, grinning ear to ear. 'I'm getting a new car!'

Okay, cool for her. Very irrelevant to me.

'Oh, well that's awesome.' I smiled.

'It is! And I spoke to dad and they've agreed that they'll buy my car off me for you. Isn't that great!?'

I was legitimately stunned. I knew they'd bought Callie her first car when she was my age, but it wasn't something we had discussed, even when I had gotten my license. My parents bought me a lot of things, in their weird way of trying to find a balance between Mum's drinking and my happiness. I think, in their heads, money was the answer, so I didn't ever go without. I had regular "pocket money" paid into my bank by Dad for helping at home and they bought the bulk of my clothes and shoes. I knew I was lucky to have that. Sometimes I felt guilty for accepting the random gifts they gave me, the obvious *sorry for screaming at you* presents. A car though. A car was a solid step towards freedom. I'd be able to leave. I could use what I was saving entirely for a gap year or to travel and not worry about a car.

'There will be some rules, Astor. Callie had rules when she was your age and so will you,' Dad's gruffer voice cut into my sunbathed open road daydreams.

'Yeah, of course. I...thank you?' I stuttered out.

'You're welcome. No driving after 10pm. I don't want you out on the road when all those idiots you call friends are hooning around.' I nodded obediently. 'No one but you drives it. Not Megan. Not Dylan. Not whatever person of the week you're dating. You.'

I fought a visible recoil at his implication that I got around. I didn't know if he thought I was a slut or if he simply didn't care. Like Matty. Either way, my heart squeezed at his words and the fragments of sadness they caused.

'Okay,' I forced out.

'And you're not a taxi service either. Got it?' Dad raised his eyebrows questioningly, like there was a chance I wouldn't agree to his rules. Mum left to get dinner on, her interest in my future mobility approximately zero.

'Yes, definitely. I can do that,' I smiled, glad this was seemingly painless. 'Um, when can I have it?'

'That is why I'm here!' Callie exclaimed. 'I thought you could come home with me tonight. We could have a girly night and watch trash. Then tomorrow we will go get my new car from the lot and you can have mine then and there. I bought the transfer paperwork too.'

My thoughts tripped along an uneven plain, trepidation holding them back. Callie and I had never taken part in things such as "girl time" or "sisterly bonding" activities. Our age difference had always acted as a barrier, keeping Callie in a life box I couldn't reach. But I wanted it, I wanted to go and just, be a teenager with her sister doing pedicures and face masks like a cliché Hallmark movie.

'Okay. Let's do it,' I smiled at her, excitement and nerves playing together in my stomach.

Callie was practically vibrating on the drive to her place. We lived on one side of town, sort of rural, and Callie was clear across the other side, not too far from the coastline, which meant sandy beaches and sea breeze. I hadn't been there a great deal, just because school and weekends with Megan sort of limited that, but Mum went there all the time.

'I am so excited for this! I wasn't sure you'd say yes, but when Mum said you hadn't gone out this weekend I stocked up. A sneaky bottle of vodka—do not tell mum—and some junk food.'

She flashed me a quick smile, not able to take her eyes of the road as we wound down various streets.

'I don't really drink,' I said, not wanting to explain further and sour the happy buzz filling the car. *My* car. There was just something about drinking at home in front of the television that felt too much like Mum for me. It wasn't the same as being out with mates.

The look she gave me was pure disbelief. 'I'm serious. Usually just one or two if it's a hangout thing or whatever.'

'Pfft. You're sixteen and never home. I was your age too, remember? I'm not going to tattle on you drinking yourself blind in some sleazy guy's garage,' she said, rolling her eyes, like the concept of a sober 16-year-old was completely wild. 'Oh! I got orange juice for it too. It'll be fun!'

She looked so happy and so genuinely excited to spend time with me, of all people, so I let it go. We talked about what we could watch that night and the different movies we liked. I was seriously surprised we had so much overlap.

We pulled into her driveway, and she neatly parked in front of her sliding front door. Callie lived in a downstairs flat. The upstairs was clad in a bright cobalt blue weatherboard, a deck wrapping around so the owners could sit outside and undoubtedly look out at the ocean. You could hear the faint crashing of the waves there, but we were a street or so back from the shore, so couldn't actually see anything without a major height advantage. Callie's little home was cinderblock on the outside, painted an off-white and she had a couple of wilting plants in terracotta pots nestled against the wall.

Inside was all Callie. Scuffed wooden floors that creaked in odd places, pale walls and mismatched art. A rainbow of throw pillows huddled together on her third-hand sofa, the grey fabric worn and welcoming. I sat down and pulled a purple cushion onto my lap. I was definitely more relaxed than I had been, but I still worried that there would be more awkward silences than conversations tonight. I need not have worried at all.

Callie dropped down beside me, piling her hair on top of her head with a scrunchie.

'Okay. Game plan. Pjs, food and drink. Do you want to pick the first movie?' she asked, handing me the remote.

I shook my head. 'Nah, you can. I'll go get changed while you decide.'

I got out my clothes, long pink pants with little ducks on them to keep my mauled thighs hidden, and a t shirt big enough for me, Callie and the family upstairs to live in.

'Just get changed here, it's just underwear. How do you feel about Cameron Diaz?'

She was absently flicking through films, barely pausing to take in each title.

'Erm, I need to pee so I'll just. Do that too. In there,' I pointed to her bathroom, in her own house.

'Suit yourself. I'm feeling like *The Sweetest Thing* could be the one. Hurry up.'

She queued the film up as I slipped into the bathroom, changing at warp speed. By the time I got back, she had poured us both a drink, the orange juice watery and to the brim.

'Feel free to start drinking.'

Callie hit play and settled back with her glass, not a care in the world. The vodka was barely diluted, hitting the back of my mouth and burning how bad of an idea this was into my throat. I forced my doubts about drinking at home down, sending Matty and that god awful night with them. I was determined to enjoy my night with my sister.

The movie was funny, I'd seen it before with Megan and it never failed to send me spiralling into fits of laughter. Callie's laugh was more of a shriek, unbridled and explosive, and I don't think I had heard it so often in my life.

'God, the ending is so cheesy, but I just love it.' Callie grinned at me, her Tic Tac-white teeth stark in the faded light.

I had left the bathroom light on, not willing to test myself with the dark right then, but she didn't seem to mind, or notice. We giggled our way through another film, one of those so-bad-it's-good types. I was relaxed for the first time in days. Vodka flavoured my thoughts, keeping them in the present and mundane easily. A whisper told me I would regret this tomorrow, but I just plain did not care. I had some peace at last.

When the credits rolled on possibly the worst movie I had ever seen, Callie got to her feet, shaking out the legs she had been curled up on.

'You going to bed?' I asked.

'Yeah, I'm old. Old and tired. You can watch something else, though; my bed being round that little corner means it won't bother me.' She gathered up the snack rubbish and our glasses, taking them into the kitchen. 'Here. Drink some water, you can't drive tomorrow if you're still drunk.'

'I will. I'm fine though. Just a little tippy. Tipsy.' I gratefully accepted the glass she offered. We sorted the sofa into a makeshift bed and I climbed in, putting old *Scooby-Doo* cartoons on and snuggling down into the blanket.

'I'm really happy you came, Astor. We should do it more often, ya know?'

I nodded and gave her a smile, watching as she moved out of sight. The bathroom light was still on, and my mind was hazy and quiet. I let Shaggy, Scooby and the gang pull me into sleep, not fighting it in the slightest.

When I pried my eyes open next, daylight had flooded the room. I moved my head, testing for a headache. Not so much as a twinge, and I smiled smugly to myself. Callie was in the sunny kitchen, scrolling on her phone and drinking what I assumed was coffee.

'Is that coffee?' I asked.

'Oh hey. Yeah, want one?' She looked up at me, eyebrow raised. Singular eyebrow. *Bitch.*

'God no, I'd sooner dehydrate and die.'

'Not dramatic at all,' she said, scrolling and sipping.

I shuffled to the toaster and set my day officially in motion. We took turns showering, chatting off and on as we got sorted. She asked about Megan and school, but I deftly steered us back to the safer waters of her work colleagues and friends. I was always eager to hear details of her life, always searching for ways to connect us. By 11, we were on our way to pick up her car.

'So what sort is it?' I asked as we pulled up to a set of lights.

'Huh?'

'Your car. What sort is it?' I looked at her puzzled face, searching for and failing to find similar features to my own.

'Um. It's silver?' her voice kicked up at the end like a question.

'Silver,' I repeated.

'Yeah. Look, I took dad with me and he did the mechanic thing, okay? Don't judge me.'

She sounded flustered and I bit my lip to suppress my laugh. Of course she wouldn't know what type.

The car yard was standard fare, primary coloured triangular bunting strung up along the fence and a white banner proclaiming the best deals in the area stretched along underneath. Thankfully, we were in and out. Her 'silver' car was ready to go, so with a lot of excitement from both of us, she accepted her new keys and handed me mine. I had packed my bag up before we left; I wanted to go down to the beach and then go show Megan that I was now, in fact, quite mobile.

'Thanks for this, Callie. Really. I hope we can do it again.'

'Of course! Enjoy the car, she was good to me,' Callie smiled fondly at the beat-up Honda I was now sat in, gave me a little wave, and skipped over to her new shinier car.

Ten minutes later I pulled into a parking space on the beach front.

I left my shoes in the car, cuffed my jeans and stepped onto the sand. The sun was high in the sky, its middle-of-the-day position making it a feature in the picture-perfect blue. The shore was dotted with people, colourful umbrellas forced into the sand and gaudy towels marking out each little group. Bikinis and bellies were out in equal measure. Kids with buckets and boogie boards made sandcastles and paddled in the shallow water. I wove through them all, taking in the sounds and ignoring the heat of the sand on my feet.

'Astor?'

I smiled at his voice. I didn't need to look to know that Dylan was walking towards me. I turned around, shielding my eyes with my hand. His blue-black hair dipped into his eyes, the little bit of wind pushing the strands around and showing his brown roots growing back in. He had his Vans in hand, washed out black jeans pushed up his calves and a TOOL shirt stretched over his teenage boy chest.

'Hey! What are you doing here?' I was never sad to see Dylan.

'I was meeting a mate, but they bailed last minute, thought I'd come stand in the water for a hot minute before the slog home.' He jerked his head to the side, asking if I wanted to keep going. 'What about you?'

'Oh, I stayed with Callie last night so I could take her to get her new car. She's let me have hers and now I am a free woman.'

We fell into step, making our way down the beach and out of the throng of families.

'Sweet! We can carpool!' He smiled his perfect Dylan smile, eyelashes batting.

'Why would I drive you to school when you have a car?'

'Dad needs it for work. Hey wanna get tacos? There's a little hole in the wall place here.' He pointed across the road at the strip of stores painted in bold colours. Most of them serving something edible, judging by the small forest of chairs. I wasn't fool enough to turn down tacos.

We ran across the road, ignoring traffic rules and earning an angry horn. The pavement was literal fire compared to the sand, and I danced in place, not wanting to burn either foot. Dylan shook his head as he watched me out of the corner of his eye, pretending he was focused on the menu board. He had been able to slip his shoes back on.

'I'm going to need to dip my feet in the ocean. I'm surprised they aren't smoking it's so hot,' I griped, still hopping like an utter fool.

'Just go back now, find us a place to sit that isn't in the umbrella sea and I'll bring it over.'

'Are you sure? I can help,' I offered, though my brain had already decided I would be taking him up on his plan.

'I'm sure, I don't need to be carrying you around when you can't walk for blisters,' he laughed.

'Dickhead. Thank you! I'll be over that way,' I pointed in the direction we had come from and took off, dancing on my toes like they would somehow be spared the heat of the ground.

I was standing in the foaming water, watching it surge forward and drag back when he found me, paper bag in hand. We sat down and he kicked off his shoes, digging his pale feet into the sand. Dylan was one of my oldest friends, and though our relationship had changed over the years, from playdough and paddling pools to casual sex and school bus rides, he was still comfortable. Sitting with him was easy, and his frequent smiles and easy laughs drew my own out.

We inhaled our lunch, picking through the fries and wandering the memory lane we shared. He threw a fry at a lone seagull. The universal invitation had half a dozen more descend in front of us, squawking and looking for more. Dylan, of course, obliged.

'Fuck off Carl, that's my one!' he said, making his voice high and cartoon like. 'No! It's mine you feathered rat,' he said, lower, but still like he had sucked down half a tank of helium. 'Give it or I will throw you into the ocean.'

'Are you...pretending to be the seagulls?' I fought to keep the laugh out of my voice. He was utterly absurd. Wonderfully so.

'Maybe. I can't imagine they say anything worthwhile though.'

'Can't say I've given it any thought, you're the only weirdo here,' I ate another fry before they were all bird food.

'Live a little, As.'

He tossed a couple more, watching them scramble over each other. Two of them getting particularly violent, wings flapping and nipping at each other.

'Sharon!' I seagull-spoke, 'I think it's finally time we try pegging!'

Dylan burst out laughing at my very poor attempt at a seagull's voice. I definitely sounded more like *Miss Piggy* than I had intended.

'That's fucking filthy, Astor,' he tried and failed at disgust.

'Hey, you never know what they could like. Don't knock it 'til you try it,' I grinned.

We watched their little grey-white bodies hunt around for more, laughing and tossing out more and more absurd lines for them, until they dispersed when no more food magically appeared.

The air shifted as the laughter washed out of familiar space between us.

'Hey, can I ask you something?' Dylan asked, more serious than he had ever been.

'Sure, whatever,' I shrugged. I pulled my legs up and wrapped my arms around them.

'What happened with Matty?'

Our gazes locked, my head resting on my knees. Unease curling down my spine.

'What's he saying?' I swallowed, concentrated on breathing, and fought to keep my voice neutral. I'd heard the rumours, but I didn't know what he'd said to Dylan and the group itself.

'He said you guys had sex, that you were shit and embarrassed, so he dropped you off,' he smiled at me, lifting his eyebrows up and down. 'Experience tells me that isn't true.'

I felt hollow, my mind dragged back into the dark were fear simmered. His casual words to describe a night that turned me inside out hurt, so much more than I should let them. Reminding me I had thought I was something to him. My eyes found Dylan's and I wondered what he saw as the smile vanished from his lips. His voice softened and his brow furrowed, concern started to edge in. 'Astor, what happened?'

Even if I wanted to tell him, I didn't think I could. If I closed my eyes, I was back in that car, exposed and unwilling, the dark filled with my shame. On the beach, in the present, I stilled. Muscles tight and throat dry as my body fought to keep all the sordid details inside.

'That's not...we...I didn't want—'

Each word felt scraped from my chest, another sacrifice of mine to correct his lies. His eyes were on me and I wondered if the truth was there for him to see. 'I didn't want to,' a whisper, four words that had all the meaning in the world, yet somehow carried no weight when it came to those who made decisions like who to believe and who not to.

He looked away, out at the ocean, his harsh exhale the only outward sign he gave that he had heard me. He had looked away from me and it was a physical pain. Could he no longer look at me? Could he tell I didn't fight enough?

'I'll fucking kill him,' he hissed.

Four words that undid me. I ducked my face into my knees, tears flowing freely and sobs cutting through me. I felt his arm wrap around my back, his hand curling around my shoulder and pulling me into him. It didn't occur to me to resist, and I folded into him, my hands twisting his shirt as my body shook from the force of my crying. He pulled me onto his lap properly, awkward limbs and tangled hair. I was useless and broken and I needed him right then to hold me together. He rubbed my back as I let every emotion I had locked away pour out, my head tucked into the crook of his neck and my fingers pressed into his body.

His whispered words were breadcrumbs and I followed them slowly, each one a stitch in this open wound, settling my tears until all that I had left were burning eyes and graceless sniffs. I wiped my nose on his collar bone, not willing to move yet.

'Please don't tell anyone,' I quietly asked. Minutes passed and I listened to his heartbeat and scrunched my toes in the sand, my legs locked around him.

Finally, he spoke. 'Okay.'

I heard the unspoken "for now" clear as day.

Children tore up and down the beach around us, parents with missing flip flops and red noses set up and pulled down their umbrellas. It all moved forward in bursts and screams and seagull shrieks. Moments from that night, now free from the box I tried to keep them in, flickered behind my eyes and threatened to tear me apart again.

But Dylan sat with me—his legs undoubtedly going numb—as his fingers traced shapes on my back, keeping me in the present with him.

CHAPTER FIFTEEN

I wouldn't miss taking the school bus, I could say that with confidence. I sat in the school carpark, reading a few pages of my book until it was an appropriate time to go in. Yesterday at the beach had been draining, I'd sat wrapped around Dylan like a stage-five clinger for a while, eventually clambering off. I thought I would have been absolutely drowning in shame after, but that hadn't been the case. He seemed to recognise my need to keep my mind busy and had filled the air with his voice. We talked about all the things we skipped over typically, movies and books, and random childhood memories. At times wading into the ocean and soaking our hastily rolled jeans, and childish people-watching games, assigning strangers lives and jobs with no reason. Dylan had kept me busy and distracted until the horizon reached out to gently tug the sun from the sky.

Megan knocked on my window and I felt my soul leave my body. She pulled my door open, and I tried to settle my heart rate.

'Christ, Megan,' I said, swinging out of the front seat.

'Well hello to you too,' she smiled, quietly pleased with scaring me. 'How was your weekend? Aside from inheriting this beast.'

'Be nice to my beast. It was okay. It was, like, good to spend time with Callie? Though I spent most of yesterday at the beach.'

'What, alone? You don't like the beach,' she said, scrunching her nose.

We were crossing the road now, the school gates looming. Each step was like a match to my anxiety, setting it alight as we got closer.

'Oh. No, with Dylan.'

I hoped a new batch of gossip was ready from the weekend, letting mine fade into the background as we cross the boundary and into the grounds. I snuck glances at the students around us, trying to work out if it was me they were looking at, if I was the name on their lips.

'Dude, are you okay?' Megan asked, soft and cautious.

'Yeah, I'm fine. I'm good,' I made myself smile, blocking out the imagined whispers around me. 'What did you do on the weekend then? I barely heard from you.'

I watched her face change, concern morphing into something else I couldn't quite place, streaks of red across her cheeks.

'Just stuff with dad. He wanted some time together,' she said, eyes pulling away from me.

Lie.

'So what did you do?' I pressed, curious.

We were outside our form class, Megan seeming to know without words that I needed to prepare myself to walk into a room of students.

'Just, went out and stuff. Nothing major…' she trailed off, pulling her phone out and swiping away. I wanted to know what she was keeping from me, but I didn't want to fight with her again, not when she was the only guaranteed person I had here.

We slipped into the room, found our seats at the back, and tried to ignore the not-so-subtle glances that followed.

I made my way through morning classes, frustrated with myself. Last week, each lesson had served up distraction on a silver platter. Notes and textbook passages smothering the buzzing in my head effectively. Today had been an uphill battle. I found myself tuning into the chatter around me rather than the lesson being taught or the pages I needed to read. Each class was a fight to keep myself focused, my eyes locked on the board at the front of the room as I strained to hear any hint of my name in the swell of conversation around me. It was a relief when one class ended, though the walk to the next was an exercise in avoiding Matty, in person and in name.

It was all exhausting.

When the bell sounded signalling the beginning of our lunch break, I sent Megan a quick message and scurried to the closest bathroom, eyes down. I rounded the corner of a block of classrooms, the doorway to the toilets mere steps away, and came face to face with both Matty and Tash, as well as few assorted faces from our grade. I swallowed a painful croak of surprise and ducked through the doorway, hands shaking.

Only two of the six pale yellow cubicles were occupied so I didn't have to wait, thankful to shut myself into a little box alone. The bathroom smelt like bleach and old shoes, and I focused on that as best as I could. I wasn't sure I would ever get used to seeing that perfectly styled hair and sharp jaw in person, and not just when I closed my eyes in the depths of the night.

When I came out, somewhat calmer and ready to find Megan, a familiar blonde head with shaved sides and Viking-style braid was washing her hands. Her sharp feline eyes caught mine in the mirror, a smirk twisting her glossy lips as we both watched my eyes widen.

'Well hello Astor,' she said, grabbing a paper towel for her hands as she turned. She leant her butt against the chipped counter, effectively a barrier between me and the exit.

'Hi Tash,' I replied, and forced myself to walk forward and turn the water on. She straightened and watched, clearly intent that we had this conversation.

'I don't understand you, you know,' her voice was all curiosity, and I had no idea if it was genuine or not. I didn't know what I had done, to set her against me. I hadn't thought she was interested in Matty, since she was supposedly dating that girl Milla that she worked with, but maybe I had been wrong. I turned to face her, pulling my shoulders back in some sort of pretend confidence. Fake it til you make it and all that.

'What do you mean?' I asked.

'You and Matty,' she said, tilting her head. Nausea flipped in my stomach at our names linked like that.

'I don't know what you mean.'

'Matty. He takes you out. We all know you were gagging for it.' She rolled her eyes, barely stopping to exhale before barrelling on. 'You fool around and what? It's shit? He said you were a mess after. And Nic said the same, that she had to call Megan.' She studied my face, fishing for reactions I wasn't sure I'd provide. 'Are you mad he's told people you were a bad lay?'

'Mmmm,' I looked down, unsure what I was meant to say. I knew what he had told people exactly, thanks to Dylan. I focused on the chipped tile floor, willing the tears to stay back. I really needed to get out of here. 'Can you move. I'd like to go.'

'No. I want to know why you're being a freak about this. You suck in bed, who fucking cares. Dylan's at your heels constantly so he clearly doesn't.' She stood taller, arms crossed. 'Half the school is looking at Matty like he's scum, and it's cause of you.'

This was news to me. It felt like everyone and their mother was looking at me and whispering as I went past. Was she imagining things, or was I?

'I don't want to get into it with you, Tash.' I pushed past her, desperate now.

'You're pathetic Astor. Get over it, it's just sex. You obviously wanted him, you got him.'

I spun around.

'It was not "just sex", Tash. You have no fucking idea. Shut your god damned mouth,' I yelled at her, the fury and sadness I felt fighting for control of every word. I fled the bathroom, pushing through students, and fumbling for my phone to find out where Megan was. The words "just sex" wormed through my mind. Confusion wasn't exactly a new contender in my mind, but boy was it winning.

Megan was waiting for me by the music room as usual, phone in hand and a smile played across her lips. She looked up as I approached and dropped her phone into her purple backpack.

'Hey, are you alright?' she asked, potentially sensing I was in fact, not.

'I just had a run in with Tash.' I pushed my shaky fingers into my hair, trying to make sense of what was happening in my head. Megan stepped closer, forcing me to look at her properly.

'Are you okay?'

'Yes. No. I don't know. Tash said—' I took a calming breath, which did no calming whatsoever. 'She said that half the school is treating Matty like shit and I should get over it because it was "just sex" and I just...I don't know.' My hands dropped to my sides, and quietly, the words barely formed in their whispery state, I asked: 'what if I am overreacting, Meggy?'

I bit my lip, watched her watching me, and tried to work out what she was seeing on my face. I was doubting myself, doubting my memory of that night. Maybe I hadn't been clear with him, or maybe I wasn't remembering right. I had said no. But I had also climbed into the back.

'No As. It wasn't just sex.' Her voice low but sure.

'But Meg, wha—'

'Stop. You know that it wasn't. You know it. It would be a lot easier if it was just sex. But it wasn't.' Tears swam in the corners of my eyes and I tried to let her words sink in. 'Don't let her twist what you know is true, As.'

'Twist what?'

Megan and I jumped apart and I swiped at my eyes. Dylan looked from Megan to me and back again.

'Astor had a run in with Tash,' she explained, pulling her phone back out and swinging her bag onto her back. 'What are you doing here?'

'Ah, well, I decided I'd hang out with you two. If that's okay?' He smiled sheepishly, hands wrapped around the straps of his bag.

'Oh? What's wrong with the others?' Megan asked, eyebrow raised.

'I may knock Matty's teeth out, and I promised Astor I wouldn't do anything,' he smiled at me, his own teeth on display. I laughed, but the sound wasn't quite right, more strangled mania than joy. Megan and Dylan exchanged a look, and I just didn't care. I didn't want to be here. I wandered between them as we walked around the school. They spoke over my head to each other, in between bites of food, trying to draw me into conversation again and again. But all I could hear was Tash's words, metronomic and scathing. When the bell finally rang for the start of the final period, I parted ways with Dylan and Megan, heading directly to my car and home.

I didn't want to be here anymore.

I stepped out of the shower, skin raw from the obscene water temperature and another round of intense scrubbing. I checked my phone, my early absence hadn't been noted and now that it was after dinner, Megan usually checked in. Only one text from Callie, however. We had exchanged a couple this afternoon, and I felt like the weekend had built some sort of little bridge between us. This time she had sent me a photo, a little fluffy kitten she wanted to adopt. I sent back heart eyes and pulled on my pjs, deciding on tv once again over a book. I didn't want to try and focus on words right now when I could watch idiots on a screen, as I had been doing since I got home.

Dad was reclined in his chair, his grey socked feet crossed at the ankle and the remote resting on his belly. Mum had her teacup on the table next to her; the wine bottle she filled it from tucked next to the leg, like being on the floor had made it invisible. She had only finished her third teacup full, which was a massive change as by now she had typically neared the end of the bottle and was looking toward a second. I settled into watch, talking to Dad about the different changes the couple on tv made to their home. Mum scoffed each time, her tone shifting from uninterested to anger steadily.

'Helen,' Dad chastised her, and my anxiety stepped up a notch. I pulled his attention back to me, not wanted them to get into an argument. I was so happy that rehab was soon, and happy that she was trying to cut down how much she was drinking. But the trade seemed to be that her anger was on a hair trigger and anything set it off.

'Yeah, that would be right, wouldn't it,' she said as Dad laughed with me at the tv, a hint of alcohol followed each word.

'What are you on about?' Dad asked, as confused as I was as to where this was headed, but not as cautious.

'It's always you and her, isn't it?' she spat. Unease, my familiar friend, seeped into my bones.

'Enough, Helen.'

'No. Look at you sitting here laughing, you're pathetic.'

She poured more wine into her cup, the final dregs of the bottle. Dad didn't say a word, and I knew it was best if I went to bed. I stood up and tried to slip out unnoticed.

'Where are you going?' she slurped her wine and asked.

'Just leave her alone Helen. Astor, go to bed.'

'I am,' I smiled at Dad, happy to leave.

'I don't have to leave her alone, she's my daughter. I had her just for you, didn't I?'

Her tone rose at the end, her words familiar. I was well aware she had me for Dad. She had been content with just Callie; one perfect, pretty child. But Dad had always wanted one of his "own" so here I was. Alcohol and resentment didn't really go hand in hand in terms of happy times.

I walked out, slipping into my room as their voices grew louder, though this argument was familiar. I barely had any space in my head for Mum when I had Tash's words to keep me company already. They'd waited in the background all afternoon, letting me think I had this infinitesimal win. Now I stood alone in the bedroom I had been in my entire life, both my ceiling light and lamp on, and the rise and fall of an argument rolling off the walls behind me. That's when they crept back in, the two words that had me prodding at the details of that night to gauge their accuracy. I settled into bed, book in hand, determined to ignore it all and let another world take me. After I tried and failed to start four separate books, however, I was willing to admit defeat. I couldn't focus, I'd read a paragraph, a page even, and then I'd slip. A word or phrase somehow dragging me back to that car and the way he spoke.

I turned off the main light. The lamp was one I couldn't part with, so I curled up on my side and turned my face into its soft glow. The silver was almost a mirror in the half-lit room, my salvation and depravation in a perfect box. Under the lamp light I could close my eyes and I did, letting the barrier down and those two short words loose. For once, instead of fighting it, I let the film play out. My green skirt and his styled hair and my desperate pleas of stop.

But did I struggle enough? Did he think I was kidding or that I wasn't serious? Did he think the fact that I lay there in silence while he moved above me meant I was okay with it, okay with him using my body that I had not freely given. Maybe I wasn't clear enough. Loud enough. Determined enough.

My pillow was damp, absorbing each wave of tears as they fell. Tears I didn't try and halt, knew I didn't have the chance to stop. Fingernails made half-moon bites in my palms and my chest ached. Physical pain and heartbroken agony as I remembered how it felt to feel nothing and how nothing wasn't what I had imagined it to be. There was no black void, no hole in my memory. Just a drip of condensation and the shuffling of clothes as my brain saved this unwanted snapshot for later but kept my mind blank in the moment.

I felt so defeated.

I cried until I couldn't. Wrung out and exhausted, sad, and weak. I didn't want to be, I didn't want him to win. I didn't want "bad sex" to be the start of my end, for Matty to have pulled those strings and set it in motion. My eyes fell to the box, silver and square. Comforting.

An idea stretched, all willpower and determination and a better mental box. I didn't have to be this pathetic imitation of me if I didn't want to be, and frankly I didn't want to. I weighed the silver box in my palm, letting my thoughts trip into one another. Tomorrow, I would go to school and I'd ignore everyone there. I would get on with my life. I just had to shove Matty so far down, all the emotions and flashes of fear. I could do that, I knew I could, if I tried. With help. First thing that had to go, though, was the lamp. It was just my bedroom after all.

I groped for the switch, set at some arbitrary point of the power cord and plunged the room into pure darkness with one sure click. My pulse faltered then took off, my ears throbbing as the blood flowed at twice the pace and gulps of panic spread from my chest. I hurried to find the cord again, running my shaking fingers along it to the switch and restoring the pale glow.

I'd work on the lamp.

CHAPTER SIXTEEN

'New day. New Astor,' I said, as I checked my eyeliner in the rear-view mirror. 'Well, the old Astor. Again.'

Talking to myself wasn't a new low, but it wasn't exactly a high either. Getting out of my car was the next step and that was fine. I was fine. I shut the door and straightened my uniform, brushed my fingertips along the hem of my skirt. Habitual. Covered.

Megan had messaged to say she'd meet me at the gate, so I plastered on what I hoped was a reasonable smile and—with music blaring in my ears—that's where I headed. I spotted her as I crossed the road, ignoring everyone around me, and I watched her laugh as she talked to someone on her phone.

Firstly, who was she talking to that lit her face up like that? And secondly, who the fuck spoke on the phone?

I stopped a few steps away and just watched. Her free hand waved about as she spoke, no doubt moving with the rise and fall of her voice. I wondered when I had last seen her so happy, and guilt whispered in my ear. How hard was it to be my friend, sucked into my misery. If even a sliver of me had been on the fence with dragging out my old Astor mask, this had been the moment it evaporated. She spun around on the ball of her foot, cheeks pinked and glasses slipping. Her eyes widened when she saw me and she twirled back around, severing her call with a breathless goodbye.

'Hey,' she smiled. It wasn't the same as before. Still Megan, genuine and warm, but not so light-hearted.

'Bonjour friend. How are you on this fine day?' I smiled back, opting to not ask who she was talking to.

'Uhm...I'm fine. You seem happier today?' she questioned, puzzled.

Understandable. I was a basket-case yesterday—and for many days before, *let's be real*— but today, not so much.

'I am,' I said.

'Right...okay?' Studying my face, Megan seemed unable to lift the information she desired straight from my mind. 'I don't get what changed?'

'Nothing. I just accepted that it was just bad sex,' I swallowed the repulsion I felt at those words. '...and that I needed to get over it,' I shrugged.

As I'd been speaking, Megan's eyebrows had made a steady climb into her hairline.

'You accepted...I just. Bad sex. What the fuck?!' her mouth was open, eyes wide and pure disbelief rolled off of her.

'Yeah,' I nodded. 'I'm good. Should we go in?' I shifted my bag on my back and walked away, trusting she would follow and not bring this discussion with her.

No such luck. *Shock*.

'Astor. I'm fairly sure that it doesn't work like that.'

'It's fine. I'm fine. Can we not do this?' I forced a smile. 'Have you seen him today?'

'Have I seen who?!' Her voice had hit shriek territory and I had the distinct feeling her head was about to pop off.

But I needed to know where he was. My blood crawled with the need to know.

'Matty,' I said.

'Are you fucking serious? Why do you want to know where that piece of shit is? I swear to God if you go and talk to him I wi—'

'No, no. I just want to know where he is. So I can be elsewhere.'

Her face had flushed red at his name, her anger palpable. I closed my eyes for a moment and willed everything I could feel bubbling up inside to stay still, calm. I couldn't risk even the barest strand of how anxious I was coming undone. How afraid and close to falling to my knees. The delicate dance of secrets and feelings and darkest thoughts were right there, balanced on the edge. I pulled on the strand, tying it off. I wasn't weak and I would be normal. I just wanted to know where he was.

The bell sounded, signalling it was time for class.

'I have no idea where he is, but I don't like this. This whole denial thing you've got going on,' she said, eyeing me sternly.

I didn't say a word, there was nothing to say. I took a deep breath to ready myself and followed her into our form class.

It turned out it was a lot harder to fake it than I had anticipated. As I moved through the motions of the day, muscle memory taking me from class to class, I found myself continuously searching for where *he* was. In class I forced myself to take notes, blindly writing down the information being taught, which had no chance in hell of being absorbed, not on this day. I smiled at anyone I made eye contact with, said hello to the "sort of friends" I had in my classes, choosing to ignore the wide eyes and startled responses. I was exhausted, my mind hummed like a radio left on low, singing words you can't make sense of. I wasn't convinced I didn't look half mad, but I was doing it.

During our first break I threw myself into the conversation between Dylan and Megan, their mutual interest in B-list film was something they fell back to frequently, as they tried to work out their new persistent close proximity. During a particularly riveting breakdown of the film *Holy Rollers*, I excused myself to the bathroom. Dylan had confirmed that Matty and his cohorts were clear across the school, so I felt at relative ease making the short walk to the toilet block. I ducked round the corner of a classroom and wiped my palms on my skirt, conscious that they were sweaty. I was uneasy, the background noise in my mind had cut off and I didn't know when it had. The constant hum was now a hollow echo of meaningless sound. Loud and empty all at once. I stopped outside the door, hand lifted to open it, and I couldn't do it. I didn't want to be stuck in there again with Tash, even though I knew she was on the other side of the school. I told myself to just...push the door open. Willed myself forward. I just couldn't. I turned on my heel and fled back to Megan, trying to walk normally and also at twice my normal pace.

What the fuck was wrong with me? I had been shut in my room, chased with a knife, trapped in *that* car. Yet the thing that had my hands shaking and clenching, and my heart racing was a school bathroom?

The closer I got to Megan and Dylan, the less I shook. I came to a halt at her side, quick sharp breaths, and eyes huge, I knew I looked unhinged. They had both looked up at my return and Megan didn't miss a thing. Her narrowed eyes were presently burning into the side of my head. I gave Dylan a wobbly smile and felt relief as he drew Megan back into conversation, providing me with the bubble I needed to get myself under control.

When the bell finally went off, Dylan took off with a wave, leaving me with my best friend and her squinting side eye.

'What happened?' she demanded.

I would have been okay if she knew me a little less well to be frank. This was not part of my back-to-normal plan.

'I am quite unsure what you mean,' I quipped, pulling my bag on and walking away. Her hand wrapped around my arm and she yanked me back.

'Don't be a fucking dick. What is going on? You've been creepy-happy all day and then you go to the toilet and come back looking like you saw the ghost of Dolly Parton in there. Tell me.'

Her tone was dead serious, angry and concerned. I wanted to tell her, but I felt like an idiot. I looked at her, avoiding her eyes, and took in the furrowed brow and hard set to her mouth. 'Astor,' she sighed.

'I couldn't go into the bathroom,' I said quietly. The anger lifts off her face, confusion and concern front and centre.

'Why? What do you mean? Come on, keep walking or we'll be late,' she linked her arm with mine and lead the way to her next class, thankfully it wasn't too far from mine.

'I...got to the door and couldn't go in.' She raised an eyebrow at me, so I ploughed on. 'I got scared, I think. I don't know, I just couldn't go in and I freaked out.'

She didn't say anything, turning it all over in her head I presumed. She pulled me to a stop again.

'Well, come on, then.'

'What?' my turn to be confused. Though recently confusion and I had gotten better acquainted.

'I assume you still need to pee, so let's go. I'll come in too or wait outside. I don't care.'

She shrugged and walked off, still dragging me with her. She stopped at the doorway, pretending she didn't notice the way I tensed. 'Do you want me in or out?' she asked.

I closed my eyes and waited a moment. I felt like an absolute idiot.

'In please.'

She tugged me through the doorway and I didn't explode, which felt like a start. I slipped into a cubicle and desperately wanted to cry. 16 and I needed my friend to take me to the bathroom.

Megan was at the sink, she had turned the taps on and was on her phone as she waited. She didn't say a word as I washed my hands but just outside the door, back in the fresh air, she stopped me.

'We'll figure this out, As. I'll come with you every time. But maybe you should tell my dad. Panic attacks aren't a joke,' she spoke quietly, seriously.

Immediately I wanted to run. Or scream. A panic attack.

Is that what this was? How did this make any fucking sense? Why was I panicking about a school bathroom and not cars or wine bottles? I was such a fuck up I couldn't even panic right.

'I don't want to tell your dad. Or anyone. Can we just keep it between us?'

Plain as day she didn't like that. I felt awful asking her not to tell her dad. I felt awful about a lot of things, it would seem. I still didn't want to tell anyone else.

'I just think he could help—'

'I don't want to, Jesus Christ,' I snapped at her. 'Sorry. I just. I'll be fine, I just need a bit of time, okay?'

'Fine. Okay. I don't like it, but it's up to you,' she nodded, not happy. 'I think this fake happy shit is crap too. Just for the record.'

'Noted. And thank you.'

'Yeah, yeah. We're bloody late now.' The grounds empty of people now that class was in. 'Also, let's sleep in the fort this weekend. I want time with my best friend.'

'It's still up?' I was genuinely surprised. Builders we were not.

'Fuck yes, it is. I'm a genius. Now go to class,' she dismissed.

I said goodbye and fixed a neutral smile on my face, braced for more "old Astor".

Every single day after was pure exhaustion, start to end. Each day I needed Megan to come with me to the bathroom, and each day I needed to know where Matty was. More than wanting to know where he was so I didn't have to see him, I wanted to know who he was talking to. Who was he sucking into his vile little world. It was becoming an obsession. Matty was a "good guy", easy to like and fall for. I was not a good anything. When I let myself imagine the scenario where I reported what had happened, I knew how it would play out. The police would turn my life inside out, they'd comb my social media, interview my "friends", and ask what I was wearing. How long was my skirt? Did I wear make-up? Perfume? Had I kissed him before, let him touch me before? What was my reputation like? Was I a party girl? Did I drink or smoke weed or sneak into the bathrooms of house parties to have quick casual sex with a friend, or stranger?

So it was better this way, I just needed to see him and know he was where he was meant to be, or at least get reliable intel as to his location. Every so often, if I did see him in between classes or whatever, he simply ignored me. Tash provided enough filthy looks to compensate for his lack of them. I spent my days forcing my scattered mind to focus on class, smile at people, say hello and be present.

Every night this week at home had been unpredictable. Mum had stopped trying to drink at a later time and was mostly back to her regular schedule. The closer we got to her rehab admission the angrier the wine made her. Her handprints smeared across my shoulders in scarlet and purple, - bruises from slamming me into the bathroom door the night before last. All at odds with the weeping apologies and declarations of love of last night. Nowhere felt like a refuge anymore.

Except Megan's. The moment I stepped into the unrestrained chaos of her room, I felt calm. The need to be someone I wasn't, to mind my words or force a smile was gone and it was just relief.

We were on her bed, *Rocky Horror* on the tv and passing a bag of chocolate caramels between us, when Megan spoke.

'Hey As, can I talk to you?'

She didn't pull her eyes off the screen, and I wondered if this was it, the moment I got to find out what she was keeping secret.

'Uhm, always?' I forced a little laugh. I couldn't pretend I wasn't nervous to hear what she was hiding. She opened her mouth to speak, and I braced myself for whatever it was.

Both our phones lit up and vibrated simultaneously. The relief rolled off Megan and we grabbed our phones. I wasn't thrilled with the secret reveal interruption even if she was.

'Troy message you too?' Megan asked, eyes on her screen.

Apparently, drinks were happening tonight at his place. Another bonfire, same people. Sundown.

He'd also sent a video of a grown man impersonating various dog breeds which had zero relation to the invite.

I hoped.

'Yeah. We should go,' I said, mulling over the idea, more sold on it by the second. Megan's secret forgotten in the wake of this new information.

'Are you serious? You know he will be there?'

'Well, it is his house, dude.' I knew she meant Matty and not Troy. I wanted to see Matty, from a distance. Make sure he wasn't wrapping his arm around someone unsuspecting. That he wasn't offering rides to anyone else.

'No, like. This is not a good idea.'

She ignored my obvious attempt at ignorance and sat up properly, crossing her legs.

'I'm going to go Megan,' I looked around for my bag so I could change into jeans. 'You don't have to come, I have my car.'

'Fucking hell. Nothing good will come from this.'

She was right, we both knew it. But I couldn't escape how badly I needed to see him; it was like a compulsion now. At school I had become obsessive about knowing where he was. I needed to make sure I didn't run into him by surprise, but also, to make sure no one else was taken in by his charm. I just wanted to keep an eye on him. There was no harm in that.

I pulled on my battered converse and let my hair out of the elastic keeping it in place.

'Look, I know it makes no sense, Meg, but I just. I need to go,' I said. I wasn't sure how to make her understand the marrow deep need to go without sounding like I'd gone off the deep end. Though to be fair, I like had gone off said end.

She sighed loudly and flopped back into a starfish, legs popping out.

'Fiiiiine. Find me my jeans with the things on the things and I'll come.'

'The what?' I had no clue what she was on about. Shock. 'You don't have to come, I can go alone. Actually, can I borrow a skirt?'

'I'm not letting you go without me, don't be a dick. And those jeans with the ass sequins.' She was digging through her floordrobe for said jeans. 'Wear whatever, I don't give a shit. Now help me search.

Chapter Seventeen

We had taken my car, since I'd parked behind Megan's after school. We drove with one of Megan's playlists pumping through my little Bluetooth speaker; her taste was...eclectic at best. We would be dancing to some obscure pop throwback and screaming familiar lyrics one second and then a sea shanty would shuffle on. There was apparently no particular rhyme or reason for such a mix, just the absolute fucking maze that was Megan's brain.

The closer we got to Troy's house, the darker the sky had fallen, as night truly settled in. My focus solely on getting us from point A to B meant it wasn't until I'd turned the car off and the constant thrum of the engine and music had gone that it hit me.

It was really fucking dark.

The desperate desire to find a light source was hard at war with the need to check Matty was where he should be. I was a jittery mix of emotions. I could have a little drink, loosen up. Plus Megan was here. My phone had a flashlight. I could do this.

'Come on, the bonfire will be warm...and well lit,' I said to Megan. She tapped out a message on her phone at the speed of—not currently present—light and slipped her phone in her bra. She raised her arm and flicked the interior light on, and I felt like an idiot for not having done so myself.

'We can just go home. No one will care,' she shrugged, not pointing out the fact that I was 16 and afraid of the dark, in addition to high school toilets.

'Nah, come on.'

I climbed out of the car and turned on my little light. The bass from the ghastly music and shouts of delight were my new soundtrack and a guiding sound to find Matty.

Megan was at my shoulder in a moment. Her denim jacket clashed horribly with her jeans, and her hair was in a single braid down her back. She slipped her hand into mine without a word and lead me through the patchwork night.

Two laps weaving through various people with their curious beer hazed eyes told us he wasn't there. Anxious and mostly unsure what to do with myself, I had a drink. It was just a little one but how I so wanted another. But when I reached for one, something mother-shaped reared its head in my mind and I decided I'd just have juice.

But I didn't want juice.

I could drink and not be like *her* though, couldn't I? I'd managed perfectly fine with Callie. I'd already downed the first one, so what harm could another do? One more wasn't going to make a real difference. I pulled my shoulders back and walked to the where the drinks were. Determination would win out, surely.

Two drinks in and I could feel the slack in my limbs, as tension started to slip away with every sip. Megan and I found a spot to perch on the logs Troy had permanently set out and I waited for Matty. Part of me wanted to find Troy and demand to know where he was, but I also knew that wasn't the best idea here. So I sipped and watched and waited. Megan was tap tap tapping away when I grabbed my fourth, oblivious to my offering her one.

'Tap tap Megan. Who are we messaging?' I tapped her forehead with my finger. I felt better than I had in ages. She looked at me with her big blue eyes and smiled.

'You know what? Tomorrow dude. I'll tell you tomorrow.' She swiped my drink and had a mouthful, handing it back with a scowl. 'I fucking hate rum.'

'I LOVE rum. It is warm and...pirates, Meggy.' I watched her eyes roll and the dots connected in my sluggish brain. 'Tomorrow?'

'Yeah dork. I think you should slow down with the drinks too,' she suggested.

And I ignored.

Troy dropped down next to me. He held out a cigarette and I shook my head. The cologne he seemingly bathed in choked me.

'Astor. Megan. Fancy seeing you ladies here.' He cupped his hands, lighting his smoke with a practiced lighter flick. 'Matty will be here soon. And Dylan. How will you possibly choose.'

'Oh fuck off,' Megan bit out before I could even process what he had said. I would definitely need another drink to cope with him.

That's what some people were saying though, I knew that. That I had fucked Matty to make Dylan jealous and now I had him at my heels. People were fucking stupid. Dylan and I had a long-term arrangement and it wasn't a secret. But apparently now, it was gossip worthy. Anger tickled the edges of my thoughts, but I couldn't drag it to fruition. Probably because of the rum. I considered another turn around the bright, blurry bonfire. Just to see if the object of my obsession was here yet. It was just a lot of movement, and it was warm here, and Troy was a little funny if I didn't look directly at him. Not that I was having much success focusing on things.

Dylan found us, or rather, me. He made his way over, a frown on his pretty face. He was such a nice guy, a wouldn't-hurt-a-fly guy. He kept frowning at me, and I couldn't work that one out either.

'Lover boy's here, guess I'll go find your other one then, eh?' Troy laughed. He got up from beside me and engulfed Dylan for some sort of dude bro hug. Dylan didn't move. Well, his frown moved, but that was all. I hoped he had brought me a drink.

'People can be just friends, though I doubt you'd know what an actual one was,' Dylan bit out.

'Chill dude, you know I like her, Christ.' Troy said.

I was fairly sure they were talking about me. Spidey senses were tingling. I definitely had those. Troy handed me his beer and wandered off, so I drank that too. A deep-down sober Astor whispered that this felt like the top of a slippery slope, but that was a harder voice to hear. All I wanted was to check where Matty was and feel nothing. Now sandwiched between Megan and Dylan, I was safe and content, I let it all go. The warmth and bright light of the fire washed over me. People walked past and waved or said hi. I accepted drinks and didn't feel a thing. This was easy and I could do this.

At some stage on drink number...I-didn't know, Nic sat down next to me. I wanted to flee. Dylan had gone to the other side of the group to talk to some people from school but every so often, his laugh cut through the roar of flames and people, and made me happy. Megan had run to the bathroom, only after asking ten thousand and twelve times if I would be okay on my own for a minute. I had, of course, ensured her that I would remain seated at all times and keep my seatbelt fastened until she returned. She had definitely not found that as funny as I had. So, I was sat on my log with my rum, sipping away and Nic had sat down. She looked about as thrilled as I did, which was to say, not at all.

'Hey,' she said. 'Are you, uh, okay and everything?'

Smooth.

I took another chug of my drink, delaying the need to answer. I wasn't sure what to say. She had been amazing when I'd shown up on her doorstep, had looked after me, and been sweet. But at school she was glued to Tash, and I didn't want to let myself forget that.

'Hello. I'm good. Great even,' my voice was full of enthusiasm. Fake enthusiasm, I didn't really have any of that. She nodded, the air between us was so tense you'd need a sword. Or to just relocate, away from the tension. Somewhere tropical maybe?

I had another long sip.

'So, how's it going ,then?' She was quiet and clearly uncomfortable. I didn't really get why this was so fucking hard. We had talked a million times. I looked at her and pity, pure unadulterated pity was all over her face. That explains it, then.

'You know what, Nic? I'm actually really amazing, ya know? So I'm great. Fabulous even!'

She nodded, not saying anything more. So we sat in silence and anxiety. Sip, sip. Where the fuck was Megan? No one took this long to pee, surely.

'Look I just wanted to say that I'm sor—' she started, but Megan had reappeared and I felt relief.

'Christ, that toilet line was ridiculous.' She climbed over the back of the log and sat down. 'Hey Nic, still following Tash around?'

'Megan!' I chastised with a drunken giggle.

Nic flushed bright red, her face lit up by the fire glow. 'I know...I'm sorry she's awful to you. She really isn't usually that bad, you know that.'

I didn't give a shit what she had to say anymore. Whatever Tash thought or thought she knew was bullshit. I went to have another drink, but I was all out. I staggered to the open bin of ice and drinks and poured myself another. I wanted her to leave while I was gone.

Megan and Nic were now enjoying a delightful, strained silence. I leaned my head on Megan's shoulder and pretended Nic wasn't there. I knew she wasn't so bad, that she was being loyal to her best friend. She had looked after me, after all. This was an anger I couldn't just drop or forget about. So I drank to keep my mouth busy.

A couple of solid minutes passed us by. Me drinking, Megan scowling at her phone, and Nic looking as though she was on a date with a perpetually late and grouchy lobster. Finally she decided she'd had enough and wandered away on a sigh. Presumably to find Tash. I couldn't say I was upset, so I celebrated with another drink. I was happy again now, unsure why I hadn't been. It was all just muted. Rum erased. I could get used to this, even though I shouldn't.

'As, let's go. He isn't here and you're fucked.' Megan was in my ear, and I forced my heavy eyes to hers. She was a little fuzzy but still her.

'Hey,' I said. I think.

'Hey yourself. Let's go. Dylan, can you help me with her?'

'Dylan!' Oh I was happy to see him. Had I already seen him? He was nice. *So* nice.

'Hey As, I'm going to help you back to the car, okay?' he spoke slowly, each word careful.

'Yup. But I can't drive,' I said, helpfully. Some of the words bumped into the others but it seemed to make sense.

'I have your keys, don't worry,' Megan again. Lovely Megan. I didn't deserve a Megan. I may had said that out loud.

The walk up the hill, away from the shouting people and warm fire was sobering. I knew it was Dylan's arm around me, that we were following Megan and my car was the goal. The ground wasn't smooth anymore, it had changed since we had arrived. Someone had added holes; I was absolutely sure. My feet wouldn't cooperate, and my mouth wouldn't shut up, and suddenly it was dark. The crest of the little hill and the trees blocked the fire glow, and it was so very dark. My knees locked and my hands shook and there was a hand on my waist that I didn't want there. Everything ached and my insides turned as fear and undiluted panic set my blood alight. Why was I out here? Who was pulling me along? I didn't want to go. I didn't want to be in the dark. I gagged, bile and rum choked me, and I couldn't get a word out. Tears burned my cheeks as I struggled to breathe. I closed my eyes, willed my body to move and clutched at the grass while my mind whispered that I'd never be safe anywhere again.

The interior light clicked on. The sound was familiar but not at the same time. I hadn't had the car long enough to know the exact click that was mine. I wasn't outside. Wasn't on the hill. I had been sat in the passenger seat of my car, sideways so my legs were out the door. Dylan was squatted down in front of me, not touching me at all but his eyes were focused on mine. Megan was behind me in the driver's seat, her hand was warm on my back under my top.

'Can we go home?' I asked out loud, slurred and whispered. My words tasted wrong.

'I'm going to fucking KILL him!' Megan growled and threw open the door. I didn't know what she had seen, or rather who. The quiet 'oh fuck' from Dylan turned my eyes to where he was looking. It took me a minute to piece together what I was seeing.

Matty and a few of the group from school had arrived. I wasn't sure who, and I couldn't tell if it was the alcohol or my fixation on Matty's presence preventing it. Tash had been at the bonfire, I knew that. She had stayed on the opposite side though, and I could pretend she wasn't there at all, so I knew it wasn't her in the mob. It mostly looked like guys. At least now I knew where Matty was. I felt as relieved as I did sick. The world was spinning violently and I was ready for bed. I didn't care much about Matty now. I'd found him. I could leave.

Megan was in his path now, hands curled into little fists at her sides. Tall and willowy, she was about as deadly as a caterpillar. I snorted at the thought of caterpillar Megan. Gosh I was tired. I hoped she hurried up, I wanted sleepies.

And then I heard my name. Thrown from his lips with disgust.

'Shut your fucking mouth, Matty,' Megan shouted. 'You have no idea what you've done to her.'

'From what I hear, she was pretty fucked up before I got here,' he laughed. 'Well fucked too.'

I curled in on myself, not wanting to hear what else he thought of me when I had thought the world of him.

'She could sleep with the whole fucking town and that still doesn't mean you can rape her, you vile piece of shit!' A stunned silence fell, but just for a second.

'Rape? Are you fucking insane?' Matty had dropped the humour and his words were acid. 'She was gagging for it. I had to basically fight her off in the park and she jumped into my car that night without a problem. You can't rape the willing. Get a grip.'

'Getting into your car isn't consent, you fuckwit.'

I found the shape of Megan in the sort of dark, the headlights of another car obscuring her and making the night darker outside of their yellow beams. I tried to make her words make sense. I didn't want to listen to this, I knew that much, but I didn't want to miss it either.

'You weren't fucking there, you bitch. Let me break it down for you. She climbed into my car, then into the back and she lay the fuck down. No one made her, I didn't hold a knife to her throat. She did it. On her own.'

Matty was smug. Confident in his righteousness.

'She told you *no* though, didn't she?'

'She didn't mean it, I could tell. Make-up on her dough face, tiny little skirt? Gagging. She reeks of desperation and everyone knows it,' he laughed again, the guys around him making sounds of support that melded together in a low rumble. 'Just fuck off, Megan.'

Matty tried to walk past her, his followers seemingly done with Megan too. That apparently was the final straw.

'You're disgusting. All of you. You think you know her? You know nothing. Nothing! Astor deals with more bullshit than any of you. Her mother is a drunk, did you know that? Shoves her around when she feels like it. Her sister, her idiot sister won't listen. Her dad who doesn't give a fuck. She has no one. And then you! You just think you can—'

I felt as though someone had turned the worlds volume to zero and all that was left to hear were the stark and honest words that Megan just let rip. There was no other sound I could make out. I knew they were still arguing. Yelling. I could feel everyone's eyes on me, their gazes crawling along my skin as they measured and judged. I wanted to disappear. I wanted the bloodstream overflowing with alcohol again, as mine felt a lot less saturated now. The static in my head snapped off as I picked out more words designed to tear me apart.

'...she cuts herself to feel better too?' his voice was babyish, mocking as he cut Megan off, though more blows landed with me. 'Knew the bitch was messed up when I saw that freak shit on her legs,' Matty laughed, and the others joined in.

Everything in me squeezed tight, and Dylan's fingers brushed my bare knee. I tried to look into his eyes, hoping there would be some sort of escape plan I couldn't see that he could, but he was focused on my thighs.

Imagining the mess of my skin, remembering a more innocent version of it. Trying to see through the tweed style pattern of my borrowed skirt. I tried in vain to pull it down, trying to feel the hem line and make sure I was covered. My fingers twitched, hands shaking and tears flowing.

'Take me home, Dylan. Megan has my keys,' I pleaded. He helped me up and lead me away, his car further up the road than mine.

My perfect secrets were just dragged out for half the world to hear, and I couldn't take them back. No matter how much I wanted to. Dylan was watching me; the fact that it was all just laid out in public clear as day to him too. I looked around to Megan, her back was to me now. Blonde plait swaying as she continued to berate Matty, who wasn't listening to her. He was looking at me, a bored look on his face. He shrugged, palms up, like a cartoon character who didn't understand how they were where they were. But he had done this. Caused this. Then Megan...Megan had blown it all up.

'That Astor over there, is not my Astor, you piece of shit. You ruined her,' Megan's voice carried to us, furious and determined. Cutting and overstepped.

'Maybe the town bike should consider who she gives rides to, if she's going to cry about bad sex.'

That wasn't Matty's voice, which meant the others were weighing in, making their opinions known.

Dylan turned his lights on and leaned over to clip my belt. 'Don't listen to them, they're trash,' he said.

'*I'm* trash Dyl. Please just take me home,' I croaked. I felt his nod more than saw it.

I didn't want to cry. I was sick of crying about Matty, but it was unavoidable. This was Megan now. My best friend in the world had emptied my life onto the ground for vultures to pick through.

All I wanted was to be as far from here—and Megan—as possible.

Chapter Eighteen

Dylan stopped at the end of Megan's drive. I hadn't been entirely aware of where we were going, as I had assumed he would take me home. Wrong, again.

'Megan has your keys, so I thought we'd come here first. I doubt she will be far behind us,' Dylan said. Reasonable. I hadn't considered that issue myself.

'Yeah, okay. Thanks. I don't want to see her, though.' I was determined to not lay eyes on her anytime soon, that was for sure. We sat in awkward silence as I sloshed all the terrible words around my tired mind.

'You need to talk to her,' he said quietly. He'd turned the interior light on when we stopped, and I looked at his face. He didn't look at me and I wondered what he thought of me now. If he'd say anything.

'I don't want to. I just want to go home and go to sleep.'

'She's your best friend, man…' he thunked his head against his seat and turned to me. A little burst of anger flared. I didn't want to see his pity after all, and I didn't want to be told I had to talk to Megan.

'Fine. Fine!' I threw open the door and practically fell out. I had sobered up a fair bit, but apparently not entirely. Dylan came around the front of the car, hands in his pockets, resigned to situation.

'I'll come and wait with you, so you're not alone.'

'Don't bother. I'm fine.' I was seething. I didn't want to talk to Megan in the slightest and Dylan's placid done grated on me.

'Don't be silly, As, come on.'

'No. You got me here, where you wanted me to be. So just leave.'

'Astor. Come on. You need to talk to her.'

'I don't need to do anything. I don't need you to fucking save me. I don't need anyone. I don't need *you*. Leave me the fuck alone!' I turned my back on him and staggered down the short driveway, grateful when the security lights clicked on and lit up the front of the house. Dylan slammed his car door and took off and I didn't give a fuck.

I dropped onto the front step, leaning against the red brick walls, and waited. Every couple of minutes I had to move an arm or a leg to activate the sensor so I wasn't sitting in the dark, and I was sure my ass had frozen in this stupid skirt. Each minute made me angrier and more sober. Forty minutes it took, according to my phone, for my own car to screech to a halt haphazardly in Megan's driveway. The headlights blinded me somewhat, but when I stood, I could see her open-mouthed face and the angry set to her eyes. She got out of the car and took a step towards me.

'I have looked everywhere for you,' she stated. Not a yell or even with anger. Just fact. I didn't need to have a conversation with her. I would get my keys, and I would go home.

'You have my car, where the hell did you think I'd go,' I said, not hiding the bite in my voice.

'Oh I don't fucking know, Astor. Frankly, I didn't think you'd go anywhere. But here we are, since you left me basically in the middle of nowhere.' She matched my tone, and it was like flipping a switch.

'WHAT the FUCK were *YOU* thinking!?'

'Okay. I may have overreacted but—' sensing my anger, she tried for calm. It did not help.

'May?! You MAY have overreacted? Jesus Christ, Megan! You told everyone how fucked my life is! The cutting! Fucking hell. MAY have overreacted.' My hands shook. We had never had an argument like this. I wanted to leave. Right now. I held out my hand. 'Keys, now please.'

'I just lost it a bit, okay? I know you're doing the denial thing right now, but I can't pretend that piece of shit didn't fucking hurt you. I can't ignore it like you are!'

'IT'S NOT FOR YOU TO SORT OUT MEGAN!' I screamed. Anger and frustration twisted, drowning in betrayal. I felt betrayed.

She took another step forward, her determination matching my anger. 'Yes, Astor it is. Of course it is. I will never let this go. You're my best friend and I won't let this go until you're okay again.'

'I won't *ever* be okay.'

The reality of my words cracked the tension between us, making way for the overwhelming grief. I had thought those words a thousand times but never had they felt truer than in that moment.

'Don't say that, As, please don't. You're my person,' she whispered the last words, and I knew she was crying. I was crying. 'I'm so, so sorry. I just want to fix this for you. I'm sorry.'

My anger dissolved and I pulled her into a hug, hands digging into each other as we held on. She was just Megan. Slightly smoky scented from the fire, completely crazy, and my best friend. I was hurt still, very hurt. But I knew she hadn't meant to hurt me, that she hadn't meant to let everything else slip out. She just wanted to fix me, an impossible task. But she didn't know that. She kept whispering apologises into my hair and we were both an ocean of tears.

'It's okay Meggy,' I said into her neck. I couldn't say that I had forgiven her, but I would, eventually. I just needed to process it all, let it settle in. I knew she was sorry.

She pulled away eventually, wiping her nose with her hand and then on her jeans. Her face was blotchy and I was sure we were both equally wrecked.

'Let's go in. I'm surprised Dad hasn't come out, really,' she said. She opened the front door and turned the entrance lights on before quickly parking my car properly. I waited in the front room, feeling awkward for the first time in her house.

We silently changed into sleep stuff and climbed into her bed, faces still painted and hair tangled. She had left her wardrobe light on, door open, so the room was softly lit. We lay on our backs, the blanket at our necks and looked at the fabric fort ceiling. The awkward feeling faded with her close to me.

She was the first to say something, breaking the silence and repeating her words from before.

'I am sorry. I didn't mean to go that far.' Her voice was raspy, catching at the end as she started to cry again. I wasn't sure what to say.

I hated this. Megan was technicolour and I was grey, dragging her back with my misery and drama.

'I'm sorry too. I seem to just...rain all over your life.' I whispered.

'No you don't, and even if you did, it's okay.'

'No, it isn't. I'm so fucking tired of this. Tired of needing this. I'm sixteen, almost seventeen, and you have to hold my hand to get me through life,' I sniffed.

'I'm always here for you, gladly. Whatever you need. I'm here.'

She found my hand and gave it a squeeze, but I pulled away.

'But you shouldn't HAVE to be! This isn't fair to you. It's fucked up. I fucking hate that I need you this badly. I love your face so damn much, but I am so tired of being a burden.'

I rubbed my eyes, tired and gritty from crying. The never-ending fucking crying.

'Dude that's what I am here for. That's what being a friend is.'

'It's just so one-sided. You're forever propping me up, always having to put your shit aside because I'm some sort of dysfunctional magnet for more dysfunction. I just want to be there for you too sometimes.'

I didn't want Megan to have hard shit in her life, not at all, I just hated that I was a permanent fucking wreck. I hated that I brought her down to my level.

She didn't say anything more, but wriggled closer, so we were arm-to-arm. I could feel her thinking, turning something over and over in her mind. My eyes were heavy and I willed sleep to take me.

Megan, however, got leapt of the bed suddenly, and stood next to it, hands on her hips and her hair standing on end. Which wasn't improved by her running her fingers through it and pacing. I propped myself up on an elbow and waited. Concerned, a little scared. But I knew her, and I had to wait. She finally took a deep breath and turned back to face me, her eyes crazy huge in her face without her glasses on.

'Okay, I'm going to tell you.'

'Oh dude, no. You don't have to tell me anything until you're ready.'

I sat up fully now. As much as I desperately wanted to know what she wasn't telling me and who she was talking to, I didn't want it like this.

'Nah. I was going to tell you tonight. Or rather last night, before the party. Just, give me a second.' She looked at the ground and I waited. Happy to give her all the time in the world and absolutely terrified of what she could say. 'Okay.' She looked back at me.

'Are you sure you want to? It's fine if you want more time, I can wait. Don't just tell me now cause I'm a fuck-up.'

I didn't want this secret out of pity.

'I uhm. I think. No, I *know*. I'm non-binary.'

I stared at her, my best friend in the entire world. Non-binary.

'Dude.' I hedged, 'how do you feel about that?' I was happy if she was happy, that's what mattered. 'Oh shit. Pronouns? What should I use?'

'They/them please,' they smiled, the same smile I had seen a thousand times. 'And I'm good. I'm happy. It feels...right? Like me.'

'Well fuck. Then I'm happy too. Can I ask who you've been speaking to?' I threw back the covers, inviting them back in. Mostly for selfish reasons, I was very cold, and they were a human heating blanket.

'Well, I wasn't sure I guess. I've never felt like a proper "girl" really, but I like skirts and make up sometimes still. So I was just, really fucking confused. So I went on Reddit,' they said, snuggling back in close.

'Of course you did. Of course it was bloody Reddit.'

I had to laugh. Fitting.

'Shush. Reddit is perfect. Anyway I posted about how I was feeling and got a reply from someone named Ellie and she really has just. Helped a lot, you know?'

'So that's who all the messages and phone calls were to? Are they non-binary too?' I couldn't pretend I wasn't put out that they had found someone else to talk to about this, because it definitely hurt a little. Maybe it was a little jealousy too. But I could squash that for Megan, it wasn't about me.

'Yeah, so Ellie is trans. But that's her business, she just really listened to me and told me about her own journey. Answered all of my never-ending questions.'

'Well, I'm happy you had her, then.' I kissed the side of their head. I had a few questions myself, but I didn't want to be overwhelming. We had time. 'Have you told anyone else?'

'I told dad. I wanted him to know first. He's been great.'

'Duh. He's always great. You're lucky to have him,' I said.

We slipped into silence, each of us lost in our own thoughts. Tonight had been a lot and we were both exhausted and cried out. I felt sleep creeping in and let my eyes fall closed.

'I didn't tell you, even though you're...not straight, because it just felt so huge, and I was so unsure about everything.' Their voice was soft against my shoulder. Familiar and warm. 'It's just. It didn't feel as simple as being gay or bi or whatever. Not to say that's easy either. But like. It's my entire being, my gender.'

'You don't have to explain, dude. You've got me for life, no escape.'

'I know. I just don't want you to think I doubted you or something. It was just something I needed to figure out my own way,' their voice was sleepy now too.

I didn't need the explanation, but it did soothe my errant, selfish worries.

'Megan, you're completely fine. I promise,' I said. 'Oh, shit. Is it still Megan or...?'

'Still Megan. I'll tell you if it changes.'

'Okay Meggy,' I smiled, ready to sleep now.

'Absolutely fucking not Meggy, you arse.'

I fell asleep with their quiet laughter in my head and that was more than okay with me.

Megan and I spent Saturday in recovery, we barely left their bedroom and just accepted plates would be added to the general décor until we could be bothered moving them. I peppered them with questions during the day, wanting to learn more about them and the mysterious Ellie. Megan happily indulged me, and by Sunday afternoon everything felt mostly normal with us. Neither of us had heard from anyone from school, so there was no telling how *The Great Confrontation* had gone down, or if it was even being talked about. Megan didn't care but I, for one, was not thrilled about the prospect of school, especially with my whole "faking it" plan.

Mum was cooking dinner when I walked in the door and threw me a *hello*. I noticed the familiar cup next to her on the bench, and had to resist the urge to check the time. I knew it was early.

By 8pm, mum was well and truly wasted, and I escaped to my room. Dad was away overnight and although he wasn't much, he was somewhat of a buffer at times. I showered and got into bed, book in hand, ready for some escapism when mum came into my room. Leaning against the wall to stop her swaying on the spot. I waited for her to say something, but she just blinked at me, a frown on her face.

'Hi...?' I said, a question rather than a welcome.

'Why do you read all the fucking time?' she slurred.

'What?'

'It's bullshit. All you do is read.'

She was red-faced and baiting me. I knew she was baiting me. She also had some bizarre hatred for my reading. When I was little she would take my books and send me outside to play, never asking if I actually wanted to. I never have worked out why she hated it. But I wouldn't rise to her.

'I just like it. But I might go to sleep now, okay? Goodnight.'

I shut my book and flipped off the lamp, trying to keep the panic quiet in the dark. Once she left I could turn it back on and it would be fine.

'You're such a fucking loser,' she said, more slurring.

'Please get out,' I asked. *Bad* move on my part.

'Get out? No I fucking won't. It's my house!' I rolled over, ignoring her. I just wanted her to go so I could turn the light on. I didn't hear her move, too focused on my own simmering panic. She wrenched me onto my back and grasped my chin in her hands, nails digging into my skin. 'It's my fucking house. Got it? I can stand here forever if I like.'

I could taste the wine as she breathed on my face, the cigarettes an after taste. I didn't dare move an inch and tears sprung to my eyes. I spent *a lot* of time fucking crying lately.

'Are you listening, Astor?' She squeezed my face tighter, and I nodded as best I could.

'Yes,' I managed to force out. She let go, a brief pause and then slapped me. I bit down hard on my cheek, desperate to not react.

'Good. Go to fucking sleep.'

She picked up my book and left, slamming my door on her way out. I scrambled for the lamp, desperate to be out of the dark. The second it clicked on, I dissolved into sobs until I eventually fell asleep. Curled up on my side with my cheek on fire and half-moons cut into my skin.

When I woke up, she had already gone to work. On the kitchen bench sat a plate of pancakes, under a plastic wrap cover so they were protected. My book sat next to it.

I had cereal.

My desire to go to school had completely abandoned me, and one look in the mirror confirmed that today would best be spent at home. I had gotten better at controlling my thoughts of that night, the memories no longer a constant loop. But I kept busy anyway. I showered, sorted through my clothes, read a bit, and eventually lay on the couch to watch British house-hunting shows. The thoughts I couldn't stop were the "where-is-Matty" ones. I hadn't seen him since Friday night, and the more time that passed, the more I was concerned where he was. What if he was making someone else think he was Prince Charming? Fooling someone else with his charm and wit. I knew he was at school, Megan and I had messaged on and off. My plea of unwell hadn't been challenged by them at all, even if they likely didn't believe me. But I knew Matty was at school. I was pretty sure anyway.

50% sure.

I tried to make myself focus on the show, the search for a house at a reasonable two million pounds or however much was needed to buy a thatched roof cottage the size of a stamp in England, but I couldn't stop checking the time. School was out soon. Matty would be out.

This tickle of an obsession blew out into a full-blown itch. I grabbed my keys and shoved my feet into shoes. If I left now, I could be there when school ended and I could just...take a quick look at him. Make sure he was where he should be. I was the only one who knew how bad he really was, so I knew I had to be the one to check.

Twenty minutes later and I had parked down the road from school. I knew the gate he came out of as I had been avoiding it like the plague, not wanting to talk to him. I checked my phone for the time, ignoring all messages, as I had all day. I'd deal with that later. Megan would understand. Five minutes 'til final bell. I sat and waited. My leg bounced anxiously, and I couldn't look away. I didn't want to miss him.

I didn't hear the bell, I was too far away, but when students clad in navy started to pour out of the gate, I knew it was time. I squinted, searching for his familiar shape in the crowd of somewhat clones. My pulse was flying, terrified I would miss him.

But there he was.

I watched as he threw his head back and laughed with his friends. With Tash too, Nic at her side.

I watched as he walked in the opposite direction, separating from the group as they went their own ways or to the buses.

I watched as he turned the corner, a few girls in front and a mixed group behind.

I turned on my car.

This was insanity. What the fuck was I doing? I needed to go home.

I pulled out into traffic. I told myself to turn right, the opposite direction, and go home. I had seen him, and he had no one with him. He was walking home.

I got to the intersection and turned left.

Chapter Nineteen

I hadn't made it home until after dark. Mum had been a ball of drunken fury, but I just couldn't bring myself to care. I'd sat outside Matty's house for hours, just staring. Waiting. No idea what for. What the fuck was wrong with me? As I drifted off to sleep, confused and unexpectedly worn out, I swore I wouldn't do it again. I wasn't that person.

Crazy stalker girl.

My insistent phone vibrating eventually woke me. When I managed to squint at the screen it was to see a half dozen missed calls and triple that in texts from Megan. Apparently, my absence was noted. It had just gone nine and I had the whole day free. There was a relief in not being at school, even if I did hate missing out on lessons. I didn't have to pretend I was ecstatic to be alive when I was home alone. I didn't have to smile or force myself to pay attention. I didn't have to look over my shoulder constantly. I dove back into my book, savouring the uninterrupted escapism it afforded me. When I had turned the final page and reinterred the world I actually existed in, reality was not as forgiving. I tried another book, my Kindle, music. I'd have cleaned if there was anything left to do. It wasn't long until I was anxious, antsy to get out of the house and do something.

I showered, not over-scrubbing my entire body raw every time I did. I wasn't sure I ever really would be. I had googled a little, just trying to find how people moved on after...that sort of thing. It was utterly depressing. By my third forum thread about...*assault*...I had closed it all down.

I wasn't like them.

I hadn't been threatened with death or beaten. I wasn't sure what category I fell into, really. I'd looked at my face in the mirror, trying again to figure it out. The glass was fogged with bathroom heat and it obscured my face to a blur of pink. I felt nothing but confusion. I swiped my face away, knowing mum would flip out at my hand streaks on the glass, but I didn't care. I threw on some clothes, brushed out my hair and haphazardly lined my eyes in black. Then I climbed in my car and drove to school as if on autopilot.

Autopilot my ass. I'd known exactly where I was headed from the second I'd stepped out of the shower, but I was willing to claim otherwise.

For now.

Class was in, so I had to wait for a bit to get a response from Megan. They were a good little student. Like I used to be. Waiting wasn't going well, I couldn't keep my legs still. If I was on an edge, tipping off it was a real possibility right now. Scrolling through my messages. I saw my sisters name and impulsively sent her a message, asking what time she took her lunch break. Maybe a little Callie time would be nice. It was nice last time.

I heard the bell and watched the little navy ants pour out of the buildings, searching for my particular ant. I spotted them striding my way, a firm set to their mouth that was visible from the moon. I momentarily considered locking the doors.

Megan slipped into the passenger seat and slammed the door shut, blonde hair tied back in a pony and glasses in place.

'Hi,' I said.

'Oh yeah you look really fucking sick,' Megan crossed their arms and sarcasm positively poured from each word. 'What the fuck, man. I have barely heard from you in two days but you're...fine? I thought it was me. I thought you'd gone off the deep end. Fuck. I almost called your mother.'

They were right, I had been a shit.

'Oh God. It's not you. I'm sorry Meg, I promise it isn't you.'

'It's fine, honestly,' they said. It didn't feel fine.

'Fuck, I'm ruining everything. I am sorry. I'm such a shit friend. Just. Look,' I faltered a little, rubbing my forehead. I didn't want to tell Megan what I had been up to last night. I didn't want the judgement, the condemnation or the sure to follow lecture. I knew it was hard to understand exactly what my fixation was with him, and no matter how I tried, I couldn't explain the bone-deep need I had to know he wasn't sucking someone else in. No one else knew so completely what he capable of. It was just me.

'It's okay, As,'

'I just...can't do the "fake it" thing anymore. It's too hard. I just need some time to, I don't know, sort my stupid brain out.'

It wasn't an outright lie. The false positivity was hard. So fucking hard and so exhausting. The relief at not having to do it? Next level.

'Right. Okay...but maybe you could come to school and just be miserable?' they said, not even remotely convincingly.

'Yeah bro, that's what I want. To be miserable and around people. Shit, can I still call you bro?'

'Bro is fine. Okay just. Stay in contact, for God's sake. I had no idea if you were okay. I hate when you're not here.'

Megan pulled out their phone, smiling at whatever was on the screen. There was a teensy flicker of jealousy knowing it was likely Ellie.

Idiot.

I quickly checked my own, noting the reply from Callie confirming lunch. Time to get to the point, I guess.

'So uhm, is Matty there?' I bit my lip, shooting for casual indifference and managed to land in stalker territory. What a surprise.

'Astor. Stop.'

'It's just a question,' I sighed, frustrated.

'You need a bloody therapist.' They held up their hand to stop my denial. 'But yes, he is at school. Honestly, no one's even talking about him, or you, anymore. Come back.'

'I will. Just...not yet, okay? Just let me have this week.'

Bargaining. Classy.

'Fine. I have to go back, I'll let Dylan know you're alive too.'

Oh hello, guilt. I hadn't replied to him yet. Chalk it up to things that made me an awful person. Lord knows it wasn't a short list.

'Love you, Meg.'

'Yeah, yeah. Love you too.'

They rolled their eyes and got out, walking back into school without me. I was beyond any doubt, completely unhinged. And I had absolutely no idea what to do about it.

Callie had suggested a café that was half-way between her work and school to meet. When I walked in, she'd already been seated in a little booth. There was a row of them, all polished dark wood benches, and matching tables. Fake potted plants and square salt and pepper shakers adorned each setting. A café like every other one in this town.

'Hey,' I waved, somewhat awkwardly as I slid into the seat opposite.

'Hey yourself! How are you? Gosh you look bloody tired. Is that why you're not in school?' Callie word-vomited into the space between us.

'Oh uh. Yeah, I've been sick but I'm good now,' I hedged.

'Well, make sure you exfoliate or use a day cream, you look ghastly.' She turned the little menu card over, words of wisdom imparted.

'Thanks?'

'You're welcome! How's school? How's Megan?' Callie basically vibrated and had we not been in a booth I feared she'd have ended up on the ground. It was a café where you placed your order at the counter, so I kindly side-stepped her questions by offering to sort out ours. She was still bouncing when I returned with our order number and drinks.

'Okay, what's up? You're buzzing.'

If we talked about her, I wouldn't have to talk about me.

"Oh my gosh I'm getting a promotion! I'm going to be a senior receptionist and admin assistant!' she smiled ear to ear. I smiled back, genuinely happy for my sister.

'I didn't think medical places had those?' I asked. She was a medical receptionist at a private centre that covered a wide range of specialties, so not just a regular general practice sort of deal. She had been there since she left school and seemed to love it, and it fit her in a weird way.

'Oh Astor, of course they do.' And she was off. Talking a mile a minute, happy as anything to fill the space with her explanations of her job and what was to come. I nodded and made sounds of agreement when required, shovelling bites of salad into my mouth once it arrived. 'Anyway, I'm thinking I might have a little celebration dinner on Friday! At my house, of course.'

'With just Mum and Dad?' I frowned.

'Yeah of course! And you. You can skip your little friends' parties and stuff for one Friday, I'm sure.'

She rolled her eyes. Like *that* was my concern.

'What about mum though?' I asked. Traditionally, we didn't do dinner time things outside the house as getting a drunken Helen home was often an uphill battle.

'God Astor, she'll be fine. It's just a dinner. And she said she's cut down with the wine, rehab soon and all. I thought you'd be happy for me.'

Callies face twisted a little, a pout turning into a frown.

'No, I am happy for you. She just, uh, hasn't really cut down,' I explained. I didn't want to start an argument. 'Well, she did for a bit. But not anymore.'

'She's fine. It'll be fine. I want you all there, okay?' She checked her phone and pushed her plate away, her words were final. 'So school? Megan? Ooh and that boy! What's happening?'

She looked at me expectantly, her eyes all sparkly and *Bambi*-like. Great

'Uhm. School is good. Same old. Megan is also good. Still loopy,' I said. I had no real desire to expand on any of that, much happier to talk about her.

'And the guy? It was a guy this time, right?' she prodded.

'Yeah. A guy. Mmmh yeah just. Not a good match.'

Understatement of the century right there.

I pulled my phone out, checking the time. 'Oh shit, I better go. I have to meet...Megan.'

I stood, grabbing my virtually untouched drink to take with me and brushed at non-existent crumbs on my jeans, eager to leave.

'Oh okay! Well this was fun! We should do it again,' Callie said.

'Absolutely!' I called over my shoulder as I high tailed it from the building. School was over in about an hour. I'd have a quick check in and then go home. Easy.

I followed him home again. I'd told myself I wouldn't. I was utterly convinced I wouldn't. Then I'd seen his stupid slicked back hair and I had to. I was fucking losing it. The small—and rapidly shrinking—logical part of my brain knew that this was wrong. That I wouldn't be able to do anything even if he was dating someone. He was allowed to go and do whatever the hell he wanted. But the rest of this brain needed to see him and check where he was. Maybe I *did* need therapy.

I'd been able to follow easily today, now that I knew where he lived. I watched him walk to his front door as I parked, slipping my oversized sunglasses on in a sad attempt to conceal my face. I absorbed the scene in front of me, sipping my smoothie through the bamboo eco straw. His house was cute, sickeningly like a postcard. Rose bushes and hanging baskets. Perfectly mown lawn. There was probably a gnome somewhere too. *Disgusting*. None of it matched the piece of shit he drove, or his nauseating breath and roaming hands.

Next to his blue front door was a little sign, white wood with dark letters in a bold font. I was too far back to make out the words, so I did the next best thing. I googled his address.

MELISSA COLLINS. PSYCHOLOGIST. FAMILIES, YOUTH AND TRAUMA

I couldn't stop the jolt of hysterical laughter if I'd tried.

How fucking fitting.

I had no actual idea what the difference between a psychologist and a psychiatrist was, so back to Google I went. Apparently, one could prescribe meds and one did "talk therapy", it would seem. One was a doctor, and one wasn't, and in Australia, one needed a doctor referral, and one didn't.

Interesting.

I sat in my car a while longer, turning my phone over in my hands and thinking through an utterly insane idea. A quick look at the time effectively shoved me into making a choice, and I hit the number on my screen.

'Good afternoon, you've reached Collins Psychology. How may I help you today?' I had expected a woman to answer, but it was a man. Not Matty.

'Hello, uh, I was wondering how I can make an appointment?' I stammered, nerves skittered and slowed my brain.

'Have you been here before?' the receptionist asked.

'Mmh no...'

'Have you been referred by your doctor and have you got a mental health plan in place?'

He was quick and to the point, but not rude. Likely having had this conversation numerous times.

'No, but I googled and saw that I can refer myself?' I was no longer confident in my googled advice. 'Is that not right?'

My heart raced, now that I had half-way decided on this idiotic plan, I wanted to see it through, desperately. Megan's words from earlier in the day had stuck, it would seem.

'You absolutely can, however, I need to tell you that if that is the case, you won't be entitled to any rebates from Medicare and will be responsible for the out-of-pocket costs.'

Hope flared.

'That's fine. I can do that. Can I make an appointment?' I bounced my leg as impatience and anxiety met.

'Let's see,' he paused, obviously looking at the upcoming schedule. 'I have a time available in three weeks, Monday 11th or I can do that Thursday which would be the 14th. Does that suit?'

Three weeks? I didn't know what the hell I thought I'd achieve by talking to Matty's mother, but I knew that three more weeks of this...stalker bullshit would destroy me.

'Oh okay. Uhm,' my voice was thick and teary. I paused, trying to think. Trying to not sniffle into the phone. I could just hang up. The receptionist made an odd sort of noise, a sympathy laden sigh.

'I know, it's a while away. So, how about I do this for you. I'll make a note and if I get a cancellation for sooner, I'll give you a call. What's your name?'

'No that's fine. I don't think I can wait that long. Thank you,' I hung up on a sob, irrationally furious and upset that I wouldn't get to look into the eyes of the person that had raised the architect of my nightmares.

I sat outside their house until the dark popped it's head up and I was forced to drive home. Out of the flames and into the fire.

Thursday morning, I woke to Helen leaning over me. Ideal.

'Your head of year called me yesterday asking how long you'd be off for. Imagine my surprise.' She threw my uniform at me and turned to leave. 'I don't know what bullshit you're playing at Astor, but go to fucking school.'

She slammed my door behind her. Can't say I blamed her. I hadn't been to school all week, placating Megan with text messages throughout the day and fighting the urge to watch Matty's house. Which so far had been a fight I had lost. Somehow my obsession with what Matty might do and with whom, had shifted into what sort of person could have produced him. I still needed to know where he was, but the need to see *her* was enormous. Surely, given her profession, she knew what he was like. I didn't know what the fuck I thought I was doing, and each night had become a tightrope performance when I got home. Avoiding mum and her rollercoaster moods but showing my face enough she didn't seek me out. In the confines of my room I was free to let all the extreme, conflicting, and confusing thoughts I was experiencing breathe. I came home and I paced, unable to distract myself. Full of self-loathing at what I was doing, angry with myself for being so weak and confused. Why couldn't I stop? I didn't understand that any more than I understood what had happened to me. It had all become twisted and snarled, every thought I had dragged the words of other people with it. Bad sex. Sexual assault. Rape. *Stalking.* I paced until I couldn't, then cried until I slept. Desperate for the seconds of amnesia morning brought.

I stood next to my car, uniform on, bag over my shoulder. There were not enough words in the English language to articulate how severely I did not want to go in. I checked my hemline, fingertips skimming their familiar path.

'So you're alive, then?'

Ah fuck.

'Hey Dylan. Alive, yep.' I turned to his voice. His usually open, relaxed face was cold with anger.

'Figures,' he said. He gave me a once over, like he was actually trying to verify my life status, and walked past me. Without looking back. I had some grovelling to do.

'Hey!' I matched his pace. 'I'm sorry, I know I've been...fucking shit. I just, I don't know.'

Good work, Astor.

He kept walking, didn't speed up or bolt, so I knew he was at least willing to hear me out. The problem was I didn't know how to explain, any of it.

'I was worried. You basically dropped off the face of the earth after being a fucking bitch. And given everything...'

'I know. I'm sorry. I *was* a bitch. I just. Can I blame the alcohol? And everything else. I just needed some time, I guess. Fuck, I don't even want to be here now.' *Here* being the school that loomed in front of us. Had anyone else noticed I was gone?

Dylan stopped, so I did too.

Sighing, he said: 'Look I get it. You could have told me, though. I'd have left you alone.'

I was an awful friend.

'I'm sorry Dyl,' I said.

'Yeah. Okay.'

He nodded and kept walking, leaving me behind. I stood and watched as he passed through the gates, into the navy sea.

I pulled out my phone and opened my chat thread with Megan. It was a graveyard of messages I hadn't replied to, dotted with an occasional "I'm fine" from me. *Guilt.* A new feeling to add to the mess in my head. I tapped out a message letting them know I wouldn't be in today and got back in my car. Maybe if today I got a look at her, it would be enough. I could get over this and then I could be better. That made sense. Mostly.

I tried to vary where I parked, so it wasn't noticeable that the same car had been parked outside repeatedly. Today I had settled for slightly past the house. It meant I had to watch in my rear-view mirror or turn around, which was a bit annoying, but I had a plan. I had seen her a couple of times, so I knew from a distance who she was. So as soon as I saw her, I would get out and bump into her. Then I could see her up close and that would be enough.

It would have to be enough.

My ass had fallen asleep after the first hour, and as I popped cherry tomatoes into my mouth, eyes still on the house, I knew I would have to go find a bathroom soon. The knock on my window however, almost turned my car into one.

Bent at the waist, her tanned face at my window, was Matty's mother.

'I think we should talk,' she said. Her eyes crinkled when she smiled. Like she did it a lot. I had no idea why but that didn't line up with the person I had built in my mind. I swallowed my mouthful and got out of the car.

I was getting what I wanted for once, and now I wasn't sure I wanted it at all.

Chapter Twenty

I was sure I would throw up on her patent pump clad feet. Her blue shoes matched her button-down blouse, dotted with a delicate flower pattern. Her black pants were three quarter length, overall making her look professional, approachable, and normal. So normal. I leaned against my car, unable to look into her eyes but completely fixated on her.

'Can I ask why you've been sat outside? I've seen your car a couple of times now, but you never get out. I don't want to have to call someone.'

Call someone. Police, she meant. Her voice was calm, friendly even. A normal conversation in an entirely abnormal situation. I tried desperately to think of words that weren't "I'm stalking your son" and came up blank. My eyes burned, frustration and desperation wanted to spill over, but I fought for control.

'I was hoping to see a psychologist,' I managed. I knew she was taking in my appearance, as I had with her. She had undoubtedly noted my uniform, gauged my age even. Had she wondered if I knew her son? I looked into her eyes and they weren't his. They were brown like his, but not the same. Not a copy like I had feared they would be. Her hair was strawberry blonde, grey creeping in at her temples and beginning to weave into her ponytail. She nodded, short and sharp, for herself and not for me.

'Okay, well, you have to make an appointment like everyone else. You can't just sit here like this,' she explained calmly, like this was a common occurrence for her. What did I know, maybe it was? 'What's your name?'

'Astor,' I said automatically. Reflexively. I had planned to use Callie's name, mine being too different to go unnoticed.

'That's pretty. Okay Astor. Do you want to come in and we can see about getting you an appointment?' she smiled at me. A genuine smile, pushing soft lines into her cheeks and crinkles at her eyes. Could she tell I was damaged? Was there some sort of clue to the outside world that I woke up each day because the hardwired need to survive kept my body going, and not because I wanted to? She smiled, kindness and patience for the destroyed girl in front of her, and I crumbled.

What the hell was I doing?

She didn't touch me, didn't placate me. She waited until I was done, her focus on me even when she held her hand up in the universal signal for "wait a minute" to someone I didn't see. She just let me cry, half bent over on the sidewalk in front of my beat-up car.

'I'm sorry,' I sniffed, snot and tears dripped repulsively, and I pulled a tissue from my pocket. 'I'm going to go, I'm sorry I bothered you.' I fumbled for the car door, more than ready to leave.

'Come inside for a bit, I don't have a client for another...' she checked her watch, simple and silver. 'Ten minutes or so. You can clean yourself up or I can call someone for you.'

'No, I'd rather just go.' I opened the door, not sure what to say. She had been far nicer than I expected. And yet her son was Matty.

'Well, you call and set a time up then, okay? Or see your GP and have a chat,' she said, her voice somewhat unsure. I turned to get into my car but paused and looked back.

'Hey, uhm. You seem...really nice.' I took a deep breath, unsure what my next words would set off, if anything, but needing them out. 'Matty. Your Matty. He didn't stop when I said "no". When I begged.'

The words were strangled and choked, but they were out.

'He wouldn't *stop*.'

I looked into her eyes, the kind brown ones that weren't his, and watched as shock flashed in them. Confusion, understanding, and then shock. Plain as day in hers as she looked into my own. Could she see the truth in mine? Red-rimmed and raw with honesty. I jumped into the car and left. Melissa Collins stood on the sidewalk, arms loose at her side, and watched me go.

I hadn't known where I was going really until I had stopped.

It was different in the daylight. There were no sweeping shadows that plunged everything into darkness, no people doing nefarious things, not even a speck of litter. Just a quiet hilled lane with mown grass and mailboxes. Trees that linked together with their branches looped tightly stood on each side, interrupted only by the handful of driveways that lead to houses I couldn't see. There was a little lookout at the end, like he'd said that night, giving a view of the valley below. A waterfall—no taller than I was—fed into a small stream, mostly concealed by overgrowth and trees. It was quaint. Pretty. Probably a place where giddy teenagers went for first kisses and clumsy make-outs. Where they built memories they could look back on in a decade and laugh at.

I spun in a slow circle, taking it all in and wondered how somewhere so innocent and unassuming could be the setting for what had happened to me. I had no idea what I had expected to find, but this wasn't it. Closure maybe? Some sort of answer. Something that made sense of everything.

How had I gotten to this point, alone in a back lane in the middle of the day, trying to make the impossible make sense. There was no way to get back what I'd lost. What I had given him, willingly or not. I hadn't tried hard enough, had I? I hadn't screamed, run for help. I hadn't fought with everything I had. I'd frozen, deer in the headlights, and he'd used me. After I had climbed into the back. I had. So what was this? Was it bad sex? Regret sex? Was it more than that? It felt like more, so much more. I hadn't wanted it. I'd said no, I'd begged. I'd cried and pleaded. But I'd climbed in the back. I'd kissed him. I'd laid there. I had a reputation. How could I be forced when I freely gave it up so often?

My entire body ached, from my marrow out. I had thought I was out of tears when I'd left Matty's mother, but apparently the supply was endless. I climbed into the drivers' seat, head against the steering wheel and pleaded with a God I had never once in my life believed in for an out.

I woke up and it was still daylight, the steering wheel impression on my forehead would probably last longer than I had been alive, and I had no idea what century I was in, let alone the time. Disorientated from my impromptu nap. Crying was exhausting, I knew that well, as it was a staple of my current bedtime routine. Maybe I was conditioned to now sleep after an emotional breakdown?

I pulled my phone out of my skirt pocket and had a message from Callie, asking if I liked eggplant for dinner tomorrow night. Completely oblivious to how utterly chaotic my life was. *Do you like eggplant?* The world kept spinning despite my personal hell. I let Callie know I unequivocally hated them and drove home.

I could hear the yelling before I had stepped foot out of the car. Dad was home early today evidently.

'Helen, you are fucking going!' Dad's voice was a boom through the air, and I knew instantly what they were arguing about. Rehab.

'Oh fuck you. I'm not going. Get over it,' Mum said, her tone was decided, final.

'Either you go, or we are done. I'm not watching you drink yourself to death anymore.'

I stood outside the faded yellow door, not wanting to walk in on their fighting and cop it myself, but I couldn't stand out here forever.

'Fine. Fuck off then. There's the door,' she said, indifferent.

That would be as good of a cue as any. I opened the front door, face schooled into neutrality, though my eyes were still red from crying. Not that they'd notice.

'Hi,' I said.

Mum didn't look up and Dad mumbled something that could have been a hello, before pushing past me and to his truck. Leaving me alone with my freshly pissed off mother. I smiled at her, even though she still hadn't looked at me, and made my way to the hall, more than happy to spend time in my room.

'You'll be happy, won't you?' Mum's words followed me, bitter and sober. I stopped, turned back. I didn't understand. It sounded like rehab wouldn't happen, and that definitely did not make me happy.

'What?' I asked.

'Your father. He said he'll leave. That'll make you happy, won't it?' she still hadn't looked at me, just continued to wash the dishes and stack them on the counter to dry.

'No.' *Yes.*

I didn't wait for whatever her reply would be. I had no doubt she'd find me if she really wanted me to know. Instead, I went to my room, closed the door, and tried to mentally sort through the rollercoaster that was my day.

In the middle of the night, as I lay staring at my ceiling and impatiently waiting for sleep, I heard Dad come home. He hadn't returned for dinner and mum hadn't cooked anything, so I'd made myself some toast, eating over the kitchen sink so I didn't use a plate. Mum had swayed in her chair, cup of wine in hand and called his name endlessly into the otherwise quiet house. I had no idea where he'd gone and seemingly, she didn't either. She'd called his name over and over, her words slipping into slurring, until eventually she'd staggered to bed. That was about an hour ago.

Dad's footsteps were heavy, uneven, and clumsy. Judging by the various sounds he was taking the hallway like the ball in a pinball machine. As he loudly got into bed, I could hear them talking, not as clearly as the yelling from earlier, but the low rumble of two voices mixing. Slurred. I darted out of bed and opened the door a bit, just enough to hear.

'I can't leave you, I love you,' Dad said, so clearly drunk and teary. 'No matter what.'

I didn't wait for whatever Mum managed to say back. That was more than enough. For some reason he couldn't leave her, and she would never quit drinking.

I crawled back into bed, my face in the lamp light and, for the first night in a long while, I didn't cry.

I was back in the carpark, sitting in my car with my uniform on. This time however, Megan sat next to me. I had woken up that morning, thrown myself together and driven to their house. They were less enthusiastic about my sudden appearance than I had hoped. But they'd gotten in my car with barely an eye roll, and I'd driven straight to get them coffee. Smart.

'Bribery is a new low, As,' Megan said, blowing on their drink.

'But is it working.'

'Well yeah. I wasn't mad at you anyway,' they shrugged, 'Just, worried. Dylan, however, he is mad. Or hurt. I don't know.'

'I know. I'm shit. I get it. It's such a mess,' I groaned.

'Dude, yeah you ghosted a bit, but you also don't owe him anything. If you couldn't deal, you couldn't deal.'

'Yeah, but I could have let him know I was alright. And you.' I closed my eyes. Shame it wasn't permanent.

'Did you want to hurt us?' they asked.

'What? No. Course not. It was just too much. It still is.'

'Then it's fine. You've said sorry right?' I nodded in response, not even sure they were looking. 'Then it's okay. Give him some time. As for me, coffee is adequate.'

'I'm such a shit friend,' I whispered, half hoping they wouldn't hear.

'Nah. You're not. Stop being dramatic and let's go in,' Megan said and opened the passenger door. I looked at my best friend, my person. I couldn't do it. The urge to see where Matty was, that was still there. A background burn that could be put out with a particular piece of information. Seeing his mum yesterday, how lovely and put together she was, I didn't blame her for what he was. I hoped she had taken my parting words seriously, but as I'd lain in bed last night, I had known it was more than certain she wouldn't. No one would believe that of their child, just like that.

The bell rang and Megan looked at me.

'I can't do it. Not yet,' I said, desperately. They looked at me for a moment, a heartbeat.

'Where are you going then? You know the school will call your mum.'

'The library,' I pulled out of thin fucking air. 'I'll deal with mum later.

'Fine. Whatever. Message me, okay?'

'Meggy?' I called as they were about to shut the door.

'Yes, I'll let you know if he's here.' A long-suffering sigh carried their words to me.

'Thanks.'

I watched Megan cross the road, phone in hand. I wished I could go with them, that I could tell them how messed up everything was inside me. How I had followed Matty and what I had said to his mother. But I couldn't, I couldn't get the words out and I couldn't make myself go into school. I turned my car back on and made my way to the library. I'd try again next week.

The day positively dragged in the library. Reading usually kept me focused, my mind sucked fully into whatever I was reading, but no matter what I tried, I found it wandering. By late afternoon I had amassed a pile of books I had started and discarded, unable to concentrate. The library was louder now, the carpet muffled the footsteps of people that filled the space, but it couldn't mute the low buzz of their conversations and I found myself zoning out listening to their nothing woes. When I next checked the time, I realised I would be late if I didn't move my ass. Somehow the day had gone from not moving to flying. I put all the books back, silently apologising that they weren't in the right places exactly or that some weren't the right way up. Twenty minutes later I pulled up to Callie's, parking on the side of the road as I could see Dad's truck in the driveway.

Showtime.

'Astor! Yay! Come in!' Callie greeted me at the door, all happy and glowing. Her plants lining the front of the house had died, but inside was still the mess of colours. I kicked off my shoes and followed her in. Mum and dad were at the table, crammed in together in the tiny space. There was an almost empty bottle of wine at mum's elbow, but in use was a tall glass, in place of her teacup.

'Sorry I'm late, I thought I had the time right,' I offered and took the seat opposite mum. Ideal. Callie bustled into the kitchen, which given the floorplan, was all of three steps away.

'You're fine! Mum and Dad were early, weren't you guys? But perfect timing really, cause it's ready!'

Callie set out what appeared to be a lasagne, though it was hard to tell with how...crisp the top was. Mum scoffed, taking a mouthful of wine. Dad said nothing.

I glanced at my sister out of the corner of my eye, catching the fall in her face before she righted herself. She had an apron on with cherries all over it, her hair was falling out of the loose bun at the nape of her neck, and she was red in the face from cooking. She shrugged it off and started scooping some of the mystery meal onto each of our plates, somewhat proud of whatever it was.

'Thanks Cal. It looks...good?' I said, watching her beam and ignoring Mum.

'It's vegetarian lasagne! I used eggplant. It's super yum, I promise.'

I severely doubted that. We ate quietly, none of us acknowledging how drunk mum was or the cold war between her and Dad. Barely a word was exchanged the entire time, but mum kept the wine flowing, filling her glass the moment she drained it.

As bad as I felt for Callie, her promotion news having been lost in the silence of the meal, I just wanted to go home. I wanted to be alone, to not have to force myself to smile. So when everyone had finished, I jumped to clear the plates, each one a different colour and all still mostly full. Time to set leaving in motion. Callie, however, pulled some ice cream out of her freezer, apparently essential for the apple pie she had made. I set to loading the sink anyway. Everything needed to soak...or be thrown out. How she had managed to fuse the eggplant to the dish was beyond me.

Mum and dad were still seated, but now they were talking, without looking at each other.

'I told you, I'm not going!'

The sound of glass breaking had both of us turn around and the words were out of my mouth before I had a chance to consider them.

'For fuck's sake,' I said. 'Typical you're not going.'

I turned to Callie, about to ask where her broom was, when the sound of more glass breaking stopped me. At my feet was what formally was a water glass.

'What the fuck did you say?' Mum barked, her words choppy as she stepped toward me. I matched her and took one back.

'Mum, cut it out. Just go sit down and I'll clean it up,' Callie scolded. But mum was watching me, ignoring Callie altogether. Dad was still at the table, watching mum but not moving.

'What did you say,' demanded Mum, watery eyes on mine.

'Nothing! For fuck's sake, have another drink.'

I knew I shouldn't have said it.

'Don't fucking TALK TO ME like that. And don't FUCKING LIE to me Astor!' she yelled, spit flying from her mouth, stepping toward me. I stepped back, my butt hitting the bench top. End of the line.

'Mum!' Callie yelped at the same time as dad called 'Helen!' across the room. But neither of them moved. Fear took off, screaming its panic through my body, setting my pulse to double speed. Nothing good was coming.

'I haven't done anything!' I yelled, self-control out the window.

She took another step, slicing her heal on the broken glass as she did. Dad got up and came up behind her, ready to investigate the cut on her foot. But she looked at me. She looked at me, then down at her foot and however she connected them, came back as being my fault. She exploded forward.

I screamed as her hands clawed at me, as they wrapped around my arms and slammed my body back. My head snapped against the upper cupboards in Callies sunny kitchen, my lower spine into the bench top. Her nails bit into my forearms, my neck. I tried to push back, to get out from her reach but she was in a rage, pure rage. Her hands made it to my throat, pressing in with all of her strength.

And then she was gone. Dad had pulled her away as her hands had snaked around my throat. He was yelling. At her, at me, I had no idea. I didn't care.

'I've called the cops,' Callie announced, her voice shaking and tears streaking down her face.

'Why bother?' I said flatly. I picked my way through the room. Dad had mum on the couch as she shouted about rehab and wine and how much she hated me. How I was, why she was like that. I shakily pulled on my shoes, touched my keys in my pocket and ran my fingers along my hem.

'Fuck off you bitch, before I get you,' she screamed, face twisted. Dad held her back. I wondered if this was enough for him, finally.

It was enough for *me*.

I stopped at the door, looking at Mum in her unfocused hate-filled eyes. 'If I see you before your own funeral, it will be too soon.'

I walked to my car, snapping on the interior light the second I got inside and drove home. I couldn't do this anymore.

I was done.

CHAPTER TWENTY-ONE

I turned the lights on as I walked through the house, muscle memory guiding my shaking hands to each switch. The entire drive home I had contemplated calling Megan, or even just going to them rather than back here. But I wasn't sure that I should go to them, I didn't want to bring all of this chaos to their doorstep. I could just sleep in my car, until I worked out what was next. I wanted my things, though. I didn't want to come back here tomorrow in the light of day and pretend tonight hadn't happened. I wanted out. Was I about to become a cliché? Teenage runaway. Not where I thought my life would be. None of this was how I thought my life would be.

My bedroom was as I had left it, bed made, everything in its place. A snapshot of a perfect little life. I flung open my wardrobe door, pulling out a spare overnight bag and a couple of jumpers. I grabbed some clothes from my drawers, jeans and shirts and underwear. I wasn't being picky. I realised I was still in my uniform, and it was such a sharp reminder that I was sixteen. Sixteen and about to leave my home to escape the wine-fuelled words and, at times, the hands of my own mother.

My hands shook as I pulled my shirt over my head and unzipped the skirt, letting the blue tartan pool at my feet. On the inside of my wardrobe door was a full-length mirror, surrounded with photos of Megan and I, bands I liked, and stupid book quotes that gave me hope when I thought I was at my lowest. Who knew I could get lower?

I stopped, taking in my own appearance. Plain blue bra, mismatched with grey underwear. Cotton and boring. Not sexy. My skin was always pale, and secretly a feature I tended to like, only marred by a few errant freckles. Just a normal girl, not fat or thin, ugly, or exceptionally pretty. But my mask had slipped, slipped as often as my hand had these past couple weeks. Astor who was always happy was gone. Astor who could bite her tongue and swallow her words. Astor who gave into the bite of a razor only when she couldn't cope anymore, when she had reached her absolute limit, was gone. The Astor in the mirror with her pale skin and hollow eyes had tried to cope, to deal with her days and keep her mind turning over. She had tried so very hard. She traced a line on her leg, and I felt it in my fingertip. My leg. One angry red and raw line. One amongst dozens, insistently criss-crossing their way from my hip to just above my knee, where my school skirt would end. My thighs were a matched pair, crusted and angry as they scabbed and healed. It was impossible to see where some began and ended, each cut made as a silent plea for peace, a trade for my sleep.

My hips, slightly rounded and peeking out the top of my underwear, weren't free from this self-inflicted punishment either. When I'd run out of space, when the pain had become too much on my thighs, I'd moved up.

No thought beyond needing the world to stop for a moment so I could sleep each night and get up each morning. I had destroyed myself.

I was repulsive, so beyond saving that my own mother knew I was a waste. This was all I would ever be. She would never love me. *I* would never love me.

How would I ever be more than something people used and threw away?

What was the point? I wasn't a good daughter, a good sister. I wasn't a good friend. I was selfish and reckless, and who would possibly want that? Who *needed* that?

I forced myself to look. To take in the evidence of how pathetic and tragic I was. I'd etched it into my skin so I could never forget.

My fingers ached to pull out a razor, to paint my skin with the words I knew fit me best, so I wouldn't forget them either. Repulsive. Disgusting. *Worthless.*

The silver box was safe in its usual spot, waiting for me. I knew I could feel better. I could feel better permanently.

I sat on my bed, still in my underwear. I was well practiced at ignoring the way my skin pulled in pain. I reached for the box, desperate now for its familiar feel.

I held it in my palm. Ornate silver, almost weightless. I couldn't remember where it had come from, who had given it to me. This little silver box that was the keeper of my secrets, held my means of escape. My arms were mostly clear. Not that it mattered in the end, really, but they were. My old scars were pale and waxy, criss-crossed across my skin in a sickly game of noughts and crosses. Except I was the only player, and I never seemed to win. I didn't think winning was on the cards for me. I held the razor carefully, not worried it would cut my fingers, but that I would drop it on the floor. This small piece of metal was the answer. I didn't need to be here, I didn't have to continue forcing my existence on people. It could be peaceful. For me and everyone else.

I slipped down onto the floor, the familiar carpet against my exposed skin itched. My stomach twisted. Was it anticipation that set my skin alight? Knowing that it was going to be over, that the persistent cycle of fear and anguish was at its end? That I was at my end. This was the best option, the one that fixed it all for everyone.

Pushing the blade to my skin—like I had done many times before—I waited for the relief. The oblivion. The sharp burn as it broke through, the tiny drop of blood. But I needed to press harder, to *mean* it. I closed my eyes, forcing tears out before they were ready to fall as I did. I swallowed a sob, making a cut into my skin.

It *hurt*.

My skin prickled, mottled with cold and fear. I was scared. I didn't want it to hurt at the *end*. Peace wasn't meant to be painful.

I couldn't do it. I couldn't pull the razor down my arm, like I had done a thousand times, but harder. With purpose. I was fucking *scared*. Scared of what happened after. Scared of what I would miss. But God, I didn't want to be *here*. I didn't want to wake up each day and drag myself through life. No one wanted me here and I didn't want to be here. I wasn't worth it. I was disposable. But I couldn't fucking do it.

Coward.

I let my head fall back against my bed, ignoring the tears that fell to meet the pinpricks of blood on my arm. I was such a fuck-up.

My phone vibrated and chimed, abandoned on my duvet when I'd come in. Habit? Curiosity? One or both had me reaching for it. Troy. A video message and a text. I was half-naked and bleeding, wanting to die. Surrounded by haphazard piles of clothes, face streaked with tears, and I just wanted some peace in my worthless life. And I got Troy.

Why the fuck did the universe hate me.

The video was from Instagram. A duck jumping off a little bridge into a stream, her ducklings jumping with her for the first time. The text was an invite to a party, promising drinking and drugs and oblivion. It was in the next town over. There was no connection between the two messages but when did Troy ever make fucking sense.

I looked at the state of things. The little silver box, my thighs that looked like they'd been through a paper shredder and tapped out a reply. Maybe I could find peace another way.

Troy was already in the school carpark when I pulled in. I'd thrown on some clothes, dry-shampooed my hair, and slapped on basic make up. My backseat held my worldly possessions, which amounted to clothes and books. Such a thrill, I was. As I walked over to him, all I was focusing on was that in 20 minutes-ish I'd be in a different town with people who didn't know *fucked-up little Astor* and throwing back some shots.

Hello numb.

'Well, well, well. Fancy seeing you here!' Troy teased, leaning against the front of his black two-door car.

'We literally planned this. Half an hour ago.' I stopped in front of him, folding my arms.

'Okay but I didn't think you'd come. You know it's not school people, right?'

He smiled his big toothy smile, the one that said nothing was ever truly serious in his world. Casual and cavalier and an annoying ass. That's Troy alright.

'Yeah. Good. Can we go?'

I moved to the passenger side, wrapped my hand around the door handle, and paused. I was about to get in the car with a guy, alone. At night. It hadn't worked out so well last time.

But what did it matter, really. As quickly as the fear reared up, I had smothered it. I didn't care anymore what happened to me. Maybe this was what I deserved.

Defiantly, I yanked the door open and climbed in.

Troy turned the car on and pulled out, fiddling with his phone as he did. *Eminem* poured out of his speakers, tinny and lacking bass.

'Where's your shadow tonight?' he asked, heading out of town.

'What? Megan?'

'Yeah, you don't tend to appear at a party without her. Did you have a fight or something? Cat fight? I'd want to see that.'

He smiled his stupid smile and I wanted to smack him. It annoyed me I couldn't correct his use of 'her', but it wasn't for me to tell.

'How'd you hear of this party anyway? Next town over and all.' I ignored everything he said.

'Ah, my dad still lives there so I have friends there too. It's not like our usual ones. They often have a DJ or a live band. It's epic.'

'Sweet,' I nodded, keenly aware that I had no idea where I would end up tonight.

25 minutes of his shit rapping, and we stopped in an industrial area just outside the next town. There were other cars parked carelessly along the road, chain link fences and tall dark box-shaped buildings loomed in the watery orange streetlights. I followed Troy to what looked like a shed, or a rundown warehouse. Wavy tin walls painted matte white vibrated with the bass of the music.

'Ready?' Troy asked, eyebrow cocked and smile wide.

'Seriously, what is this place? We're both underage for a club.'

I was curious. I'd never even heard of parties like this.

'Don't be a fucking stick in the mud. I don't know, but some kids at the school here put them on, and that's all that matters. Okay?'

'Yeah. Okay.' I shrugged.

Troy pushed open the door and we walked right into a blonde girl at a little desk, sipping vodka premix from a bottle and bobbing her head to the band screaming on stage. Someone had rigged up a couple of cheap strobes and the lights danced across the walls and ceiling. A rainbow on a power trip. Troy gave the girl a tenner, and we entered the mass of bodies. I'd taken a bottle of rum from the back of Dad's wardrobe, where he "hid" it from me in case I took up either of the family traditions: binge drinker or chronic alcoholic. Troy shimmied away from me, off to find his friends and a source of alcohol, I assumed. He had beer in his car but knowing Troy, he'd drink other people's first.

I took a gulp of straight rum and wanted to spit it out. It was hot and burned going down, fouler than I thought it could possibly be. How the fuck did people do this daily?

I pushed into the crowd, forcing another sip. I wanted to feel that floaty feeling I felt with Callie and at the bonfire. The music was a band, boys with greasy hair and tight jeans jumped around, and a thin girl with a big voice screeched about pain. I could get behind that, even if it felt a decade out of fashion. Pain was always on trend, wasn't it?

Another mouthful. Less disgusting this time. Still hot and a little burn as it went down. Bodies pushed in behind me, in front of me. My skin crawled at the feeling of people against me, and the air was thick with sweat and smoke. Another mouthful. One more. The music was a beat that I had heard before, or maybe I hadn't. I danced, moving my hips and arm up, the other clutching my bottle to my chest. The crowd yelled and I did too. Another mouthful, another song. The strobes danced through the throng of bodies and my eyes hurt so I shut them. Anonymous bodies danced with me, jumping in time to the beat. Hands on my sides and I ignored the shudder of disgust I felt. Sweat dripped down my skin. It was hot in here, but I had a drink. In my hand, fingers wrapped around its neck. *Thank God*. I tipped my head back and swallowed it down. Missing the burn a little bit.

A guy pushed a smoke into my hand—already lit—and I put it to my lips without hesitation. A different burn, familiar smell. He had a nice smile, though his front teeth crossed a little bit, I still liked it. I offered him my bottle, happy when he accepted it.

His hand was on my hip and I wasn't repulsed. His touch was something I saw but couldn't feel. It was nothing, not a hint or a whisper. But his hand was on me. Maybe this was how I got better? How I could be normal again. My head was swimming and woozy from the heat. I was thirsty. So I had another sip, let the guy with the overlapped teeth pull me closer, and danced. He didn't know who I was, didn't *care* who I was. *I* didn't care who I was. Right now I was nothing. Nothing but movement and bass and I didn't need to feel anything.

I didn't know what time it was.

Why was my bottle empty?

Flashing lights and suffocating heat and music tore through me.

Someone pressed a drink into my hand. Beer, in a can. Warm. Revolting. I was revolting.

No.

I took another drink. Forced a smile and danced. Forced a laugh until it wasn't forced anymore, and I couldn't work out what I was laughing but *oh*, it was funny.

'I want you,' was whispered in my ear. Low and sultry. Was he attractive? Did it matter?

I smiled and nodded, feeling the floor move as the world spun. Or *I* spun.

He wrapped his hand around mine and pulled me through the crowd. A murmur of apprehension fought through the alcohol maze I'd created to tell me to stop. That this wasn't a good idea.

But why wasn't it?

I'd done this before. I enjoyed it. It was expected, wasn't it? This is what I was worth.

It was what I wanted.

I think.

The night was colder than I expected. His arm slipped around my side, under my ribs and he pulled me close. Walking was hard, our feet tangled and I laughed. Loudly and bent over, like it was exploding out of me with such force I couldn't possibly be upright. He leaned into his car and handed me a bottle of beer, opening one for himself. We clinked them together, yelling *cheers* up at the taut black sky. His house wasn't far, he told me.

'Astor!' came from somewhere behind me. The voice sounded confused and familiar. I turned to the sound, smiling wide. I was happy, wasn't I?

Troy cocked his head, asked if I was okay. Concern on his face that didn't belong, and I couldn't work out why it was there. I waved him off. I was with my new friend. This is what I wanted.

We got into his car. Tools in the back seat. High vis jacket and hard hat. Who was he?

Did it matter? This is what I was supposed to do.

He turned up the music, a band I didn't know. The bass vibrated through my body and I drunk my beer.

His house wasn't far. Our feet tangled again as we walked up the path, as he fumbled for his key. I laughed as we fell through the door.

I took another drink, the last for this bottle.

I was numb and alive. In control and free.

Chapter Twenty-Two

My mouth was like cotton. Rubbish bin-soaked cotton at that. I groaned and buried my face in the pillow and the scent hit me. Sweat and unclean skin. Bile shot up my throat faster than anything and I gagged, forcing it back down. Absolutely was not in my room, or any room I had seen before in my life. I was naked—except for my socks—and last night was a blur.

Lord above, what had I done.

The squelching in my stomach was more than alcohol, it was liberally mixed with panic and shame. This is who I was and what I was worth, rum and a stream of "yes" had led me here. The crimson sheet, with a thread count lower than my questionable IQ, was wrapped around the torso of my bed mate. His skin was tanned, gently freckled and there was a little mole under one of his shoulder blades. His hair looked sandy, styled with grease, I assumed. My heart accelerated and I sat up properly, looking around for my shirt. The mattress we were on was on the floor, butted up against a corner with a window on one neutral white wall above us. The floor was a sea of who the fuck knows what. Clothes and takeaway rubbish competed for space on the navy carpet, and I wasn't sure which would win. Who the hell was this guy and where was I exactly?

I pulled on my top and dug in my jeans pocket looking for my phone. Dead. I tried not to panic, tried to keep calm. Last night tore through my mind in fragments. My leaning into this guy, following him out to his car. Rum. Beer. Laughing like I'd lost my mind. Maybe I had.

I felt all grimy, filthy. My outside finally matched the inside. My clothes stunk of alcohol and smoke and sweat. I leaned over and gave *Mystery Man* a prod in the back.

'Hey,' I said.

Nothing. I pushed a little harder, spoke a little louder.

He exhaled and rolled over, sheet slipping down as he did and, like a child, I threw my hand over my eyes so I couldn't see his dick.

Mature. Hitting all the high notes lately.

He stretched, scratching his soft-looking belly, and yawning, loudly. He opened his eyes, a perfectly nice hazel, and looked up at me. He took in my face, eyes sliding down then back up and frowned slightly. I assumed he wasn't as up to scratch with the details either.

'Hi,' he smiled. The overlapped front teeth, I remembered those. 'How's it goin'?'

'It's uh...going. You don't happen to have an iPhone charger, do you?'

Every minute I sat here, in this rubbish bin featuring a mattress, was too long. This was the measure of my life right now and I wanted to leave. I wanted to go to Megan.

'Yeah, over there,' he gestured to the other side of the room where his chest of drawers stood, every drawer open and empty. The familiar white cable was plugged in next to it. Would it be rude to put my shoes on before I crossed the trash pit to get there?

'And...maybe a bathroom?'

He waved over at the door, and I assumed that meant one was out there. *What a helpful fellow.*

I picked my way across the room and shoved the charger in place. It took a few attempts, since apparently a hangover didn't improve hand-eye coordination. A little semi-circle was trash-free by the door, allowing it to open with ease. *Lovely*. Thankfully, the sunny hall on the other side of the door was clean, not an apple core or a chocolate wrapper in sight. I ducked into the bathroom opposite and shut myself in, clicking the lock into place.

What the *fuck* had I done. Really. Matty thought I was some easy moron who slept with anyone because that was what people at school thought. Dad probably hated me now. Mum thought I was nothing. And I'd lived up to all of that last night, hadn't I? Tears burned at the corners of my eyes, full of the truth that I was nothing. I brushed them away harshly. I couldn't give in to them here.

I refused to look in the mirror as I washed my hands, eyes focused on the way the dark fingerprints from my mother's hands wrapped around my arms. Bold and brutal. Would she care if she saw them? Would she feel any guilt? Remorse? I shut off the water, wiped my hands on my jeans, and scoffed. She wouldn't; this was what I deserved after all. Not that I planned to see her again.

I just needed my phone to turn on and then I would call Megan. Then, I could work out what the fuck I was going to do next.

Outside the bathroom, I walked straight into the guy I'd crawled into the floor bed with. Still shirtless and smelling like an ashtray. He was kind of cute, though.

'Sorry,' I said.

'It's all good. I'm Scott. Don't think we got to names last night!' he laughed in that carefree way people did and my skin crawled. Not because of him. He hadn't done anything wrong, aside from having questionable taste in sexual partners and booze, as far as I knew. I hadn't even stopped to get his name.

'Astor. Look, I just want to get some battery and I'll go.'

'Astor? Nice. Yeah all good. I'm gonna shower.' He pointed over my shoulder to the room I'd just vacated and I quickly side stepped my way past him. 'Hey, you okay?'

'Yeah,' I forced a smile, 'I'm great. Just places to be.'

He nodded like he understood my busy schedule and shut the bathroom door.

Fifteen minutes later, I was sitting at a bus stop around the corner from the house waiting for Megan. When I'd picked up my phone, I had been inundated with messages from Callie, Dad, Dylan, Megan, and even surprisingly, Troy. I'd ignored them all and messaged Megan, asking if they could pick me up from here. *I need you* was actually what I had said first. My head was throbbing, a thousand monkeys with cymbals clanging away in there. I'd scooped water into my mouth in the bathroom earlier and it was not enough to fight the disgusting post-party death I was suffering right now. I had been staring absentmindedly at the park opposite, when Megan pulled to a stop in front of me.

'Fucking hell, you look like shit. What are all those bruises? Jesus. What's going on? What happened? Why are you in this shithole town?' Megan pelted me as I fell into the passenger seat.

'One at a time,' I mumbled, losing my battle to keep my eyes open in the daylight.

'Nah dude. I got a dozen calls and messages last night about you. What the fuck is going on?'

I looked over at them, sloppy ponytail and track pants. No care in their appearance but concern marred every inch of their face. I took a breath to steady myself.

'Mum came at me at Callie's, Dad pulled her off. I bailed. Troy texted about some party and brought me here. Went home with some rando who doesn't have a bed. Scott.' I frowned at his name. He hadn't been awful.

I was so disgusted with myself. I didn't want to look at Megan and see that reflected back at me. One minute stretched into five and I kept my eyes closed for every second of them.

'Google a pharmacy, I don't know where any are here.'

'What?' I looked over, automatic in my confusion.

'You need the morning-after pill dude. It's over the counter. Google.'

I blinked, stupid.

'What makes you think I didn't use protection?' I asked, though I didn't think we had.

'Well, did you?' their words stood between us, stretching in the silence I let grow. Crickets, essentially.

'Don't I need a parent or something?' I sighed, moving on.

'No, you don't. So google.'

I gave the first direction and Megan swung the car around to head back the way they'd come. Small town meant a short drive.

Sitting outside the pharmacy—a bright yellow chain one that boasted being open 24 hours—I felt sick. I had no idea if we'd used protection the night before. Not to mention if he had any STIs. Just another thing to add to my list of fuck-ups.

Inside was painfully bright, a hundred tiny artificial suns trying to melt my brain as enthusiastically as the real one. A pharmacy like every other except—being a chain—it was bigger and bolder. Every aisle adorned with tags pronouncing what was on sale this week. We made our way up an aisle of foot care to the counter where the actual pharmacist was, and music pumped out of speakers we couldn't see.

'Who the fuck puts *Paris Hilton* on for music at a pharmacy?' I asked under my breath.

Did anything make sense anymore.

'Excuse you, *Stars Are Blind* is an absolute banger and grossly underappreciated.' Megan remarked as though I'd just insulted their grandmother. I chose to ignore that.

We reached the counter and my skin prickled, anxiety skipped freely through my nervous system. What would they think of me, asking for emergency contraception because I was too fucking useless to use anything last night? I wondered if they'd be able to tell I was at rock bottom, if it was clear on my skin showing me for what I was. Or rather, wasn't.

I wondered why I cared at all.

It was our turn and I stepped forward, stealing myself to look up.

'Astor?'

'Mr. Sanders?' Of all the places I would have expected to see our old neighbour, this was not one of them. Somewhere in the depths of my melted mind, I knew he worked as a pharmacist, but I never pictured him...actually working. *Fucking wonderful.* 'This...is where you moved to?'

I couldn't be more stunned at this point. He was taking in my appearance, lingering on the bruises and fuck knows what else. Whatever he was thinking wasn't clear.

'How can I help you?' he asked briskly, business-like.

'I uh...just—' I tried to force the words into the open, but nothing came out and I was stood gaping like a fish. I looked at Megan, unsure what to do and they gave me a shove.

'Go outside, As,' they said to me, then turned back to the counter. 'Hi, I'd like the morning-after pill, thanks.'

Megan had put on the same tone their father used when he was not taking no for an answer, and I escaped down the hair product aisle to the exit. This town was bigger than ours, and the pharmacy was in a strip of shops, sandwiched between a newsagent and a hair salon in all its clown-yellow glory. I paced as I waited and tried to not think anymore ahead than I had to.

Megan came out ten minutes later, a little paper bag in their hand.

'Thank you,' fell from my lips before they could even get a word out.

'You'd do it for me. That dude is a dick, though. They'll have water there.'

I followed Megan a few doors down to a little shop and bought some water and a Red Bull, then popped an innocuous little pill into my hand, barely pausing before I swallowed it down.

'Am I going to feel sick or anything?' I asked, like an idiot I'd taken it without much thought.

'Nah I doubt it, but there's a printout thing in the box. Let's go anyway. We can talk on the drive to wherever the fuck your car is.'

'School,' I said.

'What?'

'My car. It's parked at school.'

'Right. Come on then,' they said, and I dutifully followed.

Despite what they claimed, we did not speak on the drive back to our own town. Not a word, though I could practically feel Megan's thoughts ricocheting around the inside of their skull. We pulled in next to my car, my potential for escape to fuck knows where. What I was going to do now, I didn't know.

'Troy was worried about you.'

'What?' I asked blankly.

'Troy, Astor. Fucking Troy, out of everyone we know, Troy was worried about you.'

Little snips of anger were slipping out, and I knew Megan was trying to keep calm like I'd seen them do a dozen times before. They redid their hair, tight and serious, and turned to me. Both of us sitting awkwardly sideways in the little car.

'I'm sorry. I didn't mean to worry anyone,' I whispered.

'Stop saying fucking sorry. Jesus, we just want to help you.'

Their voice was kind, always so kind, and I was an awful friend. Everything was such an impossible mess in my head. Every thought I had came with a partner, and that partner was conflicting, opposite, and jarring. I barely knew which way was up. It felt like I had no one, yet Megan was here. Megan was here and Dylan had definitely messaged, and Troy was worried. I was nothing, worthless, and without purpose and yet I didn't want Mr. Sanders to judge me. I hated myself for falling out of a bottle and into a stranger's bed but how could I? Why would I hate myself if it was where I belonged?

Even my thoughts were selfish. I was an appalling friend and never considered really what I could do better. It was just all about me. I tried to string some words together, opened my mouth and tasted the salt of tears as they fell and rolled freely.

'I don't know what I've done, Megan, I don't know,' I sobbed, each word garbled and growing in volume.

'Shh, it's okay. It'll be okay.' Megan rubbed my arm and let their words sink in. 'I spoke to Callie last night. I think you should call her.'

I didn't want to speak to Callie. I wanted to shower, scrub the layers of my skin away until last night was washed down the drain and no longer my memory to carry. I wanted to crawl into Megan's bed and sleep somewhere I knew nothing could touch me, in any way. I wanted someone to swoop in and fix all of this mess and make it better. Make me a whole normal person with a loving family. Hopes and dreams and a future that was within reach. I wanted to travel with Megan and have freedom. No shredded skin and scars to remind me every single day of the pit I existed in. A fairy godmother, that was what I wanted, like a child at Disney. People had it worse...I knew people had it worse than me. I had a house and food and an education, so what right did I have to cry? That's what Mum had said to me time and again. *Someone always had it worse.* I sniffed and coughed, wiping my nose on my shirt and not caring. Just trying to stop. Stop crying, stop complaining, stop existing. It was a few bruises from Mum and some gossip from Matty and I was a wreck.

'I'm sorry Meg, I'll pull it together. I will, I promise.' My words were sobs and I couldn't stop.

'Astor. Stop.' I looked up at them, but they were a blur, and I couldn't clear my eyes fast enough. 'Not stop crying. Stop apologising. You've done nothing wrong.'

I blinked at them, big watery owl eyes. 'I don't know what to do, Meg. I don't want to go home. I don't want to go to school. I just don't know. Last night I wanted to leave the town or the country or die, and now I feel like I'm overreacting and being dramatic.'

'As—'

'No, I'm serious. I don't know how to do this anymore. I can't keep pretending I'm okay. I don't want to ever see Mum again. I don't know what to do and, honestly, what's the point?'

'The point of what?' they whispered, voice torn.

'All of this. Fucking all of it. What is the point of me if all I am is a slut and a punching bag? I am nothing and nobody and you can't change that, so why am I here, breathing and tearing my skin to ribbons just to sleep at night, so I can wake up and be nothing again.'

'Don't you fucking dare,' Megan's voice broke and tears poured down their pale cheeks, under the thick frame of their glasses. Anger and sorrow danced together with every word. 'Don't you talk like that. What would I do without you, what the fuck would my life be without you?'

'This isn't about you, Meggy. I don't know what continuing is going to get me. There's no fucking escape from anything for me, is there?'

'Of course it's about me. You are my best friend. You're my family. I'd be alone without you. Don't leave me, As. I don't want to be alone and you're my person,' they cried, pleading.

I didn't want to wake up tomorrow, but I didn't want to hurt Megan. It all twisted and turned and overwhelmed me. They'd forget me eventually, whether I lived or not. But I didn't want Megan to suffer for even a moment, and all I had done was hurt everyone who came close to me.

'I just...I don't want to be here. But I couldn't do it and I won't.'

'God, I knew you weren't doing well but I didn't think we were this bad.'

Megan's arm crossed into my half of the car, and they linked their fingers with mine. We sat in quiet, sniffing and hiccupping as our steady crying wound down. They pulled off their glasses and wiped their eyes.

'Have you got your keys?' Megan sounded sad, and I couldn't pretend that it wasn't because of me and how much of a fucking mess I was. I nodded. 'Okay well, I don't think you're okay to drive so let's just go back to my place and we will sort this out later, yeah?'

I nodded again, afraid that if I opened my mouth all my vile self-loathing thoughts would spill out and I wouldn't be able to scoop them back up.

Megan led me to their room, though I knew the way. I stopped outside the door, wanting to crawl into bed but I wanted to be clean. As clean as someone like me could be.

'Can I shower?' I asked weakly.

'Huh?' they turned to me. 'Yeah of course. Actually yeah, I have a call to make, so go shower. My bathrobe is on the hook as usual so just chuck that on.'

'Thank you.'

'As? You're worth everything to me, okay?'

I shuffled into the bathroom, crying all over again, set the water to fire, and stripped.

Megan had sleep shorts and a hoodie on their bed for me. Unfolded, because Megan was immune to folding. The shorts wouldn't cover my legs, but it was Megan, and I sure as fuck wasn't concerned last night with Scott, so why did it matter now with my best friend. I was squeezing water from my hair, when Megan's gasp had me regretting the shorts.

'Sit down. Jesus fuck.'

I couldn't look at them. Embarrassment and anguish were all I had. I sat.

'I—'

'Oh Astor,' Megan was quiet, hovering in front of me.

'It's the only way I can sleep sometimes. It's the only thing that stops everything hurting.'

My words were muted and plain. They were all I had to offer.

'We're going to get you sorted, okay? Dylan is going to get your car with Troy, and Callie is going to call you tomorrow morning.'

They pulled back the covers, dislodging a hundred random items they'd tossed on the bed at some stage in the past year, and motioned for me to get in.

'Right now we are going to watch *Priscilla* and I've ordered some food and then you can sleep.'

'Thank you,' I said softly. 'I don't deserve you.'

Megan turned on the tv and climbed in bedside me, wriggling in close even though they'd have to get up when food arrived.

'You're my best friend. Now watch the queens and shush.'

Which was what I did.

Chapter Twenty-Three

I'd known as soon as I'd opened my eyes that morning had come and gone. I didn't remember falling asleep, everything had still felt out of touch and full of conflict. Today, now, I felt numb. Megan wasn't next to me, and likely hadn't been for a while, so they didn't know I was awake. I could close my eyes and sleep the rest of the day away and try again tomorrow.

Except I needed to pee.

I was almost back in my blanket nest when I heard the all too familiar sound of my sister, though both her and Megan were speaking quietly. I didn't want to see her. I didn't want to hear her telling me how I had overreacted, that Mum was fine. That I needed to go home or be better or whatever the hell else I'm sure I needed to do. Though I had no doubt that Megan would force me from the bedroom if they thought this was in my best interest. And I was unbelievably nosy.

Callie was perched on a turquoise wooden chair, her perfectly shaped, eyebrows dipped together in a graceful frown, as she listened to Megan's dad tell her some story about his students. Megan sat silently between them, picking at the tassels of the table runner. They all looked up as I stepped into the room, and I couldn't bring myself to look at Callie now. Embarrassment was the current winning emotion. I didn't want her to think less of me and I was ashamed by the last words I'd said to Mum. Even though I still meant them, mostly.

I wondered if she wanted to see me, but dismissed that almost immediately. She'd never wanted to see me before now, and I didn't want to see her. It was that notion of unconditional love from our mother that kept me spinning, confused. I felt almost obligated to see her and love her, even though I knew that wasn't best. The world romanticised mothers and that mythical love just as much as it made them to be villains when they didn't come up to scratch in the eyes of the public.

'Hey As,' Callie said softly, like I was fragile and might bolt. Which I might.

'Hi,' I looked up, catching Megan's eye quickly, and looking back down. The nail polish on my toes was ugly and chipping, and less judgmental than my sisters face might be.

'She's here to help, man, I know you don't want to, but just give it a minute, okay?' Megan had come to stand beside me and nudged me towards the sofas in the open planned room. I really had no desire to hear whatever excuses Callie was going to serve me. But I sat and I waited for her to start.

'I want you to come and live with me.'

The words fell from Callie's mouth without pause and I snapped my head up.

What?

'What?' I asked. My heart stopped for a moment at the prospect of a chance.

'Well, you can't go back home—'

'Oh, so they don't want me back, then?' I cut her off, outraged and far more hurt than I would ever admit at the idea they didn't want me, despite my conviction to never go back. I was exhausting myself with all the internal conflict and I'd only been awake ten minutes.

'No, they would. But I don't want you to go back there.'

I let her words seep into my skin and prayed they'd take hold. That was what I had wanted for so long. Not to live with Callie, but to not have to live with Mum. And here it was, being offered to me. I looked up at her and wondered if she could see the flicker of hope across my face before I clamped it down.

'I don't want to go back there,' I said quietly.

'What do you want? Tell me, please.'

I couldn't tell her.

She looked me over, lingering on my thighs, then my arms where my bruises were purple and obvious. I crossed my arms under my boobs and stood up, too nervous and unsure to stay seated. They weren't the first marks Mum had left on me but apparently, they were the first to be seen for what they were.

'Can we have a minute alone?' Callie asked the room and Megan's Dad stood, ushering them down the hall and pulling the door shut behind them. I was alone with my sister and the truth was suffocating. She stood and took a step toward me, and I matched hers with my own backward.

'I'm so, so sorry, Astor.'

'What?'

'You told me it was bad and I didn't believe you. Or I didn't want to believe you,' her voice quivered with each word and her eyes shone with unshed tears.

'Right. Okay.'

I wasn't sure what I was meant to say. She'd thrown a grenade into the already fraught emotional battle I was carrying with me. I had given up thinking she would ever believe me, that she would accept that when I said things weren't okay at home, I meant it. But here we were.

'I'm sorry,' she said it again, and I had nothing to give her. Was I meant to say *thank you*? *Okay*? *I forgive you*? And did she really *need* forgiveness? She'd done nothing wrong, nothing except believe the best of her mother, as most people did. I couldn't blame her for that, not really. But I was mad at her for never believing me, never seeing the bruises until now. I was her sister, her baby sister. Surely that was meant to count for something. Why hadn't it mattered until she had seen it herself?

'I don't know what to say. I'm...angry, Callie,' I said. My words were thick and sticking in my throat. 'Why do I matter now?'

'What?' she asked. Her eyes were huge in her face, surprise.

'I told you she wasn't good, Cal. Why do I matter more today than I did a week ago? A month ago?' I couldn't curb the harsh notes as I spoke. My emotions had gathered, and anger had won.

'You've always mattered,' she said, puzzled.

'Bullshit! I have been telling you! For months! Years! You didn't care then, not at all. But now she's hurt me in your presence it suddenly matters? Fuck off.'

I paced the small room, itching to scream as loud as I possibly could. Fighting the pressure that needed a release. I looked over at Callie and she had folded in on herself, arms around her waist, crying openly but quietly. I didn't want to feel guilty, but Lord, did I.

'I *am* sorry. I just didn't know, Astor. I didn't think she was like that,' she sniffed and cried.

'I *told* you she was.'

Five little words. Each one washed with pain and forced out, collected together to form the truth. I'd asked for help so many times and been ignored or told how I was wrong. So many times that, eventually, for the most part, I had stopped. No one heard me, and those who might didn't believe me. Softly, and to myself but still loud enough for Callie to hear, one more time I let the words out.

'I told you.'

I slumped onto the couch. I'd had enough. Callie was still crying and it annoyed me, though I couldn't pick why. I couldn't work out much of anything. The minutes gathered in the quiet, waiting for my sister to speak.

'So,' she started, eventually. 'You'll come home with me.' Not a question.

I didn't want to go with her, even though I hadn't any other options really, aside from here with Megan.

'I don't think that's—'

'No,' she interrupted. 'Someone needs to sort this out and I've buried my head for too damn long. You'll come back with me, and we will...I don't know. We'll go from there. I'll work it out.'

Her eyes were ringed red, face blotchy, but she looked certain. She'd made up her mind and wanted me to agree. Did I want to agree? I didn't want to go home, and I still desperately craved that sisterly bond.

'You have one bed,' I managed to say in a more civil tone.

'What?' she said, confused.

'You have one bed. Where will I sleep?'

'Well.' Her brow furrowed as she thought through the options, of which there were few. 'We can take turns. With the couch and my bed. If you like. And I'll find a bigger place,' she nodded to herself, pleased she'd had an answer.

'Okay.'

'Okay?' her smile was small and hopeful.

'Yeah. I'll be over tonight.'

I wanted the day with Megan, in this little pressure-free bubble they gave me.

'Oh, I thought we could go now and talk a bit about things...'

'I need to get my car and stuff. I'll be there by dinner,' I said. I wanted to go back to Megan now. To the bubble. To the fort.

And 15 minutes later, that's where I was. The familiar comfort of *Rocky Horror* on the screen, Megan reading class notes next to me, and the semblance of peace. Until the bedroom door was pushed open enough to admit one dark-haired head belonging to Dylan.

I slithered down under the duvet, I didn't want him to see me and pretend I wasn't an awful friend to him.

'Me and Troy got her car,' he said, speaking softly into the room. He'd brought me my car. Well, and Troy. I popped my head out. I was grateful.

'Keys?' Meg asked. Dylan squished his tall body in, taking in the landfill-like décor before tossing my keys across the room. They landed on the bed, and I scooped them up before the floor swallowed them for good.

'Thanks Dylan. I mean it.'

I couldn't look at him, but I could thank him. Would I struggle with this shame at my actions, at who I was, for the rest of my life? Who the hell would want a life like that.

Lost in my own mess of a mind, I didn't register that Dylan had moved until the mattress dipped. Megan looked between us, ignored the plea in my eyes to not abandon me with yet another person, picked up their book and left the room. Wonderful.

The silence wasn't particularly awkward, but it was heavy and very much there. I cleared my throat, unsure what to say.

'Megan told me about your mum,' he said softly.

Well that's just great. Anger flared, trying to find space to exist in my defeated body. It wasn't their story to tell. I looked up at Dylan, the downturn of his lips instead of his easy smile, and I squashed my rage. It didn't matter if he knew—not really—and I couldn't expect Megan to not give him answers if he'd asked what the fuck he was doing picking my car up for me.

'Okay.'

I wasn't sure what more to say. I didn't want to deep dive it.

'And Troy told me about the party.'

I looked away, ashamed of myself. 'As, you could sleep with the whole town, and it wouldn't matter. What Matty did, *that* was wrong. Entirely, completely, one hundred percent wrong.'

'What?' my head snapped up at the way the words sounded. Warm and without judgment. I wanted to believe him, desperately. Logically, I knew somewhere that maybe he was right, that it wasn't my fault. But it felt like it was, every single atom that made up who I was felt it was me, and I had no idea how to shut down that feeling.

'Fuck it, honestly. I'm going to go full moving-tv-drama moment now, so brace yourself. You're not to blame. For your mum, for Matty. None of it. I knew you were cutting or self-harming or whatever you want to call it. I should have asked what was happening. I'm sorry I didn't,' he paused and pulled in a breath, 'but this isn't you, As. It isn't your fault your mum drinks and it isn't your fault Matty is a rapist.'

'Matty isn't—'

'He isn't what?'

'I got into the backseat, and I'd been all over him the day before. I got into the back and let him kiss me. So...whose fault is it, really,' I shrugged.

He stared at me, mouth slightly open. 'Are you serious?'

I picked at my nails and pretended I wasn't bothered. 'I don't even know what I am.'

'Astor,' he pleaded, making direct eye contact. 'If you said no and asked him to stop, and he didn't stop, it's rape,' he said with a firmness I didn't often here in his voice. Usually his words were full of humour, designed to pull a smile out of you. Not like this. Never this serious.

'No one would ever believe that.'

'*I* believe that.'

'Okay,' I lifted my shoulders again, hinted the faintest of smiles. 'Thanks for bringing my car back,' I tacked on at the end.

'You've said thank you already.' We sat in silence for a moment or two, neither bothered by it. 'I just want to say sorry for how I was at school the other day too,' he added.

Funny how that was just the other day when my main issue was stalking. Now I was homeless and motherless.

Stellar progress, Astor. *Woo.*

'You're fine. I was being a shit friend.'

'You were being a bit selfish which, given how things are, is fine, but that doesn't make you a shit friend.'

At *selfish*, I felt the familiar prick of tears. Not because I disagreed with him, but because I agreed wholeheartedly.

'I'll do better.'

'You don't need to do better. We're fine. I'm your friend always.'

I nodded, my signature move. I wanted to believe him entirely, every word. But it all felt so out of reach. Like it really was a touching moment in a movie and not reality. Everything didn't end perfectly here, that wasn't real life. I hoped his words would take root and grow into something I could hold onto, but I doubted it.

He gave my hand a little squeeze, said goodbye and left, after making me promise to text him later if I felt up to it.

Early that evening, I found myself pulling to a stop in the same place I had been merely days before. Callie had called me earlier ,and I'd let Megan answer for me. I needed to be at the police station in the morning to give a statement for that night. To decide if I wanted a protection order. I sat in my car on the side of the road. The interior light was on even in the premature dark, though I suspected the memories that were within Callie's walls were kinder than whatever lived in the blackness outside. I didn't move for a bit. Everything felt impossible. My phone started ringing, Callie's personalised tone—*Mean* by Taylor Swift. Should probably change that.

'Hello?' I answered tiredly.

'Are you coming in?'

'Oh...yeah I was just...getting my stuff.'

She'd seen my car then.

'I've watched you sit there for—' I heard the air shift as she moved the phone from her ear to check the time on it. 'Eleven minutes now. Just come in.'

I went to reply but she'd hung up. *Alright then.*

I grabbed a bag from my backseat I was confident held at least some form of underwear, and that was basically the most fucks I could give at this moment.

The minute I walked in the door, the scene from the last time I was here played out for me clear as day. Mum's hands on my arms. Dad yanking her back. Callie crying. I pushed it all into a box and dumped my bag on the couch. Couch slash bed, I guessed.

'Hey,' Callie said, as she stepped out of the bathroom. 'I was watching you from the bathroom.'

Awesome.

She informed me I had a doctor appointment tomorrow before we went to the police station.

Also awesome.

'Why?' I asked.

'Well. I think it's time we get you some therapy or counselling. Whatever it's called for your age. Just someone to talk to. Maybe medication.'

I didn't love the idea. Medicated? No.

'Do I have to?'

'Yeah, As. You do. Look, Mum has fucked you over. You're not coping. Time to get in the professionals.'

I wanted to tell her to shove the idea up her ass. *What happens in our house stays in our house.* Had she forgotten the rules? But I had followed the rules and that hadn't got me anywhere.

'Can you do that? I mean, you're not my parent,' I asked.

She sat down next to me and I was immediately full of dread.

'Okay, I spoke to Dad. Yesterday actually.' She sounded nervous.

'Right.'

'He said he'd call the docs if he has to and let them know you're with me but I don't think it will be a problem. You're able to get a mental health plan as a teenager.'

'Right,' I said again. I didn't know how I felt. For most of my life I had been desperate for dad to help me, and it felt like now that I wasn't his direct problem, he was happy to. 'Do I have to see him?'

'No, no of course not. He agreed that you're best here, As,' she smiled.

'Okay. And Mum? Where's she?' My stomach swooped. Anger and guilt and sadness paved the rollercoaster of emotions right now.

'Um, at this stage she is going to rehab. I don't know long term. Dad is pretty upset. About her behaviour. He was adamant that she gets help or it's over. Don't know how serious it is.'

I let that sink in. Is that what I wanted? Would I have my dad if they divorced? Would he want to know me, knowing I split them up? Adding splitting my parents up to my mental list of shit was almost too much.

'Okay.'

I was crying again. I was so fucking over crying. I was angry I couldn't stop crying. Why couldn't I control any of this?

'I think a doctor will really help, okay? I know it doesn't seem like it now. But it will all work out.' She stood and patted my head, deliberately not acknowledging the disgusting sobbing I was partaking in. I just wanted off this ride, off the emotional wreck. 'Let's get takeout, then we can watch *Bridget Jones* and go to sleep. Tomorrow is day one. We're going to be okay.'

I nodded, wishing it would be okay.

I'd give anything to be okay.

CHAPTER TWENTY-FOUR

I was standing at the front door of a house I knew better than my own. Likely because I had lived in my own house for all of six months now. Callie and I had found a new place fairly quickly. It was little, but still close to the beach, and I liked that a lot. I liked a lot of things now.

I pressed the doorbell and knocked twice for good measure. And because I knew it pissed Megan off when people did both.

The door opened and I took in my friend, all one thousand miles of light blonde hair and big, thick framed glasses.

'What the fuck are you wearing?' they asked, disgusted. *Rude*.

I looked down at myself and my very carefully planned outfit.

'You're basically a hoarder, so you know what clothes are. Lord knows you've got a mall worth in there,' I tried to smile. I was still working on that one, so it was a little forced, but my feelings were genuine.

'Your pants are yellow,' they deadpanned.

'I know! Excellent, aren't they?'

'Your top is orange. Why is it orange? And tied like you're a hot girl summer farmer. You're like a colourblind *Daisy Duke* in that.'

'You're very rude today, Megan. I am clearly, a rainbow.' I did a curtsey and let them take in the full effect. Didn't want them to miss the tiny red top hat I had on my head, attached to a headband.

'God,' they groaned. 'Your socks.'

My socks were knee-high. One was green and one was blue. My shoes were purple. I wasn't sure I knew the difference between violet and indigo on the spot, so I'd gone with purple. I'd painted them myself too.

'Wonderful, right?'

Megan sighed, hand on their face. 'Can you explain why you're dressed as a rainbow on my doorstep at 8 in the morning?'

I was suddenly quite unsure of my idea. What if I was overstepping? Was this too much?

I took a breath, counted to five in my head, and reminded myself that I knew Megan.

'We're going to Pride!' I was excited, and I hoped they'd be too. Megan's mouth popped open and for a minute, there was nothing. Just their stunned expression. 'Bro, it's only like, two hours to the city. I'll drive.'

'Oh my fucking god YES!'

Happy dance.

Thank the lord. Megan was slowly coming out to people, in their own time. I didn't want to push them to do anything, but I really wanted to go to pride with them for the first time.

Megan's dad came and peered around their now bouncing self, taking in what I had on.

'What are you two idiots doing, then?' he asked bemused.

'Going to Pride, we'll be home tonight, though.'

It wasn't far to the city, so we'd have no problem getting home at a reasonable hour. And neither of us drank or anything, so no worries about being too intoxicated to drive.

He studied my face, and I wondered if he was trying to gauge my mental stability. Could he tell I was slowly resetting my tiny brain?

'Well, have fun. Don't do anything I wouldn't do.'

He stepped past Megan, kissing their hair briefly. He got into his car, gave us a wave, and left.

'Well, go get ready so we can leave too. I want to stop for snacks and Red Bull.'

I shooed them inside and made peace with this taking a while, since Megan would need a backhoe to find Pride-y clothes in that bedroom.

Miraculously, an hour later we were pulling out of the gas station with a bag of snacks and drinks on our way. Megan had managed to find a few colourful items in their hovel of a room—purple being the main one—and I'd very kindly done their hair into two French braids, with ribbon woven in to add some flair. Not as much as me, but I set a high bar. We had music on shuffle and were alternating talking shit and singing at the top of our lungs for the first hour. The sun wasn't out today. The sky was a mottled grey with its clouds hanging loosely and daring to touch the road we sped along. As the second hour of the drive hit, Megan turned the volume down. Off, really. They turned it off. Dance party over.

'Real talk minute, weekly check-in.'

They turned to face me in their seat, serious expression pulling their eyebrows together.

'Okay,' I said, bracing myself. I'd asked that we kept talking about Mum to a minimum, so weekly check-in it was. The car was just ideal. No escape.

'Your mum has been out of her treatment-home-thing for a bit now. Still haven't heard from her?'

The bottom fell out of my stomach at the mention of her, as it always did. I tried to not think about her, preferring to exile all concept of her from my mind. It was still an open wound for me, and likely would be for some time. I was making progress, slowly. Mental health here wasn't always the fastest, especially if you were waiting for the public system to care for you. I was a mess though, and was seen quickly. My psychiatrist was a younger woman and I saw her each week. She specialised in people like me, children of addicts. Self-harmers. She was also helping me come to terms with all the Matty stuff. I still hadn't filed a report with the police, and I don't think that I ever would. On paper, I knew right and wrong. Any hypothetical situation. Adding myself into the equation threw me off balance and I couldn't make it work in my head. I knew that telling the police meant reliving it all again, and that the likeliness of anything happening to him was almost zero. I also knew what he was, though, and I had to live with that too. He was still at the same school, but I'd had to change. Just living his life normally and giving me no thought. Yet, I still slept with a night light. I still had moments where I desperately needed to know where he was, so another person didn't end up like me. My entire life had slipped out from under me. But slowly, slowly I was learning that

I wasn't the cause, accepting that I was not at fault. At least, I think that was the end goal.

Talking about Mum, though. That was like opening a Pandora's box in my sessions. Cracking that lid had let out a lot of big, scary emotions, not only about her, but about Dad too.

'Uh, no. I don't think I will. From what I understand she has no desire to ever speak to me again so,' I shrugged.

'And you're okay with that?'

I thought about it, like I hadn't already a hundred thousand times before. My answer didn't change, ever, but it had grown as I'd come to understand my own mind a little more.

'I wouldn't say I was okay with it. It's...a lot. Some days I want to move to another country and change my name and pretend Astor Price never existed so she can't ever find me.' I steadied my breathing, refusing to let Mum send me into a mental spiral. 'Some days I miss her. I miss the daytime hours when she was sober.'

The times she would look at me like I was her daughter and *maybe* she loved me. Like maybe I wasn't nothing. Sometimes I desperately wanted that, to know I wasn't nothing. To know that she *did* want me and cared for me. But I couldn't have that. This was better for me, better for both of us. Despite what we are told time and time again, maternal love wasn't a given and love didn't conquer all. In this case it couldn't even conquer a bottle.

I looked over at Megan, the little lines on their forehead tipping into a frown while what I'd said settled in. I turned the music back up, shaking off the thoughts of Mum and singing along.

Until Megan turned it off again.

'As.'

'Yes Megan,' I sighed.

'Why are we going to Pride?'

I panicked a little. Was I doing the wrong thing? I thought they'd be excited but maybe they were just pretending for me?

'Oh. Uh—' I searched for words but apparently, panic ate them.

'Dude, chill. I'm happy. Just curious,' they laughed, likely at my wild-eyed face.

I did relax, though. This was easy when I didn't overthink.

'Well, you've joined the alphabet mafia now. I thought it would be neat. You might meet other enbys!' I flashed them an almost smile. 'I was a dick when you came out to me, leading up to it even. I know you had and still have Ellie, and I'm really happy you do. But I want you to know you've got my support always.'

'You weren't a dick.'

Cue eyeroll.

God I was glad I hadn't lost Megan while I was messing up my life left and right.

'I'm excited,' she said.

'Good. Plus, I've never been either, so it'll be cool to go.'

I waited a minute, giving Megan the time to ask something else, before I reached for the music again. I couldn't do a silent car. My hand touched the button.

'Can I ask something?'

Sweet suffering Jehovah.

'Yes, Megan. Anything, always.'

Patience Astor. You cannot leave your best friend on the side of a highway.

'How come you never like, "came out" to me as pansexual or anything? Am I allowed to ask that?' They did air quotes when they said *came out*, another frown on their face.

'Stop frowning or your face will stay that way,' I stalled. I felt like an outlier when it came to this stuff. I had no issue with my identity, more with how others saw me. 'Well, for me, my sexual orientation and being pan isn't...my defining feature, I guess? I did my googling and stuff, to figure out what I was feeling, but it also wasn't a big deal to me. And I know that it is to a lot of people and that's fine. It is a big deal. It changes lives and breaks down families and friendships. But for me, it wasn't like that. My parents don't care, and Callie is bisexual, so she doesn't give a fuck. I dunno.' I did an awkward little shrug.

People in the queer community had a lot of opinions about what was the "right" way to be, even though the continued message was acceptance, acceptance, acceptance. Online, that wasn't the case. The internet was gross a lot of the time.

'Okay, then,' Megan was still frowning, but more from the small info dump I'd guess. 'Do you think I was too...I don't know. Did I overthink being non-binary too much?'

'What? No. No one goes through this shit the same, dude. What is right for me isn't right for someone else. Like, you do you.'

I looked over and they were nodding, so I hoped I'd helped somewhat.

'That was the most "Astor" sounding I've heard you be in a while. That whole bit,' they said after a moment, leaning forward to turn the music back on.

'I'm trying, Meg. Being pan may be the most straightforward part of my life. Pun intended.'

'You're such a dork.'

'But you love me,' I smiled.

I managed to find a parking spot at a train station. It was easier to park there and take the last ten minutes of driving by train. City parking cost a fortune. Dad was still paying me an allowance, same as he always had. I'd spoken to him a handful of times since that night at dinner and, while I didn't think we would ever live together again, he'd given Mum the ultimatum of rehab or divorce and then stuck to it, so that was something. Sometimes he texted me, and that was okay too. I missed him a lot more than I was willing to admit. He wasn't the best dad, but he was mine.

We stepped out of the city train station finally, and into a sea of similarly dressed people. Hair was dyed and styled with rainbow bands, clips, and headbands. Flags were hanging from backpacks, stuffed into back pockets, and tied as capes. There were people with signs demanding trans rights and proclaiming that love is love. It was suffocating and I was in awe. Obsessed. Everyone there, regardless of how they identified or if they were just an ally, was full of joy. Pure unadulterated queer joy. I'd never seen anything like it. I wanted to be in the middle of it. Megan's hand slipped into mine and I turned to them. Their eyes were wide but full of excitement.

'Hey, we have to go find Dylan. He's at the post office apparently, which is just over there.'

I stood on purple tiptoe and pointed out the familiar red sign I'd spotted as we came down the ramp.

'Dylan's here?'

'Yeah, let's go.' I tugged on their hand and towed them through the ground, *excuse me*'s and *I'm sorry*'s cutting our path through the medley of colour. Dylan was leaning against the wall of the store, swiping through his phone. His freshly box-dyed hair fell into his eyes, and his familiar black clothing was broken up by a pink tutu with little sequins sewn onto it. I gave his shoe a kick and he looked up at me.

'Hey,' he smiled. Big and perfect, just how I liked it. I gave him a hug, it had been a while since we'd seen each other.

'Did you two plan to meet here?' Megan jumped in, eyeing him suspiciously. 'Like...are you together?'

Dylan laughed and I rolled my eyes.

'No Meg, Dylan comes every year. His dads are gay. And no, we aren't together. It is in fact possible to just be friends, you know,' I teased.

'With benefits,' Dylan added.

One day I would roll my eyes back and they'd be stuck there. I swear, Megan lived underground sometimes. Dylan was wonderful, but he was a brilliant *friend*.

We got something to drink each and slipped back into the crowd. Megan's head hadn't stopped moving as they tried to see everything at once.

'Do you think we'll see anyone from home?' they asked, having to raise their voice against the crowd.

'Probably not, but if we do, they'll just think you're with me,' I shrugged. 'Maybe we can go to Pride in different cities when we leave this place.'

'Let's do it. London Pride can be our first stop,' they smiled. London was top of my list for when school was over.

The human rainbow made its way down the street, loudly and chaotically, proud of who they were. It was intoxicating, in the best way and I felt like I could do anything. It didn't matter what my mother was or anything I had gone through. The scars I carried on my skin didn't matter. It was freeing. I'd never felt free.

Dylan had wandered ahead a bit, used to the scene, while Megan and I were newbies and taking our time. I could see him to the side of the mob, writing on a board that had been fixed to a barrier. I slid in beside him, dragging Megan with me.

'What's this?' I asked, putting my chin on his shoulder. He was almost uncomfortably taller than me.

'Fuck, you scared me,' Dylan jolted in surprise, dislodging my head. 'It's just a board where you can write shit. Messages and stuff. There's a few of them. This march leads to a stage and some queens perform, so they have them every so often.'

I studied the board now, white painted plywood. A plastic cup of markers sat on the ground in front of it. They'd be lucky if they lasted the day, I thought. It was covered in writing. Some people had just written their names, like our esteemed friend Dylan, but others had written little notes. "A + M", "Taylor 4 Olivia" and "Love wins" mixed in with *RIP*s remembering people who had passed away. It was lovely. Optimism and sorrow with a dash of hope, all there. I wanted to add my name. To officially be here.

Using a green sharpie I signed my name with a flourish, and looked over to see what Megan had added.

"Meggy loves Astor" was written over a purple and pink rainbow in their familiar handwriting.

'Not like, romantically, right?' I asked, feigning horror.

'You're such a dick. Of course not. You're my best friend and I love you. Fuck knows why.'

I looked at my best friend in the entire world and gave them my very best smile.

A real one.

dly. I thought. It was covered in writing. Some people had just written their names, like the Daltons' friend Dylan, but others had written little notes. "A + M", "Taylor + Olivia" and "Love wins" mixed in with RIPs remembering people who had passed away. It was lovely. Optimism and sorrow with a dash of hope, all there. I wanted to add my name. To officially be here.

Using a green sharpie I signed my name with a flourish and looked over to see what Megan had added.

Meggy loves Aster was written over a purple and pink rainbow in their familiar handwriting.

"Not like, romantically, right?" I asked, teasing them.

"You're such a dork. Of course not. You're my best friend and I love you. That's why."

I looked at my best friend in the entire world and gave them my very best smile.

A real one.

ACKNOWLEDGEMENTS

Someone once told me that this was super informal. So given that my chance of winning an Oscar is zero, but my releasing another book is almost certain, please consider this my Academy Award acceptance speech.

I'd like to thank the people who helped me (and Astor) get to this point.

The book community on Instagram; thank you to everyone who has listened to me complain about Astor, reminded me that I can do this and generally just supported me.

Jacob Demlow for reading the entire thing when I felt like no one would, even though it's extremely light on love and fluff.

Ashley Moellinger, for giving Astor her first ever review. Reading each word gave me such joy and confidence that this could be real.

Congress, my Americans as I call you to everyone else. I love our group and the unwavering support. I am grateful for every conversation, gossip exchange and kind word.

Thank you to Sera Milano for writing books that show inclusivity and diversity in such a natural way. I am so thankful you gave Astor a chance. Your advice helped shaped her final form and I am so pleased to simply know you and call you a friend.

Spencer. Spencer, Spencer, Spencer. There is no one else I'd rather make an Uber driver doubt my sanity with. I can't wait for another interstate holiday, more obsessive arcade games and laughing 'til we cry and can't breathe.

My dearest friend Kate. Canada, quite honestly, is too far away. I don't know what on earth I did to gain you as a friend; there is no one quite like you. Thank you for being so confident in me, for listening to every doubt, for being excited and cheering me on every single day. You always remind me that I can put myself first and I don't know that I would be here without you.

Michael. Thank you is not enough. You have believed in this book, in me, more than I ever have. I am so grateful for everything you have brought into my life, for not just telling me I should and could write, but for insisting that I do. Thank you for trusting me with your words, for wanting to write with me, for discussing the plot of everything with me until we are convinced that we can do it better. It means more to me than you can ever know, and I can't wait for everything we have planned. *tap tap*

And finally, Jamie. I know I believe that I can do anything, but I didn't believe I could do this. You did though, so thank you and I love you.

About Author

Amy Jane Lehan currently lives in regional Victoria, Australia, though she was born in New Zealand.
She has five kids, four cats and a Great Dane.
When she isn't writing, she enjoys a true crime podcast, a documentary, or talking about books on the internet.
Who Could Love You, Astor Price? is her debut novel.

Content Warnings

Emotional abuse

Physical abuse

Self-harm

Suicidal thoughts

Drug use

Alcohol and alcoholism

Sexual assault—this happens on page, contained to chapter eleven, though the impact is discussed for the duration of the book after.

Milton Keynes UK
Ingram Content Group UK Ltd.
UKHW041914090823
426579UK00004B/12/J

9 780645 618907